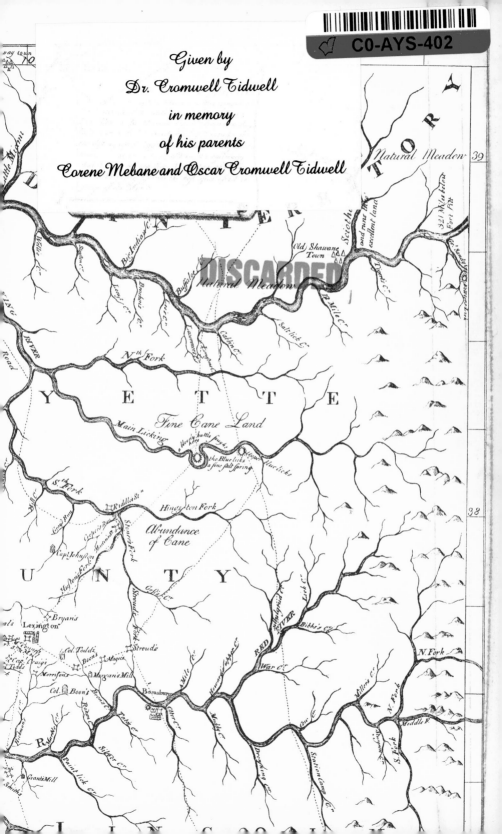

The Public Library of Nashville and Davidson County

KEEP DATE CARD IN BOOK

POCKET

The American West connotes plains, Indians and Cavalry charges. But at one time the American West—THE FIRST WEST—the frontier was that vast tract east of the Mississippi called by the Iroquois, Ken-tah-teh, land of tomorrow. In a fast-moving, informative and enjoyable narrative, Ruby Addison Henry presents a lively account of the settling of the Kentucky territory. Relying primarily on unpublished journals, she gives breadth and life to this early part of American history.

The saga opens with the legendary Daniel Boone, who was, of course, the first white man to explore and settle this tract. And what follows is an intriguing study of the problems, the hardships and the pleasures of this new colony—for colony it was, of what was to be its sister state, Virginia. It was with some difficulty that the early settlers achieved their independence from Virginia. This and many other fascinating and little known facts are part of this excellent book, THE FIRST WEST.

THE
FIRST WEST

by

RUBY ADDISON HENRY

AURORA PUBLISHERS, INC.
NASHVILLE/LONDON

Preface

Work on the manuscript for this book was begun many years ago. I had the privilege of watching some of the careful research and painstaking labor which went into it. I enjoyed the creative and balanced interpretation which the author brought to facts she had discovered and verified. Much of her research went back to old manuscripts, yellowed newspapers, and government records.

The author was particularly sensitive to democratic processes in the forming of the state of Kentucky. She also gave due attention to the influence and interaction of this area on and with the United States as it was then and as it grew to be.

Her survey of the United States in 1792 opens up an amazing picture of our country's industry, education, politics, and cultural components at that time.

Yet the author has not let statistics and statements of facts dull the interest of the story she tells. She has depicted individuals and situations with a freshness and vigor that make the reading of this book an enjoyable experience. It is history that lives.

Arrangements for publication of "The First West in the United States" were completed shortly before Miss Henry's death on February 19, 1971.

Nashville, Tennessee   Robbie Trent

v

CONTENTS

Foreword

A region, like a continent, may at some time have its great moment in the spotlight of the world's history; a moment which may vitally affect the course of human affairs. In the latter part of the eighteenth century, such an opportunity came to the wilderness south of the Ohio River, on the far side of the Appalachian Mountains.

In the early 1770s that uninhabited region had no definite name. The English colonists on the Atlantic seaboard spoke of it as the "Backlands," or "On the Western Waters." Yet in less than a score of years after the first white settlers built their cabins in one of its valleys, more than one hundred thousand Americans called it their home; and, Kentucky, the name of the new state which they had established there, was known throughout the western world.

During that time remarkable changes had also occurred on the eastern slope of the Appalachian Mountains. The thirteen English colonies along the Atlantic coast had declared and won their independence. They had organized and put into operation a new form of government, based upon the then revolutionary principle of "the consent of the governed."

The settlers beyond the Appalachians played an important, and, more than once, a decisive part in some of the events that made possible those changes in government. The region west of the mountains inevitably became a buffer zone between the British armies with their Indian allies and the American "Rebels." This area was the chief bone of contention during the treaty negotiations in Paris after the Revolution; it became the subject of violent sectional jealousy among the thirteen states themselves; and, for many years afterward, it provided a fertile breeding ground for plots and schemes to separate the entire western region from the new nation.

How those pioneers in our first "West" met the varied threats to their lives and property and made their own unique contribution to the extension of human liberties is the theme of this book.

To those pioneers, democracy was more than a theory; from sheer necessity, it became a way of life. The first clapboard roof had hardly been put in place before the Kentucky settlers insistently demanded from Virginia the right of local home rule and self-government. At the close of the Revolution, they began their long struggle for independent statehood.

While keeping strictly within the framework of the existing laws of Virginia, they vigorously exercised the rights of freedom of speech, of press, of petition, and of assembly, to achieve their purpose. Finally, after six long years and nine conventions, with their own statehood in sight, their delegates assembled at Danville in 1782 to write a constitution for the fifteenth state.

In this, their basic law, recognition of human dignity, broke a new political trail. For the first time in history, a written constitution guaranteed to every adult male citizen the right to vote and to hold elective office, without any property or religious requirements. It was the individual who could vote, not his possessions or his membership in any particular religious body. Later states might provide more, but none would dare provide less.

These Kentucky pioneers left to America a challenging record of their political development. In the midst of constant toil and danger, they somehow managed to pen letters and diaries, to keep full minutes of their many political meetings, and to write petitions and memorials to the Virginia Assembly and to the Congress of the United States.

In this book this priceless literary and historical legacy has been freely used. From the pens of those pioneers and the writings of men to whom they later told their stories, we can best learn the conditions of their daily lives, the facts about their lowly or heroic deeds, and some of the causes of their failures and successes.

I have tried to write simply, keeping in mind some readers who may have little knowledge of history. Each chapter usually has one definite theme. The tempo varies with the subject matter:

leisurely in domestic chapters; swift-paced in those concerned with war; deliberate in those where political ideas and action predominate.

My purpose, aside from accurately presenting the facts, has been to lead the reader into the mental, physical and emotional atmosphere of the place and period; to evoke a mood, create an attitude, develop an appreciation, and arouse the reader's interest and pride in his rich historic heritage.

For several reasons, I have let the people tell much of the story themselves. Their own writings and recorded statements are the stuff of life itself. They have a vividness, a sense of reality, which no rewriting can possibly convey.

I have occasionally translated reports into direct conversation to clarify a situation, but whenever I have ascribed a statement to a definite person, it is always based upon his own spoken or written word.

Ruby Addison Henry

Louisville, Kentucky

Part One

"ON THE WESTERN WATERS"

CHAPTER I

Land of Tomorrow

Conquering, holding, daring,
Venturing as we go the unknown ways . . .
—WALT WHITMAN

The first West in the United States—what was it? Where was it? In the beginning, its devolpment was only an adventure with no well-defined limits or goal, but as men acted on the inner urge to explore fresh fields of thought and action, a purpose developed within them. Hammered out by existing influences and changing circumstances, that purpose became at last a definite goal. That goal and the guideposts leading to it are clearly discernible in the growth of one—and perhaps many another—state.

The history of that first West was in the making when Daniel Boone of North Carolina met the veteran Indian trader, John Finley, in the summer of 1755. Both were militiamen in Gen. Edward Braddock's army, then slowly cutting its way through the forests of western Pennsylvania to attack the French forts on the upper Ohio.

John Finley, thirty-four years old, probably scouted far in advance of the army while Daniel Boone, twelve years younger, drove a supply wagon in the rear. At night the two men traded tales of adventure beside their campfire. Boone listened with special interest as Finley told of an experience he had had two years earlier in the little known wilderness beyond the Appalachian Mountains.

He spoke of a band of Shawnee Indians who had lived in a rich region south of the Ohio River in a place which they called

1

"Eskippakithiki." It was then the only Indian town between the Ohio and the Tennessee rivers, and no one knew how long the Indians had been there. Some said they had wandered there from the south.[1]

Finley had gone down the Ohio to trade there in the fall of 1752, taking four men with him. They had built a cabin and a stockade, opened up their packs and settled down for a winter's trading.

In January of the next year, a band of scalp-hunting Conewago and Ottawa Indians had come along. They had picked a quarrel with Finley's party and killed three of his men. Finley and the other man had fled into the woods, saving their scalps, but losing all of their goods.[2]

The next year war had broken out between the French and the English, and the Eskippakithiki villagers had joined with other Shawnees in Ohio to fight for the French. No one dared live in the Eskippakithiki region now, Finley said, for too many tribes—Cherokees, Shawnees, Iroquois, and perhaps a dozen others—claimed it.

The Iroquois called it "Ken-tah-teh," which means "Tomorrow" or "Land of Tomorrow." They planned to live there sometime, they said. The Shawnee name for the region sounded like "Kenta-ke." Finley thought it might mean "level land," or "place that is green." [3]

Finley had never seen such a country. The rolling land was covered with grass and trees and filled with caves and creeks and sulphur springs, where animals came by the hundreds to lick the earth. Canebrakes along the river grew taller than a cabin roof. There was more game than any hunter had ever dreamed of. Finley saw bear, deer, beaver, otter, and buffalo so thick around the licking places that they tromped on one another. All the tribes hunted there. Trails and war-paths criss-crossed the country like a spider web. Indians said that the trail near their place ran all the way from the Shawnee villages north of the Ohio to the Cherokee towns in the upper Tennessee valley. They called this trail "Warrior's Path." [4]

No one knew who owned the land. France and England were fighting over it, and if England won, Finley said, he meant to investigate the section. It should be easy to find that Warrior's Path, he thought, by going northwest from the forks of the Yadkin River in Boone's country.

Daniel Boone remembered every detail of that story. The picture of such a hunter's paradise as Finley described, unbroken by Indian village or white man's clearing, haunted his dreams. If England won, he, too, meant to go there and see it with his own eyes.

However, Finley and Boone had to wait seven long years for England to win the French and Indian War. Not until 1763 did "half a continent change hands at the scratch of a pen," and the British flag wave over the old French forts from Canada to the Straits of Florida on the south and to the Mississippi River on the west.

In the summer of that same year, the Ottawa chief, Pontiac, banded the northern tribes of Indians together in a desperate attempt to drive the British out of their country. They struck so suddenly and in so many places at once that they almost succeeded in their purpose.

After that short but bloody uprising was put down, the king of England, George III, issued a new order to the governors of his American colonies. This, the "Royal Proclamation of 1763," directed them to grant lands to veterans of the colonial wars who were ". . . discharged in America; and . . . shall personally apply." That would seem to invite Finley and Boone and other borderland settlers who had their mind's eye upon the rich lands beyond the western mountains.

However, there was more to King George's Proclamation. It forbade the royal governors, ". . . for the present," to grant any lands beyond the headwaters of the rivers which flow eastward into the Atlantic, or upon any lands which were reserved to the Indians. It went even further in that it ordered all persons who had settled upon such lands ". . . forthwith to remove themselves from such settlements." In addition, it strictly forbade any private person to purchase from the Indians ". . . any lands, reserved to the said Indians." [5]

The king wanted no more costly wars. He wished to please

the Iroquois who had helped the British, and he also hoped to pacify the "French" Indians by keeping traders and settlers out of the lands reserved for them.

The Proclamation of 1763 came too late to stem the strong tide of westward migration. Settlers' cabins already dotted the eastern slopes of the Appalachians from Pennsylvania to the Carolinas. Some pioneers had settled in the high valleys of the Shenandoah and the New Rivers, and some had crossed the Blue Ridge and located on the headwaters of the Tennessee River long before George III declared that region out of bounds for his American subjects.

The hardy frontiersmen built their cabins and stockades near the streams and cleared a few hilly acres for garden truck and corn. Their belled horses, cattle and sheep grazed on the mountain meadows, and their long-nosed hogs ran wild in the forests.

Once or twice a year, as hunting luck favored them, they took packhorse trains of furs and pelts down the valleys to sell in the lower settlements. They brought back salt and alum, gunpowder and lead, iron and steel, tools and rifles. Theirs was a rough, dangerous, but fiercely independent life, far beyond the reach of the hated laws and restrictions that had irked them in the older settlements.

George III finally faced the stubborn fact that no royal decree could keep such people from straying into forbidden territory and getting into trouble with the natives. He directed his agents to bargain with the Iroquois tribes for their western land claims. In the treaty signed by them at Fort Stanwix, New York, in 1768, those Six Nations sold to the king and some land companies their claims to all lands west of the mountains.[6] That land included the country south of the Ohio which John Finley had so vividly described to Daniel Boone.

The Colony of Virginia was jealously alert to anything concerning that particular region. It was no part of the king's "Crown Lands," won from France by the fortunes of war, she protested. It was within Virginia's own boundaries, as defined by the terms of its original charters.

To satisfy the Virginia colonials and to appease the Cherokees in the south, who also claimed that region, British agents made two treaties with that tribe. In the first, at Hard Labor, South Carolina, in October, 1768, the Cherokees agreed to recognize the Great Kanawha River as Virginia's western boundary.

Hundreds of settlers had already located beyond that line and to protect them, a second treaty was signed in October, 1770, at Lochaber, South Carolina. In this one, the Cherokees accepted the Louisa River (now the Kentucky) as the western limits of Virginia, but they retained their claim to lands south and west of that river.[7]

Late in the winter of 1768-69, after the first treaty with the Cherokees, John Finley knocked on the cabin door of Daniel and Rebecca Bryan Boone, near the mouth of Beaver Creek in the upper Yadkin Valley in North Carolina. Almost fourteen years had passed since the day when the two woodsmen had cut traces and fled on the wagon horses from the scene of Braddock's defeat, but their dream of adventure on the western waters had not faded.

Finley had gone down the Ohio the year before. Now he wanted to go overland across the mountains, to find that Warrior's Path, and to revisit the site of that old Indian village. Did Daniel Boone want to go with him?

Did Boone want to go! He would have started at dawn the next morning, had that been possible, but these two needed more men for such an undertaking. They also needed time and money to secure and assemble the necessary supplies, and it was the end of April before the party was ready.

Boone had found four other good woodsmen to go with them— his brother-in-law, John Stewart, and Joseph Holden, James Mooney, and William Cooley. They wore the standard outfit of the frontier, a combination of white man's and the Indian's clothing, long shirts of unbleached, homespun linsey under deerskin hunting coats that lapped double across the chest and came down to the knees, with long sleeves and a wide cape, both fringed. The outfit included long deerskin or buckskin breeches or "leggins" fringed at the sides; and buckskin moccasins, stuffed with deer hair or dry leaves and tied tightly over the leggins at the ankles.

A buckskin belt, tied in the back, made a large wallet of the bosom of the hunting shirt. In this, each man carried enough food for his next meal—a chunk of corn pone, a piece of "jerk" or boiled ham, a bag of parched corn. The wallet also held a hank or two of raveled tow of flax or hemp, with which to wipe his rifle.

Unlike the red man, the white frontiersman preferred to keep all his hair when he could. He wore it long, braided in a pigtail and sometimes clubbed up at the nape of his neck with a string or narrow ribbon. His headwear varied. It might be a handkerchief, a coonskin cap or a felt hat. Contrary to legend, Daniel Boone is said to have preferred a hat to a coonskin cap.

Each man carried the essentials for hunting or combat fastened to his belt or hung by leather thongs around his neck. These included a bullet pouch, powder and priming horns, a powder measure, small "patches" of cloth in which to wrap a bullet when loading, extra flints, and a long hunting knife in a leather sheath at his left side.

An iron bullet mold, a small supply of powder and lead, an extra knife, a roll of buckskin for mending clothing or moccasins and some extra food could be wrapped in the blanket or bearskin and tied to the back of his saddle. A small iron pot, a metal cup and an ax hung from the pommel in front.

The frontiersman placed his loaded rifle across his saddle, its long barrel cradled in the crook of his left elbow. He tied an extra rifle on the bundle behind his saddle.

At dawn on May 1, 1769, the six adventurers loaded their packhorses. First, they carefully fitted and fastened a thick pad or old blanket or bearskin on the back of each horse. Between the front and back of the wooden saddles they balanced small kegs of gunpowder and rum, as well as bars of iron and lead bent to fit the angle of the saddle. The pack also included long, stout bags of flour, meal, ham, bear's bacon, jerked venison, salt, sugar, shelled corn, and whatever else they thought they might need for food. Then they tied a heavy cover over each load and fastened another rifle on the top of it; hung a small bell on a rope around the neck of every horse and tied the bridle of each pack animal to the tail of a horse in front of it.

Then the explorers set forth ". . . to wander through the wilderness of America, in quest of the country of Kentucke." They traveled in a "westward direction." On June 7 they arrived at the Red River, a southward-flowing branch of the Kentucky, ". . . . where John Finley had formerly been trading with the Indians." [8]

Squire Boone, Daniel's younger brother, had stayed at home to plant corn and harvest the crops on their farms in the Yadkin valley. Seven months after the explorers left, Squire and a younger man, Alexander Neely, set out to join his brother's party, taking along fresh horses and supplies. Late in December they located Daniel and John Stewart, who had much to tell the newcomers.

A band of Indians had captured both of them and had held them for a week before they could escape. The savages had plundered their hunting camp and stolen all the furs and skins that the six men had collected. After that, John Finley and the other three men had left Boone and Stewart, to return to safer regions.

John Stewart disappeared not long after Squire Boone arrived and he was never seen again. Then Alexander Neely set out for home, leaving the two Boone brothers alone in the wilderness.

Together the Boones built their winter quarters, a "half-faced" hunting camp, probably somewhere near Red River. In front of a large fallen tree in a secluded place, they cleared a space large enough for a cabin floor. Then they sank the sharpened ends of two forked saplings in the ground, eight or ten feet in front of the log, for the far corners of their shelter, placing shorter forked poles between them and the log. They laid long poles from right to left in the forks and placed roof poles across these from the front to the big log at the back. On these slanting roof poles they piled slabs of bark, brush, dry leaves, grass and sod. They enclosed the sides with smaller logs, bark and brush. Then they gathered dry leaves and moss for their beds inside the cabin. The whole job was done in less than a day.

From that base, the two brothers hunted throughout the winter and spring. On May 1, 1770, they loaded the packhorses, and Squire started back east to the settlements. Daniel was left alone in the wilderness, ". . . without bread, salt or sugar, . . or even a horse or dog." He also had very little powder and lead.

Boone cave, four miles northeast of Harrodsburg, where Daniel Boone is said to have wintered in 1769-70. Courtesy the Filson Club.

Sometimes he stayed in a cave; often he slept in the tall cane-brake the better to conceal himself from prowling Indians. On July 27, 1770, he met his brother at their old camp site. Squire had sold their furs and hides, paid their debts and brought fresh supplies of food and ammunition. By autumn they had another stock ready. Squire made a second trip back to the North Carolina settlements and again rejoined Daniel in the wilderness.

Deciding that the place was no longer safe, they ". . . proceeded to Cumberland River, reconnoitering that part of the country until March, 1771, and giving names to the different waters." [9] Near Cumberland Gap they had an encounter with some Indians who took their horses, all their pelts, and compelled them to exchange their good rifles for poor ones. The Boones reached their homes in May, 1771, little better off in worldly goods than when Daniel had left two years before.

No one could rob Daniel Boone of what he had stored in his mind. He had heard from others of that far country on the western waters. Now he had seen with his own eyes the rolling meadow lands, the vast forests, and the herds of wild animals. He had crossed its mountainous wilderness from the Appalachians to Finley's old camp site on Red River. From the top of Pilot Knob he had viewed ". . . with pleasure the beautiful level of

Daniel Boone's first view of the "Great Meadow" of central Kentucky. Mural painting in the capitol at Frankfort by Gilbert White. Courtesy Cusick Studio, Frankfort.

Kentucke." He had explored the country from the Falls of the Ohio to Cumberland Gap; from the Licking River to the Green and the Cumberland. He knew its valleys and its hills, its creeks and licks and caves as well as he knew the country around his own home.[10] Daniel Boone had not wasted those two years.

Men on the Virginia and Carolina frontier reported the story of the Boones' "Long Hunt" and it became a favorite topic of conversation.

"Rich rollin' land, they say. Plenty o' game. Fine grazin' for stock."

"No Injuns live thar now. But some cotched Dan'l onct. Kep' him a week. Stole all his furs." "But he aims to go back thar. Says he means to live in that far country."

Daniel Boone, indeed, intended to go back, and take his family with him, ". . . to live in Kentucke, which I esteemed a second paradise, at the risk of my life and fortune." [11]

It took him two years to get ready for the journey. He sold his farm and everything else he owned that could not be carried on horses. He made or bought extra supplies of everything the party might need, from moccasins for their own feet to shoes for their horses.

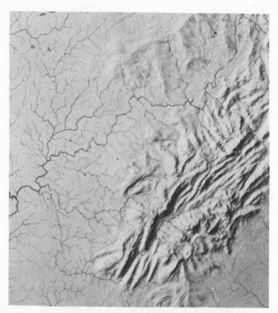

This relief map pictures the great bar-
rier of the Appalachians between the
Atlantic slope and the western waters.
Courtesy U. S. Forest Bureau.

Five other families joined the Boones, leaving the Yadkin settlements September 25, 1773. With Daniel Boone and his family,
they turned their faces towards the distant West.

This first domestic caravan of home seekers in the western
wilderness set a pattern which countless others would follow in
coming years. They wore the typical frontier costume—men and
older boys in hunting shirts and leggins; women and girls in ankle-
length, full-skirted dresses of blue or brown or black homemade
linsey, knitted stockings and heavy, homemade leather shoes, with
shawls around their shoulders and linen sunbonnets on their heads.

Mounted guards led the way, each with his long rifle across
his saddle. Their keen eyes searched the woods, noting the
slightest stirring of leaf or bush. Behind them came the long
string of packhorses, kept in line on the narrow trail by some of

the men and older boys on foot. Next came the women and girls riding astride a saddle or sideways on pillions or cushions strapped on like saddles. Mothers carried babies in their arms, with an older child astride behind them. Other children rode in large hickory baskets, nicely balanced on each side of a packhorse.

The slow-moving line of domestic animals followed, their bells tinkling at every step. The men and boys in charge of them ran back and forth to keep them on the trail. Far behind rode the last group of men, to guard from attack in the rear.

Day after day the travelers toiled over the mountain passes and forded the streams. At night they camped at a place made ready by the advance guard. October 9, 1773, they climbed Wallin's Ridge and crossed the last river on the route in southwestern Virginia. The steep southern slope of Cumberland Mountain loomed ahead.[12]

Daniel Boone had sent his oldest son, James, back to William Russell's Station on Clinch River for flour and some other supplies. Five men accompanied James on his return trip. They camped that night about three miles to the rear of the main

Monument in the Pioneer Memorial State Park at Harrodsburg, Kentucky, erected by the United States government in 1934, commemorates the founding of the first permanent settlement of the West. The map shows the route taken by George Rogers Clark in 1778 on his expedition to the Northwest Territory. Hesse, photographer.

company. At dawn, a band of Indians attacked James Boone's party and killed all except one man, a Negro who escaped.

Rebecca Boone sent a linen sheet to wrap her son's body for burial. All the dead were buried near the place where they fell; their graves were covered with logs and brush to conceal them from the Indians.

After that tragic loss, Daniel Boone and his friends dared not go on. They could not and would not return to the distant region from which they had come; yet they dared not stay where they were.[13] They had no choice but to retreat to the nearest settlements, forty miles back in the valley of Clinch River. For them, as for the Indians, the fertile wilderness on the western waters was still the "Land of Tomorrow."

CHAPTER II

Harrod's Town

All the past is future.
—ROBINSON JEFFERS

Many frontiersmen besides the Boones and their Yadkin neighbors had hunted in the wilderness south of the Ohio and had set their hearts upon having homes in it. Among them, none was better known throughout the territory than Captain James Harrod of Virginia.

Early in 1774, the year after Boone's unsuccessful attempt to settle in the new country, Harrod set out for the Kentucky wilderness with a party of about thirty men from the western part of Virginia and Pennsylvania. They floated down the Monongahela River in canoes, or pirogues, made of dugout logs. At Fort Pitt, then only a tiny frontier settlement, they turned into the current of the broad Ohio.

Sometime in May they reached the mouth of the Kentucky River. Entering it, they paddled and pulled their way upstream between banks that became ever higher and steeper. At the mouth of a little creek, now called Landing Run, they left the river and hid their canoes. Shouldering their packs, they made their way on foot westward across the hills towards Salt River.[1]

Harrod had learned about this Salt River region when he had traveled down the Ohio with the McAfee brothers the previous summer.[2] He chose a site for his party's headquarters a few miles south of the McAfee surveys. Here he made camp under an elm tree near a large spring known to every wilderness hunter. A few

13

days later, Captain Isaac Hite and eleven other adventurers from the Shenandoah Valley joined his party.

The men of these two companies scattered out from this rallying point each morning to locate and survey tracts of good land in the fertile, rolling country between the Salt and the Dix Rivers. Harrod selected for himself a tract near a place which he named "Boiling Spring," about six miles south of their main camp at the "Big Spring."

Under the laws of Virginia each settler could lay claim to a "cabin right" of four hundred acres at $2.50 a hundred in any wilderness land open to settlement. Each holder of such a cabin right had also a "preemption" right to an adjoining one thousand acre tract at a cost of about $400.00.

The law required a settler to improve his land by building a cabin and raising some corn. Such improvements usually consisted only of a three-sided, unroofed log pen and a few rows of corn planted among the stumps of the clearing.

The law, however, made no provision for surveying the land; the settlers themselves must either make such a survey or employ someone to do it for them, and the fee for that service was usually one-third of the tract surveyed. Harrod's and Hite's men worked together at that task, as they did at clearing and building. As soon as they had finished several cabins, they drew lots to decide to whom each one should belong.

Those frontiersmen knew Indians too well to overlook the risk they incurred in trying to make a settlement in that region. If they had been merely hunting, their scalps might have been reasonably safe, for the Indians were outwardly at peace that summer. "Plenty game on my river," the Cherokee chief, "Captain Dick," had once told a party of hunters. But he added, "Hunt! Kill! And *go home!*"

At their nightly meetings under the elm, Harrod and his companions decided that they must make a closer settlement for greater safety. They set up their surveying outfit on June 16, 1774, and began running the lines and laying off their "town." Its boundaries included their camp site and extended down the branch that flowed from the Big Spring. They planned to give each man in the company a half-acre town lot and a five-acre outside lot.

Their equipment was similar to that which George Washington had used as a young wilderness surveyor. Their large round compass with a five- or six-inch needle was mounted on an iron base about fifteen inches long with "sights" at each end. A skinned sapling, on which the surveyor marked off six feet (judging by his own height), served as a pole for measuring. The chain originally consisted of one hundred wire links, each about eight inches long. When one link became bent or broken, the surveyor patched it with hickory strips or pawpaw bark. A short pocket rule of ivory, several sheets of paper, quill pens, and a bottle of ink completed the surveying outfit. Boundaries or corners were marked with a knife or with powder or any convenient tree, stone, or other landmark.[3]

In the midst of surveying, Harrod's party was startled one day by a loud "Halloo!" from a distance. Looking up from their work, they saw two white men at the edge of the clearing, holding their hands high above their heads in the frontier gesture of peace.

At Harrodsburg, the fort builders had the foresight to enclose their Big Spring within the stockade walls. This view shows the spring as it looks today within the grounds of the Pioneer Memorial Fort. Hesse, photographer.

"Halloo!" Harrod called back, and the veteran scouts, Daniel Boone and Michael Stoner, strode into camp.

Eager questions met them.

"What news back in the settlements?"

"Seen any Shawnee 'signs'?"

"Whar'd you come from?"

"Whar you bound for?"

"News a-plenty," the two men replied. "Old Cornstalk and his Shawnee braves are stirring up the Mingoes and the Miamis in the Ohio country. Lord Dunmore has sent us to warn all you people in the Cantuckey country to get out before the Indians break loose.

"We've come from the Clinch. We're bound for the Falls now, where Cap'n John Floyd is making surveys for the governor."

It was serious news, but Harrod did not give the order to break camp at once. Nor did Boone and Stoner hurry away on their eight-hundred-mile tramp; instead, Boone lingered to lend a hand with the surveying. The Harrod's Town party gave him a town lot in return for his help and built a double log cabin at once on the line between it and the next lot.

July brought a second warning. A breathless runner dashed into camp one day and gasped, "Injuns!" . . . Fired on our party! . . . Killed Jared Cowan!"

Harrod hastily gathered together all the men he could and hurried to the scene of the attack. They found no Indians, but they knew that they could not disregard this warning.

As soon as all the members of their party came into camp, the frontiersmen started for their border settlements. They left a few scattered "lottery cabins," some patches of growing corn, and several "half-faced" cabins in "Harrod's Town." These bore mute witness that the white man had come into the wilderness and expected to return.

To avoid a chance encounter with the Shawnees on the Ohio, the men went home from Harrod's Town by way of Cumberland Gap. Most of them promptly enrolled in the army that Gen. Andrew Lewis was raising to fight the Indians and in October, one thousand frontiersmen under his command marched northward to join Lord Dunmore's forces at Fort Pitt.[4]

In the evening of October 9, they camped at Point Pleasant, at the mouth of the Great Kanawha River, "little imagining," one wrote, "that we were to engage the whole United Force of the Enemy Ohio Indians."

During the night Cornstalk's braves crossed the Ohio and crept up to within a mile of their camp. At dawn they fell upon the unsuspecting whites, who had neglected to post sentries or guards.

The battle raged furiously, back and forth under the trees, until dark. "Never did Indians stick closer to it, nor behave better." At night they recrossed the Ohio, taking the body of every fallen red man with them.

They had killed fifty Virginians and wounded eighty. With a smaller force than their opponents, they had all but won the battle of Point Pleasant, one of the most desperate ever fought between white and red men.[5]

Chief Cornstalk, realizing that his warriors could not possibly destroy both that army and the one under Lord Dunmore, frankly told his people that the English were too many for them. He advised them to accept the best terms that the whites offered, if the whites would promise to stay out of the Shawnee country north of the Ohio. The Shawnees took his advice. In their treaty with Virginia they agreed never again to attack white people on the Ohio. They also gave up all claim to any land south of that river and solemnly promised never to enter that region again.

The English had at last acquired the three most important tribal claims to a large part of the territory west of the Appalachians. The Iroquois had sold theirs in 1768 at Fort Stanwix, in New York. The Cherokees, in 1768 and in 1770, had given up their claim to any land north and east of the Kentucky River. Now, in 1774, the Shawnees gave up their claim to the common hunting grounds south of the Ohio River.

The hard-won victory of the Virginians at Point Pleasant thus became an event of national importance. If the Indians had won that battle, the Americans could have made no lasting settlement in the unoccupied land south of the Ohio during the early years of the Revolutionary War. Even if the colonists could have won that war without the aid of the first West, the western boundary of the thirteen United States would certainly have been set at the crest of the Alleghenies.[6]

No one could foresee how long any Indian tribe would observe the terms of a treaty. The Shawnees, with the memory of the battle of Point Pleasant fresh in their minds, might keep their pledge for a year. Possibly, if the whites did not provoke them too much, they might keep it for two or three years.

Even one year of peace would mean much to the land-hungry white people who had their eyes on the western wilderness. Explorers and settlers swarmed into it as soon as they heard of the Shawnee treaty, and the snows of the following winter had not melted before fleets of dugout canoes were floating down the Monongahela into the Ohio, bound for land "on the western waters."

On March 11, 1775, the McAfee brothers and some of their friends reached their tract of land on Salt River. A few days later, Capt. James Harrod, with a larger company than he had brought the year before, passed the McAfee party on the way to his own settlement. They camped again beside the Big Spring and reentered the empty cabins of Harrod's Town on March 15. This time they came to stay.

Permanent settlements were beginning in new territory. Each one had an influence on the adventure toward freedom and, as men learned to live—and sometimes to fight—together, that influence would spread even into what would some day be the United States of America.

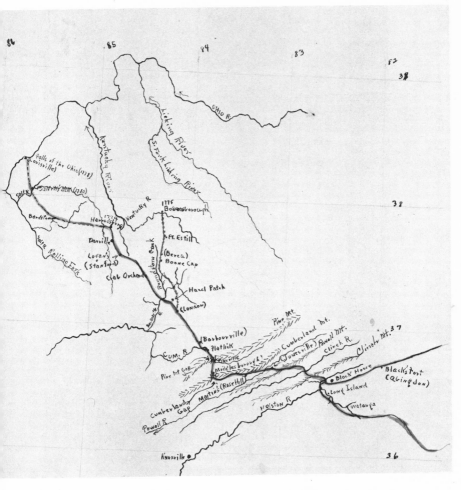

Outline map of the Pioneer Roads to Kentucky. Adapted from William Allen Pusey's Wilderness Road to Kentucky, pp. 50-51.

Bronze tablet of Judge Richard Henderson, founder and president of the Transylvania Company, on the courthouse of Henderson County, Kentucky. Courtesy Robert Worth Bingham.

CHAPTER III

Boone's Trace to the Kentucky

Every noble work is at first impossible.
THOMAS CARLYLE

Even during his participation in Lord Dunmore's campaign against the Shawnees, Daniel Boone had not forgotten the region west of the Appalachians. Soon after he was released from his military duties, he ". . . was solicited by a number of North Carolina gentlemen, that were about purchasing the lands lying on the S. side of Kentucke River, from the Cherokee Indians, . . . to negotiate with them, and, mention the boundaries of the purchase." [1]

In these words, Boone recorded his connection with a remarkable pioneer enterprise that in scope and daring rivals any promotional venture of today.

The North Carolina gentlemen" to whom he referred were members of a business group called "Richard Henderson & Co." It had been organized for the purpose of speculating in western lands. Its legal head, Col. Richard Henderson, was a prominent lawyer in the colony and had recently been one of the justices of its highest court at Salisbury. Associated with him were John Williams, his law partner, and the three Hart brothers—Thomas, Nathaniel and David, prominent merchants and plantation owners in the Hillsborough region of North Carolina.

Daniel's glowing account of the unoccupied lands he had explored on his long hunt had fired the imagination of these men and inspired them with the idea of making a permanent settlement on the western waters. The Shawnee treaty seemed to open

21

the way for them to carry out their plans. In January 1775, they reorganized their business, enlarged it to nine members, and re-named it the Transylvania Company.

The next step toward locating in the new territory was to deal directly with the Cherokee Indians for their remaining claim to lands in Kentucky and Tennessee.

Daniel Boone, sometimes accompanied by Henderson, some-times by Nathaniel Hart, spent most of the winter of 1774-1775 in the Cherokee villages, talking with chief after chief. The squaws fingered the samples of cloth and blankets, while the braves tested the edges of knives and hatchets which the Transylvania Com-pany representatives offered in payment for the tribal claims.[2]

Finally, between puffs at their long pipes, the chiefs grunted and nodded their approval. "We will talk to our people," they said. "We will meet our white brothers at the Sycamore Shoals on the Watauga after the snows melt." When Boone left the Cherokees he assured Henderson and his partners that the Indians would ac-cept their offer.

Boone recorded his next assignment from the Transylvania Com-pany—"to mark out a road . . . through the wilderness to Ken-tucke, with such assistance as I thought necessary to employ for such an important undertaking." [3]

For this task he collected thirty "enterprising men, well-armed." These included his brother Squire, his old friend Richard Calla-way, his scouting companion Michael Stoner, Capt. William Twetty, and young Felix Walker.

The group assembled on March 10, 1775, near Long Island in the Holston River where the north and south forks join. They set out at once along the Warrior's Path, across the long, parallel ranges and valleys of northeastern Tennessee.

The old trail led them in an easy, zigzag course over Clinch Mountain, across Clinch River Valley, and up a steep four-mile climb to Kane's Gap in Powell Mountain. Looking northwest over the fertile Powell Valley, the pathmakers could see the long, blue-gray skyline of Cumberland Mountain, ten or twelve miles distant.

Boone had been delighted to see the many new cabins along the route, especially Capt. Joseph Martin's "station" in Powell

Valley, about halfway between the Holston settlements and the Kentucky border. Beyond Martin's, the Path followed Indian Creek southwest to the base of Cumberland Mountain where dense forests covered the mountain's steep lower slopes. Above the trees rose "a very high ridge of white rocks inaccessible in most places to man and beast."[4]

The trailblazers hacked a path for twenty miles through thick cane and laurel along the creek before they saw the only break in that massive wall—a wide, saddle-shaped notch in the ridge. The Pinnacle, a bare, white, limestone cliff, towered hundreds of feet into the sky on the northern side. Half a mile from its crest rose a lower peak. Between them lay the Gap, the first and most important key to the western wilderness.

Boone and his party struggled up the steep slope of the mountain, clearing a trail to the pass. Pausing on the windswept summit to rest their panting horses, they looked across the valley of the Cumberland to the long straight wall of Pine Mountain. The only break for passage over it in a hundred miles lay directly north, where the river slipped through a deep, narrow water gap. The Warrior's Path headed straight for that opening, clinging close to the southern bank of the river through it and for a short distance beyond to a long, shallow ford.[5]

After crossing the river, Boone turned northwest towards the Kentucky River and set his course across a region of steep, tangled ridges and narrow, winding valleys deeply cut by a network of rivers and creeks. He had nothing to guide him through that rugged country other than the trails of wild animals and the ancient beds of streams, but Boone had visited that region more than once, and he had a photographic memory for places and landmarks.

He followed the right bank of the Cumberland for about seven miles and then turned north to Flat Lick, a little valley between the hills. From there, he went up and down one dim trail after another, taking short cuts across the dividing ridges and the streams between them.

At Rockcastle River, which the party forded at Parker's Branch, Felix Walker recalled that they killed a fine bear on their way, camped all night, and had an excellent supper. He said, "On leaving that river we had to encounter and cut our way through a country of about twenty miles, entirely covered with dead brush, which we found a difficult and laborious task." [6]

He referred to the narrow valley of Roundstone Creek towards Big Hill Range, the last foothill of the Cumberland Plateau. South of it, the waters flow to the Cumberland River; north, to the Kentucky River, thirty miles away. Crossing Big Hill at "Boone's Gap," they followed a fork of Silver Creek to the present site of Berea College.

Again they had to cut a path through thick cane and reed. In Walker's words, "as the cane ceased, we began to discover the pleasing and rapturous appearance of the plains of Kentucky . . . So rich a soil we had never seen before; covered with clover in full bloom, the woods were abounding with wild game—turkeys so numerous that it might be said they appeared but one flock, universally scattered in the woods. A sight so delightful . . . it almost inclined us, in imitation of Columbus, to kiss the soil of Kentucky." [7]

The pathmakers had traveled two hundred miles, blazing the trail and marking the "mile" trees. They had selected fords at the wide streams and made log footbridges over the narrow ones. They had cleared the trail of undergrowth and fallen trees and had burned the dead brush. Another day would bring them to the river of their dreams.

While they slept that night, unguarded, the lurking danger of the wilderness crept close. At dawn the Indians struck, killing Captain Twetty and his Negro man and severely wounding Felix Walker. Some members of the party fled into the forest or back along the trail. The whole undertaking hung upon one man's coolness and courage.

That man, Daniel Boone, had no thought of turning back. He rallied his scattered men and set them to building a log pen fort. He wrote a letter to Judge Henderson and sent it back by a messenger. He nursed the wounded youth with the care of a father, and as soon as Walker could be moved, Boone and his party pushed on towards the Kentucky.

Late in the afternoon on April 1, the pathmakers came to a buffalo "trace" about twenty feet wide, beaten down two or three feet below the level of the forest floor. The weary men, who had been cutting a trail through a thick growth of cane since dawn, gratefully mounted their horses and rode at ease, two or three abreast.

The trace followed Otter Creek, Boone told those riding in front. It would lead to a salt lick near the Kentucky River. Then, riding back to the rear, he leaned from his saddle to speak a comforting word to Felix Walker, who lay upon a crude stretcher made of sapling poles and bearskins, and slung between two packhorses.

Suddenly those in front gave a cry and spurred their horses to a gallop. The others followed, all gazing open-mouthed at a herd of two or three hundred buffalo grazing in an open, level space.

The lumbering beasts, as startled as the men, rushed bellowing towards the river. Before the riders could reach the water's edge, the buffalo had crossed the stream, scrambled up the opposite bank, and disappeared in the forest.

Some of the men had started to follow the herd across the river, but Boone had called them back.

"We make camp on this side, men, by this spring," he said. "Yon river is the Cantuckey, the end of our trail. Make a shelter breast high in the hollow here under the sycamores; and set a watch for the night."

The woodsmen went at their tasks with skill acquired by long practice. The sound of their axes shattered the silence of twilight and set the birds twittering in the branches. A number of small trees soon came crashing to the ground. The men cut these into logs, which they notched and fitted together to form a log pen, laying branches across the top for a roof.

Two men then carefully lifted the stretcher upon which Walker was lying and carried it into the rude shelter. Others gathered fallen wood, started a fire by "flashing" some powder with flint and tinder, and hung up quarters of a freshly killed deer to roast.

Another group unloaded and watered the horses and tethered them where they could graze under the trees.

Camp chores were finished by the time the meat was cooked. Each man cut what he wanted with his hunting knife and sat down to eat it with a handful of parched corn from his leather pouch and a cup of water from the spring. When he had finished and the fire had been put out, he rolled up in a bearskin blanket on the ground with his rifle under his hand and his dog beside him. While their comrades slept, two watchmen sat against a tree, as silent and motionless as the shadows about them.

Daniel Boone had completed his important undertaking. The road he had made was only a rough bridle path through the dim forest, but he had chosen it wisely and marked it plainly. For his work as the first highway engineer of the West, as much as for any other achievement of his eventful life, he could rightly regard himself as "an instrument ordained to settle the wilderness."

Boone's Trace to the Kentucky owes its unique place in history largely to its timing. In 1775 such a pathway could have been made in no other region, and even in that region, the journey could have been made only in the brief period between the signing of the Shawnee Treaty and the outbreak of the Revolutionary War. It was planned and executed by a private land company for its own use, but the trail served the cause of liberty by clearing the way to the settlement of the first West during the struggle of the colonies for independence from Great Britain.[8]

The road toward free government was making new paths. The Cherokees had promised to meet and talk with their "white brothers." In this way the two races might come to understand each other better and might find that disagreements can be settled by other means than fighting.

CHAPTER IV

The Treaty of Watauga

A dark cloud hangs over that land.
It is bloody ground.

—DRAGGING CANOE

Sycamore Shoals, the place selected by the Cherokees for their council with representatives of the Transylvania Company, was in the valley of the Little Watauga, a branch of the Holston River. The settlers in that remote region were so out of touch with their government in North Carolina that they had organized a little republic of their own which they called "Watauga." By 1775 a fort bearing that name had become the center of all the frontier settlements in the upper Tennessee Valley.[1]

Indians had begun to assemble at Watauga even before Boone and his party left to mark out the trail to the Kentucky. For a week, the Transylvania representatives and the Cherokee chieftains bargained around the council fires and on March 17, 1775, came the final scene in that historic meeting.

In the background, forested foothills with patches of snow on their slopes rose to meet a stormy March sky. Below the hills, in the curve of the tree-fringed river, stretched a wide, level plane, with Fort Watauga in the center. Scores of wigwams and dozens of campfires filled the cleared space between the fort and the river. Whole carcasses of beef were roasting over trenches of glowing coals.

A thousand or more blanketed Indians moved about or squatted around the fires. The sharp wind bore the sounds of their guttural grunts and high-pitched voices, the yelps of dogs, the tinkle of bells, and the odors of singed meat and acrid wood smoke.[2]

Just below the hills, hundreds of frontiersmen from the valley settlements stood or walked about, talking in animated groups. Each held his long rifle in one hand, the leash of his dog in the other. A score or more kept watch over their horses, tied to the trees beyond the cleared space.

A group of white men in three-cornered hats, long capes, and knee breeches huddled about a plank table in front of the fort. Behind them, inside the fort, white and Negro men were busily sorting and stacking great piles of bundles and boxes.

The feeling of tension increased when everyone, as if at some secret signal, began to move towards the central group. There sat Judge Richard Henderson, president of the Transylvania Company, in earnest conversation with John Williams, its secretary.

The other representatives stood nearby—the three Hart brothers, two soldierly-looking men, John Luttrell, Jr., and Maj. Leonard Hendley Bullock; two native Scotsmen, William Johnston, a leading merchant of Hillsborough, and James Hogg, a prosperous merchant who had been in the Colony only a year.[3]

Richard Henderson had spent years in planning and organizing this company. He and his partners had staked a goodly fortune, ten thousand pounds in English money, upon the outcome of this venture. The company's goods—blankets, cloth, knives, hatchets, trinkets dear to the Indian heart—lay stacked within the fort, ready for delivery.

The Indians had finally agreed upon the boundaries. They had kindled the great council fire in the center of the clearing outside the fort. The hour for which Henderson had hoped and worked had come.

As the Cherokee chiefs approached the table where Henderson sat, a shrill voice rose in fiery speech. Henderson turned his head quickly and looked inquiringly at Thomas Price, an interpreter for the Indians.

"That is the die-hard, Dragging Canoe, again," said Price, pointing to a chief who had leaped in front of a crowd of braves, waving his arms to hold them back.

"Why should we sell our land?" cried Dragging Canoe. "What can we expect to get for it? Not more than a blanket or a hunting

Judge Richard Henderson, a study for the mural lunette, The Treaty of Watauga, in the capitol in Frankfort, Kentucky. By Gilbert White. Courtesy Cusick Studio, Frankfort.

shirt apiece. A dark cloud hangs over that land! It is bloody ground!"[4]

But Dragging Canoe stood alone. All the other chiefs had agreed to sell. Price went to where they stood in front of their warriors, their arms folded, their eagle-feathered headdresses waving in the breeze.

At a word from him, they came forward slowly—Oconostota, their "King," old and crippled, Savanooka, the "Raven Warrior," tiny Attacullacullah, their greatest statesman, weighing not more than a pound for each of his ninety years, two large scars on each wrinkled cheek, his ears banded with silver that hung almost to his shoulders.[5]

Silent, motionless, the Indians stood at one side of the table. With dignity equal to theirs, Judge Henderson and his partners took their places on the other side. James Robertson, head of the Watuaga settlement, John Sevier, Isaac Shelby, and other frontier leaders drew near the partners. The circle of white men and Indians, crowded and massed rank upon rank, closed in about them.

In tense silence, John Williams lifted a long parchment from the table. He began to read it, slowly and distinctly. As he paused after each sentence, Price turned to the chiefs and translated what Williams had read. The eyes of the motionless Indians shifted from one speaker to the other as they listened to the words describing the boundaries of the "Great Grant."

All that tract, territory or parcel of land, . . . **beginning** on the said Ohio River at the mouth of Kentucky, . . . from thence running up the said river . . . to the top ridge of Powell's Mountain thence westwardly along the ridge of said mountain unto a point from which a northwest course will hit or strike the head spring of the most southwardly branch of Cumberland River, thence down the said river including all its waters to the Ohio River, thence up the said river as it meanders to the beginning.[6]

"All that tract . . . Kentucky! . . . Powell! . . . Cumberland! . . . Ohio!"

There was a stir, a swift intake of breath. Did those hundreds of pairs of beady black eyes close for a moment? Did the wind send a shiver through the crowd?

Williams hastily picked up a shorter document. "Your land lies between that country and ours," he said. "It is good to have the path clear and clean. We have given you more goods and guns and powder to let us cross your country. This 'Path Deed' gives us the right to pass through your villages on the Holston River, between Watauga and Powell's Mountain."

When Price had translated the last sentence, Williams dipped a quill pen in the ink bottle and offered it to him. Price held it out to Oconostota, who slowly came forward and took it. Then the old chief, followed by Attacullacullah and Savanooka, bent over the table and signed the "Great Grant" and the "Path Deed" by making his mark as Price directed.

Henderson and his partners drew a deep breath of relief. At last, their Cherokee Treaties were signed, sealed, delivered, in the presence of witnesses, according to the ancient customs and laws of the white race.

The Treaty of Watauga from a mural painting in the capitol in Frankfort. Courtesy Cusick Studio.

The red race had a different and probably more ancient way of sealing and witnessing its treaties. At a sign from Oconostota,

a young warrior stepped from the crowd, holding high with both
hands the gaily decorated stem of a large peace pipe of carved
stone. The Cherokee chieftains and the Transylvania partners
squatted on the ground in a circle around the council fire.

Stepping lightly inside the circle, the young brave held the pipe
to Oconostota's lips. The old chief drew a deep breath, then blew
the smoke up, down, around him. The bearer next offered it to
Henderson who carefully repeated the ritual. Then he held it to
the next chief, the next white man in turn, until each one in the
circle had sealed in smoke the Treaty of Watauga.

Many of those Indians had witnessed the Treaty of Lochaber
four years earlier. In that treaty the Cherokees had solemnly
agreed to make no changes in their boundaries unless they were
authorized by an agent of the king of England. As they bade farewell to the partners, one repeated what he had said earlier to
Boone: "You have bought a fair land, brothers; but you will have
much trouble in holding it." [7]

His words held a double meaning, but Richard Henderson had
gone too far to heed warnings or prophecies.[8] Other companies,
as he well knew, were dickering for grants of lands on the western
waters. His own party must be the first to cross the mountains, the
first to make a settlement beyond them during that year of peace.

His trailblazers had had a week's start. A band of adventurers
was waiting to go with him; his wagons were loaded, his horses
ready.

His next command would be, "To the West! Forward! March!"

CHAPTER V

"An Expedition to Cantuckey in 1775"

*Every person views life from his own angle, which
is different from every other man's standpoint,
and no one can see the whole view.*

—WICKS

Richard Henderson kept careful records. One section of his
journal is headed, "An Expedition to Cantuckey in 1775." From
that Journal and his letters to his partners in North Carolina, we
get the viewpoint of an anxious executive, burdened with the
responsibility for the success of the whole undertaking.

Henderson left Watauga on Monday, March 20, 1775, three
days after the treaty with the Cherokees was signed. His partner,
John Luttrell, Jr., and his young brother, Samuel Henderson, were
with him. Later, when joined by the party led by Nathaniel and
David Hart, the company included forty mounted men, besides
a number of white boys and Negro men on foot. They had forty
packhorses, a string of wagons loaded with supplies of ammunition, salt, seeds, and provisions, and a drove of cattle to kill for
food along the way.

It took this large caravan ten days to reach Captain Martin's
Station in Powell Valley. They built a cabin there and stored
the wagons. They also hid some of their lead, powder, salt and
other heavy supplies, ". . . as we could not possibly clear the way
any further."

At Martin's they met other adventurers bound for the Kentucky wilderness. Among them was the young frontier soldier,

Benjamin Logan, who had migrated from Augusta County in
Virginia to the Holston Valley after Lord Dunmore's War.
On April 5 they set out, traveling together for greater safety.

> Friday, 7th. About break of day it began to snow. About
> 11 o'clock, received a letter from Mr. John Luttrell's camp
> that there were five persons killed by the Indians on the road
> to the Cantuckey. Same day, received a letter from Daniel
> Boone, that his company was fired upon by Indians who
> killed two of his men, though he kept the ground and saved
> the baggage, etc.[1]

Boone had also written:

> My advice to you, sir, is to come or send as soon as pos-
> sible—for the people are very uneasy. Now is the time to
> flusterate the intentions of the Indians, and keep the country
> whilst we are in it.

Henderson gave Boone's letter and some of his own mail to a
messenger to take back to his partners in North Carolina. He then
ordered the line to march on.

> Saturday 8th. Started about 10 o'clock, crossed Cumber-
> land Gap. About four miles from it, met about 40 persons
> returning. Could prevail on only one to return. Several Vir-
> ginians who were with us turned back from here. Henderson's
> men were wavering and ready to go home.

If Boone himself should be among the next group fleeing from the
wilderness, then, without doubt, all would leave. Henderson
somehow had to get word to Boone that he was on the way.

Halting the company, he asked for a volunteer to ride ahead and carry a message to Boone. The men shifted about uneasily, but not one spoke or moved forward. At last, to Henderson's great relief, William Cocke, who had left his young wife in the fort at Watauga while he went adventuring, stepped out from the crowd.

"Judge Henderson, I'll take your note to Captain Boone," he said.

This offer, extraordinary as it was, we could by no means refuse. We fixed Mr. Cocke off with a good Queen Ann's musket, plenty of ammunition, a tomahawk, a large knife, a Dutch Blanket, and no small quantity of jerked beef. Thus equipped, and mounted on a tolerable good horse . . . Mr. Cocke started from Cumberland River . . . and carried with him . . . a considerable burden of my own uneasiness.[2]

Still they met people fleeing down the trail, spreading dismay among Henderson's party.

Every group of travelers we saw, or strange bells which we heard in front, was a fresh alarm . . . Some hesitated and stole back, privately . . . Many came on, though their hearts, for some hours, made part of the deserting company.

Sunday, 16th. About 12 o'clock met James McAfee with eight other persons, returning from Cantuckey.

The McAfees, having finished work on improvements on their land near Salt River, were returning to their homes in Virginia. Against James McAfee's advice, two of his brothers joined the Transylvanians and went back to the Kentucky with them.

At about the same place where they met the McAfees, Benjamin Logan left Henderson's company with one or two white men and a few Negroes he had brought with him. Choosing a trail that branched off to the west, he struck out through the unmapped wilderness to select a place for a settlement of his own.

Things soon began to look brighter for Henderson. He found notes that William Cocke had tied to saplings along the trail to tell of his progress. Two days later he learned that his messenger had reached Boone in safety.

Tuesday 18th. Traveled about 16 miles. Met Michael Stoner with packhorses to assist us. Camped that night in the eye of the rich land. Stoner brought excellent beef in plenty.

Wednesday 19th. Traveled about 16 miles, and camped on Otter Creek—a good mill place.

Another diary of that first journey over Boone's Trace was written by William Calk, the prosperous owner of a mill, a store, and a plantation in Virginia.[3] Hearing of Henderson's plan for a western settlement, Calk had packed up his surveying outfit and set forth with four friends to see for himself the much-talked-of western country. His diary, written on two sheets of parchment, gives an account of the trials and hazards, the homely details and incidents of wilderness travel.

William Calk his *Jornal*. 1775 March 13th Mond. I set out from prince wm. [County] to travel to Caintuck. On tuesday Night our company all Got together at Mr. Prises on Rapadan, Which was Abraham hanks, philip Drake, Eanock Smith, Robert Whitledge & my Self. Thear abrams Dogs leg got broke by Drake's dog.

From this start in northeastern Virginia, Calk's party had made its way over mountains "that tired us all almost to death" towards Cumberland Gap. They were delayed by snow storms. They got lost while hunting.

Thursd 30th: we Set out again and went down to Elk gardin and there Suplid our Selves with Seed Corn & irish tators . . . I turned my hors to drive afore me & he got Scard. Ran away threw Down the Saddel Bags & Broke three of our powder goards & Abrams flask, Burst open a walet of corn & lost a good deal & made a turrabel flustration amongst the Reast of the horses . . . we cacht them all agin & went on & lodged at John Duncans.[4]

They bought bacon at Duncan's and meal at Briley's mill farther on. The next night they lodged on Clinch Mountain "By a large Cainbraike & Cuckt our Suppers." On Tuesday, April 4, they arrived at Martin's Station in Powell Valley, where they overtook Henderson's company "Bound for Caintuck."

Wednesday ye 5th Breaks away fair & we go on down the valey & camp on indian Creek. We had this creek to cross many times & very Bad Banks. Abrams Saddel turned & the load all fell in. We got out this Eavening and Kill two Deer.

On Thursday, Calk's little party had waited for Henderson's to catch up with it. The next morning came a heavy snow which forced them to remain in camp, "Being in number about 40 men & Some Neagros. This Eavening Comes a letter from Capt. Boon at caintuck of the indians doing mischief and Some turns Back."[5]

. . . William Calk His Jurnal April ye 8th 1775 Satterday We all pact up and started Crost Cumberland Gap. About one oclock this Day we Met a great maney peopel turned Back for fear of the Indians. But our Company goes on Still with good courage. We come to a very ugly Creek with Steep Banks & have it to Cross several times." [This was Yellow Creek between Cumberland and Pine Mountain.]

The company remained in camp the following Monday.

. . . Some goes out ahunting, I & two more goes up a very
large mountain. Near the top we Saw the track of two indians
& whear they had lain unter Some Rocks . . . At night Capt.
hart comes up with his packs & there they hide Some of thier
lead to lighten thier packs that they may travel faster.
. . . tuesday 11th this is a very loury morning & like for
Rain but we all agree to Start Early. We Cross Cumberland
River & travel Down it about 10 miles through Some turrabel
Cainbreakes. As we went down abrams mair Ran into the
River With her load and Swam over. He folowed her & got
on her & made her Swim Back agin. It is a very Raney
Eavening. We take up camp near Richland Creek . . . Mr.
Drake Bakes Bread without Washing his hands. We keep
Sentry this Night for fear of the indians . . Next day they
found Richland Creek too high to ford.
. . . We toat our packs over on a tree & Swim our horses
over. There we meet another Company going Back. They
tell Such News Abram & Drake is afraid to go aney
further . . . This day we meet about 20 more turning Back.

On Saturday, the fifteenth, they met some men "that turns &
goes with us. We travel this Day through the plais Caled the
Bressh & cross Rockcastle River." There Calk noted that they had
fine food for their horses.

. . . Sunday 16th: Cloudy & warm. We start Early & go on
about 2 miles down the River and then turn up a creek
that we crost about 50 times [Rounstone] . . . The Eavening
we git over to the waters of Caintuck & go a little Down
the creek; & there we camp. Keep Sentry the fore part of
the night. It Rains very hard all night . . .

About eleven o'clock on Tuesday the eighteenth, they met four
men from Boone's camp "that Caim to conduck us on. We camp
this night just on the Begining of the Good land. . . ."

Wednesd 19th: Smart frost this morning. They kill 3

Bofelos. About 11 o clock we come to where the indians
fired on Boone Companey & kild 2 men and a dog & wounded
one man in the thigh. We campt this night on oter [Otter]
creek—
. . . Thursday 20th this morning is Clear & cool. We start
Early & git Down to Caintuck to Boons foart about 12 oclock
wheare we Stop. They Come out to meet us & welcome us in
with a voley of guns.

The party had reached Boone's camp in Kentucky. To William
Calk each mile of the journey had been filled with interest, each
mishap a challenge to his sturdy good humor. However, the poor
Negroes in the party, who had imagined they saw an Indian
behind every tree, shouted with joy and relief at the sight of
Boone's little unfinished cabins.

Richard Henderson president of the company, evidently shared
their feeling.

After being for one whole month . . . traveling in a
barren desert country . . . our horses packed beyond their
strength . . . no part of the road tolerable . . . our people
jaded and dispirited with fatigue, and what was worse, often
pinched for victuals. To get clear of all this at once, was as
much as we could well bear.

Riding into his wilderness settlement with escort and salute,
he questioned whether "a happier creature was to be found under
the sun." The dinner of "cold water and lean buffalo beef, without
bread," celebrated Henderson's fortieth birthday, and he declared it ". . . the most joyous banquet I ever saw."[6]

CHAPTER VI

A Place of Defense

Our fortress is the good greenwood,
Our tent the cypress tree;
We know the forest round us
As seamen know the sea.
—WILLIAM CULLEN BRYANT

Judge Henderson saw at once that Boone's half-fortified camp was entirely too small for both companies, which now numbered about eighty men. Besides, he ". . . found Captain Boone's men as inattentive, on the score of fear . . . as if they had been in their homes in Hillsborough. A small fort wanting two or three days' work to make it tolerably safe, was totally neglected on Mr. Cocke's arrival."[1]

The site of Boone's camp was a low, sheltered grove about sixty yards from the river, near an abundant spring of fresh water. Between it and the river lay the bare, trampled space to which wild animals had come for centuries to lick the salty earth around a sulphur spring. Near these springs grew three great sycamores and a large elm tree.

Henderson chose a site for his fort on higher ground, about three hundred yards south of Boone's cabins, with the lick spring and the gigantic trees between them. He put the surveyors to work staking off the bounds, while he drew a plan for it.

Such forts were of the utmost importance to the safety of people on the frontier. The outer walls of this first fort erected in Kentucky formed an oblong enclosing about an acre of ground. One long side lay parallel with the steep bank of the river; the op-

41

posite side faced the stump-filled clearing between the fort and the forest.

The back of the twenty-six one-story cabins formed a part of the outside walls, with a large two-story blockhouse at each corner. The shed-shaped roofs sloped inward. Long poles were tied to the rafters with thin, flexible strips of bark or hickory to keep the roof boards in place.

A stockade of log pickets twice the height of a man filled the gaps between blockhouses and cabins. These were set up in deep trenches filled with firmly packed earth. Horizontal wooden bars a foot or two above the ground held the pickets together. They also provided a foothold for the men in the fort to fire through the loopholes in the stockade without being seen from the outside.

The loopholes, bored in the outside walls of the blockhouses and cabins, were beveled so that rifles fired through them would have a wide range. Heavy double gates in the middle of each long side of the fort were made of split logs and hung on wooden hinges. When the gates were closed and the wooden bars dropped in place behind them, such a fort was practically proof against every possible form of attack except cannon.[2]

Remembering the Indian scares on the journey, Henderson was impatient to get his fort built. He soon learned that he had not taken into consideration the magnitude of the task or the other interests and demands of life in the wilderness. It took his workmen a week to fell and clear away the trees on the fort side. That was no small achievement with the hand tools then in use. On the following Saturday Henderson wrote in his *Journal* that they had ". . . begun a little house for magazine but did not finish it."

This small cabin, built half below ground and covered with clay, was intended as a storage place for the company's supply of ammunition. Simple as it was, and essential as it was to their safety, it could not be completed until "Wednesday, May 3rd."

Henderson moved from his tent into the first blockhouse that was ready, using it for the company's headquarters. He set up a "company store" in one of the first cabins. There the pioneers could buy for their own use powder and lead and other wilderness necessities that the company had brought from Watauga with such difficulty.

One entry on the company's books charged Michael Stoner with "7 3s 6d [seven pounds, three shillings, sixpence] for powder, lead and osnaburgs" [a heavy, canvaslike cloth], and credited him with "10 10s for work making roads to Cantucke." Another on Friday, May 5, shows that Henderson "let Mr. Wm. Cocke have five yards and a half of osnaburgs off my old tent for which I charge him 5s 6d Va Money." [3]

In spite of all that both Henderson and Boone could do to hasten the work, the year ended with the fort still unfinished. On June 12, Henderson wrote that he doubted if it would ever be completed "unless the Indians could do us a favor by annoying us, and regularly scalping a man every week until it is performed."

Yet his own *Journal* mentions several good reasons for the delay. The food situation at Boonesborough had been critical from the very beginning. Herds of wild game no longer stayed obligingly within easy range. The most skillful hunters sometimes had to travel twenty miles or more from base to find any game at all.

Wednesday . . . Hunters not returned. No meat but fat bear. Almost starved . . . Mr. Calloways men got a little spoiled buffalo and elk, which we made out with pretty well. Thursday . . . Sent off Mr. Stoner with Capt. Calloway and some of his men in search of persons above mentioned . . . 3 o'clock. Hunters came in but no news of lost men." Sunday . . . Men returned . . . had been lost. Michael Stoner, our hunter not returned; was expected yesterday; *no meat*. Our salt *quite out*—except about a quart which I brought from Harrodsburg.[4]

In addition to their concern about safety and food, Henderson and his partners kept in mind the purpose of this daring and costly venture—to promote the sale of the land purchased from the Cherokees.

They had advertised their "Proposals for the encouragement of settling the lands" as early as Christmas. That proposal offered twenty shillings a hundred acres to each emigrant settling in the country and raising a crop of corn before September 1, 1775. It was an attractive offer to frontier people.[5]

Most of the men who came with Boone and Henderson expected to "take up" land from the company on those terms. Those prospective purchasers could not be kept waiting long. On the day after the company arrived at the Kentucky, the surveyors began to lay off "town" lots. William Calk made some interesting comments on that subject:

> Friday 21st. Warm. This Day they Begin laying off lots in the town and preparing for peopel to go to worck to make corn.
> Saturday 22nd . . . they finished laying out lots. This Eavening I went afishing and Catcht 3 cats . . .
> April Sunday 23rd. This morning the peopel meets and Draws for Chois of loots. This is a very warm day.
> Monday 24th. We all view our loots and Some Don't like them. About 12 o'clock the Combsses come to town & next morning they make them a bark caneu and Set off down the River to meet thier Companey.[6]

Henderson noted that the two McAfees and some others did not want to draw at all. On the contrary, "They wanted to go down the river Cantuckey, about 50 miles, near Capt. Harrot's settlement—where they had begun improvements and left them on the late alarm. I informed them myself, in the hearing of all attending, that such a settlement should not entitle them to lands from us."

Even his own partners did not see eye to eye with the president about the relative importance of their company's affairs and their own private interests:

> Mr. Hart having made choice of a piece of ground for his own & people's cultivation. . . . I suppose, will be able to render

sufficient reasons to the company for withdrawing from our
camp and refusing to join in building a fort for our mutual
defense . . .
  Friday 28th Mr. Luttrell chose a piece of ground about ¾
mile from the fort and set three of his people to work. Two
remained with me to assist in clearing about where the fort
is to stand.[7]

How the other adventurers viewed the situation can be inferred
from William Calk's account of his own activities.

Tuesday 25th. In the Eavening we git us a plaise of Defence
to keep the indians off . . .
Satterday 29th. We git our house kivered with Bark & move
our things into it at Night and Begin housekeeping, Eanock
Smith, Robert Whitledge & my Self.
Monday May ye first. I go out to look for my mair and Saw
4 Bofelos, the Being the first Ever I Saw & I Shot one of
them but did not git him . . . When I caim home Eanock &
Robin had found the mair & was gone out a hunting . . .
Tuesday 3d, I went out in the morning kild a turkey and
come in & got Some on for my Breakfast, and then went
& Sot in to Clearing for corn.[8]

Boone's party had planted some corn before Henderson arrived.
More was planted after he came, with some men guarding those
who cleared and plowed the land. Every man, as the terms of settlement required him to do, was anxious to make a clearing and
plant "Seed Corn and irish tators" on his own "plaise" before it
was too late.
  Neither Henderson nor Calk mentions what was probably the
strongest reason for the delay in building the fort. For one entire
month, in frost and snow and rain, those men at Boonesborough
had been obliged to keep together on a long and dangerous journey.
Now, in comparative safety at the end of the trail, they had relaxed. Nothing less than the actual sight of painted Indians or the

sound of a bloodcurdling war whoop could have held them steadily at any sustained task.

No man or boy in that company could resist the charm of that "pleasing and rapturous country" in its springtime freshness and beauty. Even Henderson welcomed at times an excuse to throw off his load of care. On Sunday, May 7, he went into the woods with his brothers and Captain Boone to search for a stray horse; and, although he was no woodsman, he stayed out with them all night.

Upon his return to headquarters, he found two visitors from Kentucky's first settlement: "Capt. Harrod and Col. Slaughter from Harrod's Town on Dick's River."

As he greeted his guests, Richard Henderson must have realized that he faced a problem harder than that of building a "plaise of defence" to keep the Indians off. He did not want to talk about a question so many-sided as land titles in the new region.

CHAPTER VII

The Colony of Transylvania

All power is originally in the people.

—RICHARD HENDERSON

Harrod and Slaughter were not Henderson's first visitors from the Salt River settlements. Capt. John Floyd had come several days earlier to ask on what terms his company of young men could settle on the lands of the Transylvania Company.

Floyd was assistant to Col. William Preston, surveyor of Fincastle County, Virginia, who was violently opposed to any recognition of the Transylvania Company's title to land in the Kentucky wilderness. Floyd's request was evidently made in good faith and his company included two young lawyers and ". . . several other young gents of good families," just the kind of adventurers that Henderson would most like to interest in his company. Henderson decided that he could trust that "honest, open countenance," and made generous promises of land to Floyd for himself and his companions.[1]

The two visitors from Harrodsburg presented a very different problem. James Harrod had begun his settlement a year earlier on land included in the Transylvania purchase, and Henderson had thought of his first meeting with him ". . . not without considerable anxiety and some fear."

Harrod and Slaughter made no request for terms of settlement on the company's land. Instead, they got into an argument the next morning about their own rival land claims on Salt River, and Slaughter, to Henderson's great embarrassment, appealed to him to settle the dispute.

47

"Captain Harrod and his men from the Monongahela," Slaughter explained, "had selected the best tracts of land before we came, but they were not satisfied with one choice tract apiece. When my company came out later from other parts of Virginia, we could find no good springs that they had not already claimed for themselves."

Henderson, as a judge in court, probably would have decided for Slaughter. But here he was not a judge; he was the president of the Transylvania Company. If he took sides with either, or told them that neither had any rightful claim, by what law and by what power could he enforce his decision?

Although not one of them would openly have admitted the fact, they all knew that they were on forbidden land, under the king's law or Virginia's, or both. The subject of land titles might explode like a keg of powder. A chance word might provide the spark to set it off. Henderson cast about in his mind for a safer topic of conversation "to divert the debate of this irritating subject." [2]

"Surely there is land enough for all," he suggested. "But what will it be worth to any of us, unless we find some way to enforce law and order? How can we hope to remain in this country unless we provide for our mutual defense and stop the destruction of our wild game? I have thought of a plan, if you gentlemen wish to hear it."

Seeing that he had their attention, Henderson warmed to his subject, outlining his plan as he talked. He wrote, "The reception this plan met with from these gentlemen, as well as Captain John Floyd, . . . gave us great pleasure; and therefore we immediately set about the business."

> Appointed Tuesday, May 23rd, instant, at Boonesborough, for the meeting of delegates, and accordingly made out writings for the different towns to sign and wrote to Capt. Floyd appointing an election. Harrodsburgh and the Boiling Spring Settlement received their summons verbally.[3]

The next day Henderson's guests from Salt River "took their departure in great good humor."

On Saturday, May 20, the citizens of Boonesborough elected their representatives. On the twenty-third, the delegates from the other settlements—Harrodsburg, Boiling Spring, and St. Asaph's (Logan's)—rode up to the log headquarters of the Transylvania Company and presented their credentials ". . . as duly elected for the several towns and settlements."

Looking about for a place to hold the meetings, Henderson noticed again the beautiful tree, "one of the finest elms that perhaps nature ever produced," between his camp and the river. That "divine tree," he decided, should be their council chamber.

Seventeen lawmakers, free men elected by a majority in their communities, assembled on Wednesday, May 24, 1775, to organize a form of government for the wilderness settlements. They unanimously chose Col. Thomas Slaughter as chairman and Matthew Jouett as clerk of the assembly. The Reverend John Lythe of Harrodsburg opened the meeting with prayer.

The chairman then sent a committee to notify the proprietors that the "House of Delegates for the Colony of Transylvania" was ready for business. "And Colonel Richard Henderson, in behalf of himself and the rest of the proprietors, opened the convention with a speech."

The backwoods legislators were dressed in deerskin hunting shirts and leggings. Some of them, as John Floyd later described his own appearance, were "as shabby as a turkey buzzard in May." [4] But the president of the colony read his carefully prepared speech with as much formality and dignity as if he had been addressing the British Parliament in London.

Some of his phrases, strange at the time, now have a familiar ring to American ears. "All power is originally in the people," he read; and, as "laws derive force and efficiency from our mutual consent," they should be made for the benefit of all. In closing, Henderson assured the assembly that the proprietors would agree to any laws it passed to promote the happiness of "this newborn country." Then, after giving the chairman a copy of his address, he bowed to the assembly and returned to his log headquarters in the fort.

Most of the delegates were more at home with a rifle than a

pen, but Matthew Jouett's minutes indicate that all of them were familiar with the centuries-old procedures of English lawmaking bodies.

In a crowded three-day session, they passed nine bills with order and speed. The preacher delegate, John Lythe, offered "a bill to prevent profane swearing and Sabbath-breaking"; Daniel Boone presented two: "a bill to preserve game" and "a bill to preserve the range," the natural pasture on which both wild game and domestic animals depended for food. The other bills arranged for courts and legal procedures, for regulating the militia, and for writs of attachment and fees for clerks and sheriffs.[5]

The delegates had on their minds, however, some things that the president had not mentioned in his address. For one thing, they wanted an understanding with the proprietors regarding the rights and duties of both parties. On motion of John Todd, a delegate from Logan's settlement, the chairman appointed a committee to "draw up a compact between the proprietors and the people of this colony" that would define "the powers of the one and the liberties of the other."

The settlers thoroughly detested the proprietary system of land ownership such as the Transylvania Company planned to set up, under which a purchaser lost his title if he failed to pay a yearly "quitrent." At the time of the Cherokee purchase, most of the colonial governments had yielded to the insistent demands of their people and abolished that feudal custom, but they had continued another practice, to which actual settlers objected just as strongly. It was the custom of selling, or granting, enormous tracts of land to wealthy persons or political favorites who left all the risks of developing such land to others.

The delegates at Boonesborough feared that the Transylvania Company might do the same thing in order to interest prominent people in their venture. To prevent that, if possible, they sent a committee to ask the proprietors not to grant land to any person or group except on the same terms that they had given to the first comers.

Richard Henderson and his partners felt that they had the right to manage their affairs as they pleased. Yet they did not want to offend the delegates by an outright refusal. How could they sidetrack this new "irritating subject"?

Henderson's eye fell upon John Farrow, the lawyer for the Cherokees, who had just arrived to complete the formal transfer of the land, according to the ancient law of "livery of seizing." "We shall have the ceremony performed before the delegates," he said to his partners. "That will give us a chance to show them our title deed from the first owners of the soil in Transylvania."

The next day, accompanied by Farrow, he came before the assembly with the Watauga document in his hand and invited the delegates to make a record of its boundaries in their minutes. Then he turned to Farrow, who stooped and cut a piece of sod from the ground and offered it to him.

While both men held this symbol of ownership, Farrow said, "I hereby declare my 'livery of seizing' of this land, on behalf of the Cherokee Nation." To which Henderson replied, "I accept this sod on behalf of the Transylvania Company of North Carolina." That feudal ceremony was the only answer the delegates ever received to their request.

The committee appointed to draw up the compact made its report on the last day of the session. Americans, reading it today, would think that the proprietors reserved too many rights and powers for themselves. However, they should not fail to note one provision, a very unusual one at that time, for "perfect religious freedom and toleration." [6]

Since the next day was Sunday, Henderson invited the delegates and visitors to remain for one more meeting. The elm tree "Capitol" became their church and the speaker's stand the pulpit. Everyone in the settlement, white and Negro, attended the service.

Together, they joined in the responses as the Reverend John Lythe from Harrodsburg read the service of the Church of England. They stood to sing old, familiar hymns. Together, they knelt in the sweet, white clover and prayed "for all sorts and conditions of men." For the first and perhaps the last time, there was prayer on Kentucky soil for "His Most Gracious Majesty, King George the Third."

It had been a good meeting, the out-of-town delegates decided, as they jogged along the trails that afternoon, keeping a sharp lookout for anything unusual. However, as they drew near the first clearing of their settlements, another thought must have struck some of them like a blow between the eyes.

Just what had the assembly done about quitrents, large grants, absentee landlords, and legal title to the claims of earlier settlers? [7]

There were hard questions, to be answered as people faced the problems of ownership and the responsibilities of governing.

CHAPTER VIII

". . . The County of Kentucky"

A sense of history . . . is a sign of maturity.
—W. STEWART MCCULLOUGH

Settlers who were locating land under the terms offered by the Transylvania Company had good reason to feel concerned about their titles. As early as February, 1775, the royal governor of North Carolina had warned all persons ". . . against having any dealings with the said Richard Henderson as every Treaty with the Indians is illegal, null and void." [1]

The governor of Virginia, a few days after the meeting at Watauga, had denounced Henderson and his partners as ". . . disorderly persons" who had ". . . set up a claim to lands of the Crown within the limits of this Colony" and had threatened them with imprisonment if they did not immediately leave the country.

Every man in the wilderness had heard of those official warnings. Henderson had even referred to them in his speech to the assembly as Boonesborough. He realized that he must quickly do something to remove disturbing doubts about his company's title, but to whom or to what authority could he appeal against the king's own governors?

The Revolutionary War was beginning. Early in June a traveler brought news of the fighting at Lexington and Concord in Massachusetts. Every traveler brought later news, and sometimes papers five or six weeks old. Richard Henderson read them eagerly. Somewhere, he thought, in that strong tide of protest against the king and his ministers, he might find a clue to his question about titles. By August he had a plan ready. Leaving John Floyd in

charge of his company's affairs at Boonesborough, he hurried back
to North Carolina to consult his partners.[2]

His plan was to send a member of his company to the Continental Congress to ask that body to recognize Transylvania's title
to the Cherokee land and to accept his "Colony" on equal terms
with the other English colonies in America.

At their meeting in September in Oxford, North Carolina, the
partners prepared a Memorial to the Continental Congress, re-
questing it to ". . . take the infant Colony of Transylvania into
their protection." [3] They chose shrewd, capable James Hogg to
present it and to act as their delegate.[4]

James Hogg arrived in Philadelphia late in October. On his return to North Carolina in January, 1776, he sent Judge Henderson
a detailed report on his diplomatic mission. It would repay anyone interested in the state of public opinion and the progress of
democratic ideas at that time to read his remarkable letter. Quoted
here are some parts directly related to the fortunes of the Transylvania Company:

> Mr. Hooper [of North Carolina] introduced me to the
> famous Samuel and John Adams; and as I found their opinion
> friendly to the new Colony, I showed them our map, and ex-
> plained the advantages of our situation. But the difficulty that
> occurred to us soon appeared to them. 'We fear the results
> of taking under our protection a body of people who have
> defied the King's Proclamation! . . .
>
> They were pleased with our memorial; but . . . they ob-
> served that we were within the Virginia charter. They advised
> me to sound the Virginians, as they would not choose to do
> anything in it without their consent. . . .
>
> I was several times with Mr. Deans, of Connecticut. He
> will send some people to see our country; but he says he will
> have nothing to do with us unless he is pleased with our form
> of government. Quitrents, they all say, is a mark of vas-
> salage. . . .
>
> Some days later I met Mr. Jefferson and Mr. George

Wythe, who seriously examined our map and asked many questions. They observed that our purchase was within their charter. . . . I observed that our settlement would be a great check on the Indians. . . .

Mr. Jefferson said that it was his wish to see a free Government at the back of theirs. But he would not consent that we should be acknowledged by the congress, until the matter had the approval of the Virginia Assembly; and that, for that purpose, we should send one of our Company to their next Convention.[5]

Before the next meeting of the Virginia legislature, it received a petition signed by eighty-eight uneasy inhabitants ". . . of that part of North America, now denominated Transylvania," setting forth their grievances against the company and their anxiety about their land titles. They humbly implored ". . . to be taken under the protection of the honorable Convention of the Colony of Virginia, of which we can not help thinking ourselves still a part." [6]

Virginia, however, could spare neither time nor thought that fateful summer to consider the plight of a couple of hundred adventurers in the western wilderness. All her energies were centered at Philadelphia, where the Continental Congress was desperately trying to solve the problems of all the colonies in America.

In June, Richard Henry Lee, a delegate to that Congress, offered a resolution that the Colonies ". . . are, and of right ought to be, free and independent states." John Hancock, president of the Continental Congress, appointed another Virginian, Thomas Jefferson, as chairman of a committee to draft a document that would set forth the reasons for that resolution.

On July 4, 1776, the delegates adopted Jefferson's report, the Declaration of Independence.

About a month after that memorable event, a young man visited Patrick Henry, the first elected governor of Virginia, at his country home near Richmond. The visitor was in his early twenties, with piercing blue eyes, ruddy skin, and wavy, reddish hair tied in a queue at the back of his neck. He wore the uniform of a militia captain.

He introduced himself as George Rogers Clark, ". . . a son of your former client, Mr. John Clark, in Caroline County."

"Yes, yes," replied the governor. "I recall that you were with Dunmore at Fort Pitt in '74. Captain Clark, now, I see. Where have you been since then?"

"I went back to surveying down the Ohio. Last year, Col. Hancock Lee made me a deputy surveyor on the Kentucky. I never saw a richer or more beautiful country, your Excellency. I have just come from there now. I have a petition—"

"What! Another? From those Transylvania people?"

"Oh, no! This is from the people of Harrod's Town, Virginia settlers in the Salt River Valley. They will have nothing to do with the Henderson party. They held an election in June and chose John Gabriel Jones and myself as delegates to the assembly from the 'Committee of West Fincastle.' They want Virginia to set up a county government in that region. We started at once, but the assembly had adjourned before we could get to Williamsburg. I came on here, as I thought you might like to see our petition." [7]

Governor Henry glanced rapidly through the paper which Clark handed him.

"Very, very interesting," he commented. "I suppose you know that the assembly already has two other petitions from that region. It can do nothing about the matter, however, until it meets again in October."

"But, Mr. Henry!" Clark exclaimed. "The Indians may not wait until October! We are in great need of supplies, especially gunpowder. Can not the governor of Virginia order five hundred pounds of powder at once to defend her frontier and protect her citizens?"

The governor replied that he really did not have the power. "But," he added, "the Executive Council has. I will send you to it with a request.

"Mr. Thomas Jefferson, one of your father's neighbors, is a member of the Council," he continued, as he gave a note to Clark and wished him godspeed.

Clark found Mr. Jefferson and the other members of the Executive Council in Williamsburg interested and sympathetic, but they hesitated to grant his request.

"The law does not provide for any such action on our part," they told him. "We shall gladly lend the powder as we would to friends in distress, but you will have to pay for it if the assembly later refuses to receive those people as citizens and to uphold Virginia's title to the country."

Clark replied that he could not afford to take that risk, and again reminded the Executive Council that the power was not for himself, but to defend Virginia's land and her citizens.

At last the council gave him an order for the ammunition, but told him that he would have to bear the expense of getting it to the Kentucky stations.

Clark took the order and left. Later he returned it, with a note in which he stated that he could not accept it. He was sorry, he wrote, ". . . to find that we should have to seek protection elsewhere, which I did not doubt of getting." As for Virginia's interests, he pointedly added that ". . . if a country is not worth protecting, it was not worth claiming."

That note brought the desired results. "I was sent for," he wrote. ". . . Orders were immediately issued, dated August 23d, 1776, for conveying those stores to Pittsburg and there to await further orders from me."

Harrod's Town was a long way from Pittsburg, but Clark had gained his major point. "Being a little prejudiced in favor of my mother country I was willing to meet halfway."[8]

The final scenes in the struggle for political control of the Kentucky wilderness took place in the colonial capitol in Williamsburg. When the assembly met there in October, Clark and Jones presented the Harrod's Town petition for a separate county. Richard Henderson and William Hooper, two able lawyers from North Carolina, were present to plead for the recognition of Transylvania as a new colony or state.

To get the matter started, Thomas Jefferson offered a resolution on October 11 that ". . . the inhabitants of the western part of Fincastle . . . ought to be formed into a distinct county." His

James Hogg, representative of the colony of Transylvania, interviews members of the Continental Congress asking their support of the request of his company for admission to Congress as the fourteenth colony. Bronze tablet on the Henderson County courthouse. Courtesy Robert Worth Bingham.

resolution was discussed for two months. It was openly fought by the ambitious county lieutenant of Fincastle, Col. Arthur Campbell. It was secretly opposed by agents of the Indiana and Vandalia land companies, who contended that Virginia had no valid claim to the region.

After the House passed the resolution, its enemies managed to deadlock it for two weeks in the Senate. Finally, on December 7, 1776, that body voted to establish a new county, ". . . called and known by the name of Kentucky."[9]

At last the infant settlement on the western waters was a political entity with a legal name. It would have its own local organization and officials and its two representatives in the Virginia Assembly. Of greatest immediate importance to its inhabitants, the titles to land located under the laws of Virginia would be secure.

Kentucky was now a part of Virginia's domain. There was no higher authority to which Richard Henderson could appeal from that decision. His idea of establishing Transylvania as a new colony was dead, but the Transylvania Company still existed.

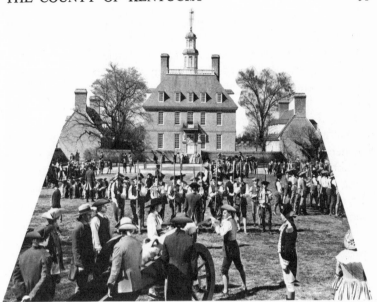

Virginia militia drilling on the green in front of the Governor's Palace at Williamsburg. From "The Howards of Virginia," a Frank Lloyd production, released through Columbia Pictures Corp.

Henderson and his partners proceeded to make the most of what was left to them. Each of them located a cabin right and a preemption claim, like other settlers, in the land over which they had once hoped to rule as proprietors. They labored hard, but in vain, to get Virginia to recognize the titles of those who had taken up land with their company and had paid the entry fees.

Virginia took no further action on the subject until November 4, 1778, when the assembly declared that ". . . the purchase heretofore made by Richard Henderson & Company, of that tract of land called Transylvania, is void."

Later in that session the assembly admitted its obligation to the Transylvania Company for opening a trail and establishing a settlement ". . . by which this commonwealth is likely to receive great advantage." It voted to grant ". . . to the said Richard Henderson & Company" a tract of about two hundred thousand acres lying each side of the Green River with a frontage of twenty-five miles on the Ohio.[10]

Richard Henderson, however, had no foreknowledge of Virginia's tardy recognition of his company's services on that dreary day in December, 1776, when he turned south from Williamsburg to rebuild his broken fortunes. Nor could he foresee that a fair and gracious city, founded by his surviving partners on a part of that grant, would proudly bear his name. He only saw that his cherished dream of empire had vanished into nothingness.

Another dream was taking shape in the mind of George Rogers Clark, a young militia major already on his way to Pittsburgh, to take some five hundred pounds of gunpowder to Virginia's new county "known by the name of Kentucky."

Part Two

THE WEST IN THE REVOLUTION

CHAPTER IX

The First Kentucky Homes

*The wilderness and the solitary place shall be glad
for them; and the desert shall rejoice, and blossom as
the rose.*

—ISAIAH 35:1

The wilderness settlements had not marked time while the
East was deciding their political status. In July, 1775, Daniel
Boone had gone back to Martin's Station to bring out the salt that
the Transylvania Company had left there for Boonesborough.

When he returned in September, sunbonneted women rode on
two of his horses and little heads bobbed up and down in hickory
baskets on others. After waiting nearly three years, his family at
last arrived at its new home in Kentucky—Mrs. Rebecca Bryan
Boone, Jemima, aged fourteen; Israel, at sixteen nearly as tall as
his father, and several younger Boones.

The families of Hugh McGary, Thomas Denton, and Richard
Hogan had traveled with the Boones to the fork of the trails.
There they followed Logan's route through the Crab Orchard
Gap and reached their new homes on Salt River on September 8,
1775, the same date that the Boones arrived at the Kentucky River.

Later in September the Richard Callaway, William Poague, and
Barney Stagner families joined the Boones. The settlement now
had a grown young lady, Miss Elizabeth (Betsey) Callaway, sixteen years old.

What a difference the coming of those families made! "The
men, especially the younger ones, immediately improved in ap-

63

pearance, for there was a sudden craze for shaving and hair-cutting."[1]

The pioneer husbands immediately went to work building log chimneys, laying puncheon floors of split logs, and making crude furniture. William Poague, who was clever with his tools, could hardly keep up with the demand for cedar buckets (one-handled

In peace or war, pioneer women did their daily chores. This is one of four marble panels in the monument to Daniel and Rebecca Boone in the Frankfort Cemetery. Courtesy Cusick Studio.

"piggins" and two-handled "noggins"), and tubs and churns, which he exchanged with the hunters for meat and hides.

The cabins soon began to look homelike. Outside there were ash-hoppers and soap-kettles and rain barrels. Within, the "fireboard" or mantel shelf held the family Bible in its wooden box, a whiskey jug, a tinder box, some packets of household medicines, perhaps an ink bottle. Gay patchwork quilts or soft-colored handwoven "kivers" covered the beds. Tiny looking glasses hung on the walls. Puncheon shelves held the family supply of utensils and tableware.

This group was posed in the cabin in the Pioneer Memorial Fort at Harrodsburg dedicated to the memory of Mrs. Ann (Poague) McGinty, the first "home demonstrator" in the Kentucky wilderness. Courtesy James J. Isenberg.

The hum of a spinning wheel mingled with old songs at the Poague cabin. Mrs. Anne Poague had neither flax nor wool, but she observed that wild nettle grew abundantly about the fort settlement. She sent Betsy Poague and her brothers and sisters to gather all the dry nettle they could find.

She soaked these stalks in the creek and prepared them like flax. Then she persuaded her husband to build her a loom on which to weave "linsey-woolsey" of silky nettle-fiber and buffalo wool.

Mrs. Daniel Boone kept her youngsters busy pounding bark for her tanning trough or curing the skins and hides for the winter supply of clothing. After they had stretched a fresh hide against the cabin wall or pegged it out on the ground, they scraped off the hair with sharp-edged stones. They then worked the raw hide in their hands until it was soft and pliable. Their mother would need many a deerskin to make shirts and leggins and moccasins for her family. And Daniel, no doubt, was somewhat hard on his clothes.

Everybody dropped all other work to help "jerk" the meat whenever the hunters brought in a supply. After cutting it in long strips an inch wide, they laid it on an oblong scaffold made of green wood. There it was dried and smoked over a slow fire. They kept this to use when the supply of fresh meat gave out.[2]

Israel Boone and all other boys over twelve were counted as fort "soldiers" and had regular porthole assignments. Each one had his own flintlock rifle and a full equipment for hunting or fighting. He carried a tomahawk in the right side of his wide belt and a long knife in a leather case on the left. A leather pouch, which hung from a strap over one shoulder, held round, lead bullets, wads of greased flax or "tow," small patches of greased linen to wrap the bullets in, and extra pieces of flint. A powder horn made of the tip of an antler hung on another strap around his neck. It held a "charge" about the size of a thimble.

When his turn came in the shooting match, a boy rested his long rifle barrel on a forked stick and took aim carefully. Not until he could hit a nailhead at forty paces would he be classed as a real marksman.[3]

While their brothers were learning the arts of war and hunting, the girls in Boonesborough received practical training in frontier home economics. They milked the cows and churned the cream for butter. They made soap and candles. They carded wool and flax, spun and wove the yarn into cloth. Sometimes they dyed the yarn before weaving it. These young women cooked and sewed. They helped their mothers care for younger brothers and sisters. They also found time for fancy work, decorating moccasins and hunting shirts with beads and dyed porcupine quills, just as Indian squaws did. Many of them could shoot a rifle as well as their brothers could.

Both boys and girls learned early to detect the nearness of Indians by such signs as the moving of brush or leaves, the restlessness of cattle and other animals, or the cleverly imitated call of a wild turkey or an owl.

Besides their home training in frontier skills, young people in the wilderness settlements usually had some schooling in reading, writing, and arithmetic. Mrs. Jane Coomes started the first school in Kentucky in 1775, almost as soon as she and her husband, William Coomes, were settled at Harrod's Town.

Each weekday morning, after her housework was done, Jane Coomes rapped a stick against the schoolhouse door to call the children. The pupils read in turn from the book in her hand— the Bible, a hymnbook, or *Pilgrim's Progress*. They spelled a few words from a little horn-bound speller. They learned to write and do their "sums" on wide, smooth chips or paddles with a piece of charred wood from the hearth.[4]

Within the forts everyone who was physically able took part in vigorous games and dances, and all were keenly interested in the frequent wrestling, running, and tomahawk-throwing contests as well as the shooting matches. As all frontier folk, the Kentucky settlers looked forward to a round of feasting and merrymaking at Christmas.

On December 23, 1775, two Boonesborough boys, Sam McQuinney and Daniel Saunders, went out to trap turkeys. When they had not returned on the day after Christmas, a searching party was sent out and found Sam's body not far from the river.

The fort people never heard of Daniel Saunders again.[5]

They learned later that Cornstalk, chief of the Shawnees, had warned the settlers against a small band of outlaw Shawnees. The tribe, as a whole, was still at peace. The men continued to hunt game and to visit from one settlement to another, but the women and children had to stay in the forts, longing for the time when they could safely venture beyond the stockade walls.

The sugar-making season brought a break in winter monotony. When a bit of mild weather came in February, the men went into the woods with iron kettles and wooden troughs. Before they returned they filled every spare keg, bucket, and large gourd with maple syrup and sugar. When the last snows had melted, they began the endless task of clearing ground for cultivation.[6]

The Sabbath was always a welcome day of rest, especially during the hot summers. On Sunday afternoon, July 14, 1776, after the Bible reading in the fort, Elizabeth and Frances Callaway and Jemima Boone got into a canoe to paddle out under the shade of the cliff. In spite of their efforts, the canoe was carried across the river by the swift current.

To the girls' horror, five Indians suddenly appeared on the bank above them. One leaped into the water and shoved the canoe against the shore. Another held a tomahawk over the heads of the girls, ready to strike at the first outcry. The others dragged them from the canoe and motioned for them to walk ahead of them.

When the girls failed to return home at milking time, a search was undertaken and the empty canoe was found, almost hidden by the overhanging cane stalks. John Gass hastily stripped and swam across the river to bring it back.[7]

The two fathers quickly organized rescue parties, Callaway leading a dozen mounted men to ford the river about a mile below the fort, while Boone's party of eight crossed over to the scene of the kidnapping to take up the pursuit on foot.

With the center man on the trail, the others at his right and left twenty or more feet apart, they covered five miles before darkness came. They made thirty miles the next day. Early on Tuesday morning they saw the carcass of a freshly-killed buffalo on the Warrior's Path, forty miles or more from Boonesborough, not far from the Blue Licks Springs. Further on they saw smoke rising above the trees.

Cautiously the rescuers spread out to surround their quarry. As they crept closer, they saw that the Indians were entirely off guard. One was roasting meat over a fire. Elizabeth Callaway sat leaning against a tree. The other girls lay on the ground on each side of her with their heads in her lap.

"Our study had been to get the prisoners without giving the Indians time to murder them after they had discovered us," wrote John Floyd. "We saw each other nearly at the same time. Four of us fired and all rushed on them. . . . We sent the Indians off almost naked . . . being so elated on recovering the three poor little heartbroken girls, we were prevented from making any further search." [8]

By the next night the rescue party and the girls were safe within the protecting walls of the fort.

All at once, it seemed, Indian signs were plentiful in the wilderness. Settlers began to flee for safety. Early Boonesborough residents, however, were busy preparing for a wedding, always an occasion for the greatest festivities in frontier life. It took place on August 7, 1776, with dark-eyed Betsey Callaway and tall Samuel Henderson as the bride and groom.

The bride's dress was probably made of home-woven linsey-woolsey; or, since her father was well-to-do, it might have been made of Irish linen. It had a closely fitted bodice and a full, ankle-length skirt. She folded a fine linen kerchief about her neck and wound her long braids of black hair around her head.

Samuel, in keeping with frontier custom, donned his best quill-embroidered hunting shirt and fringed leggings of soft doeskin. He cut a handsome figure as he galloped around the stockade at the head of a party of young men and reined his horse up sharply at Colonel Callaway's home to claim his bride!

The wedding guests assembled near the spring. While the fiddlers from Harrod's Town played "The Campbells Are Coming," Elizabeth and Samuel walked down the well-worn path to the giant sycamores that had witnessed many memorable scenes in

Boonesborough's history. There, with Squire Boone officiating as preacher, they promised to take each other as man and wife, for better or worse, until death did them part.

All the fort women helped Mrs. Callaway prepare the wedding feast. They served it in one of the blockhouses, with watermelons from their own gardens for dessert.

Then the dancing began—old-fashioned reels and jigs. There was more feasting at night, and dancing again to the light of tallow dips until the sun came up.[9]

A day or two later, the neighbors gathered to help Samuel build his cabin. By night, the chopping party had cut enough logs for the walls, hitched horses to them and dragged them to the selected site. The best carpenters on hand had felled a large, straight-grained tree, cut it into four-foot lengths, and using a broad-bladed, short-handled tool called a frow, split them into wide boards for the roof. Another group split smaller logs in half and hewed the flat sides with their broadaxes to make the puncheons for the floor.

They "rolled up" the cabin the next day. Four expert "corner men" did the notching and placing, while others supplied them with logs. After they had built up a few rounds of logs, they laid the "sleepers" and the floor puncheons. When the walls were seven or eight feet high, the corner men cut the logs shorter for the front and back in order to slope in the sides to make the roof.

Other workers had sawed a three-foot space in one side for the door, a much wider opening in the opposite wall for the fireplace, and two small, high openings for windows. They bored holes in lengths of wood three inches thick and fitted these into the openings for door and window frames and fireplace jambs, pinning them with wooden pegs to corresponding holes in the wall logs.

Another group built the chimney of small logs and clay. As soon as that was done, the masons in the party chinked the cracks between the logs of the cabin walls and the chimney with pieces of heartwood and mortar. Then they fitted large, flat stones into the back and sides of the fireplace and laid a wide stone hearth.

By the second night the clapboards had been laid on the roof and secured in place by heavy logs laid over them. The new house was finished, built without a nail or screw or any other piece of metal.

The carpenters spent the next day smoothing the floorboards and hanging a stout clapboard door and covers for the two windows. Then they made the furniture—a puncheon table, several three-legged stools, pegs to hang clothing on, some shelves, and a "fireboard" or mantel shelf.

Their final task was to make a "built-in" bed in one corner. The first step was to push one end of a long forked pole through a hole bored in the floor and fasten the other end to an overhead rafter. Then they tied one end of a seven-foot pole in the fork for the front side of the bed and a shorter one over it for the foot. The other ends of both poles were firmly wedged into cracks between the logs of the walls. Thin boards laid over the front pole and pushed into a space between two logs in the wall formed the bottom of the bed.[10]

Elizabeth covered these with a pile of Samuel's bearskins and buffalo hides and a cloth tick stuffed with turkey and pigeon feathers. On top of that she placed her own hand-woven linen sheets and covers.

It was a beautiful pioneer house, perfectly adapted to the time, the people, and the circumstances. In true frontier tradition, everyone in the community had freely given his time and skill to help build and furnish it.

The night after it was finished, the fort women and Elizabeth cooked and served the housewarming feast. Once more the fiddlers played for the dancing. Once more the sun came up before the frolic ended. The first white bride and groom in Kentucky were properly launched on the hazardous venture of making a home in the wilderness.

CHAPTER X

War in the Wilderness

*He knows not his own strength
that hath not faced adversity.*
—BEN JONSON

A few days after the Callaway-Henderson wedding at Boonesborough, a returning settler brought a copy of a Virginia paper containing the full text of the Declaration of Independence. The assembled pioneers heard for the first time the ringing phrases that have become a part of the vocabulary of American democracy—"all men are created equal . . . inalienable rights . . . life, liberty, the pursuit of happiness . . . the consent of the governed . . . free and independent states."

Even as the Kentucky pioneers celebrated their belated Fourth of July with bonfires and rifle volleys, they realized something of what the break with England would mean to them. The Revolution had begun. War would follow. For them it would be the war of the border, with firebrand, scalping knife, and tomahawk.

Not one of them doubted that England would again employ the savages as allies in an effort to subdue her rebellious American colonists and to hold the territory she had so recently won from France. They knew, too, that the first blows would fall upon the new, exposed settlements in the Kentucky wilderness.

The settlers did what they could to prepare themselves for a struggle. They worked on Henderson's fort and put the other stations in order. They gathered their crops and wild fruits and nuts. They carefully hoarded their powder, hoping each day for Clark's arrival from Pittsburgh with a fresh supply.

The year 1776 ended before that hope was realized. Clark and Jones and seven other men had narrowly escaped capture on the way down the Ohio in December. Landing on the Kentucky side a few miles above Limestone Creek, they hid the powder and hurried on to the settlements to get a larger force to guard it on the way to the forts.

Indians attacked Jones's returning party at the Lower Blue Licks on Christmas Day, killing him and two other men and capturing several, one of whom was young Joseph Rogers, a cousin of George Rogers Clark. When Capt. James Harrod heard of this disaster, he started on January 2, 1777, with forty men, to find the powder and bring it in. With young Simon Kenton as guide, Harrod's party returned to Harrodsburg without the loss of a man or a keg of powder.[1]

Making Harrodsburg his military headquarters, Clark ordered all the settlers in the country into the three forts south on the Kentucky River—Boonesborough, Harrod's, and Logan's. These forts were like little islands of settlement in the vast wilderness. The Shawnee Indians in Ohio were between them and the nearest American forts at Wheeling and Pittsburgh. Their only line for supplies or reinforcements was over Boone's Trace to the settlements in eastern Tennessee; and those were now threatened by the Cherokees.

Clark sent two scouts each week to patrol the Ohio River and to watch around the deserted station. He dispatched two young hunters to the Illinois country as spies. He also sent an "express" to Pittsburgh to ask for help in recovering a large number of horses the Indians had stolen.

Indian raids began early that spring. On March 6, James Ray, seventeen-year-old son of Mrs. Hugh McGary, heard the crack of rifles while he was working at a clearing near Shawnee Spring. Never did James Ray put his long legs to better use than on that day, when he outran Black Fish's swiftest warriors and warned Harrodsburg in time to defend itself.

In April the Indians attacked all three forts at once. At Boonesborough they fired upon two men working in a field. Simon Kenton, scouting around the fort, killed one brave, and Daniel

Boone, hearing the firing, hurried out with ten men to the relief of his scouts.

In the fight that followed, a rifle ball broke one of Boone's legs. As an exulting warrior held his tomahawk over the head of the prostrate leader, Kenton fired his rifle pointblank at the Indian's breast. Then, swinging Boone's hefty form to his broad shoulders, he carried him into the fort.

The situation at Logan's was more desperate than at either of the other forts. Late in May, one hundred Indians laid seige to it and remained in the neighborhood for several weeks.

Before the siege ended, the defenders of the station had used up nearly all of their powder. At Boonesborough, the resourceful Daniel Boone had made a fresh supply by mixing charcoal with some of the brimstone and saltpeter which Henderson had left there; but Logan, having no materials with which to make gunpowder, had no choice but to risk a trip to the Tennessee settlements.

With two companions, he crept through the Indian lines one dark night and traveled by unused trails to the Holston River. After arranging for the necessary supplies, he left his comrades to help guard the ammunition and started back alone. He reached his fort ten days after he had left it, having traveled four hundred miles on foot.[2]

His safe return cheered the anxious defenders almost as much as his assurance that four kegs of gunpowder and four packhorse loads of lead were on the way. He brought other heartening news. Virginia, in answer to their pleas for help, had ordered Col. John Bowman to take one hundred militiamen to the relief of the hard-pressed Kentucky stations.

The Indians withdrew after the arrival of the militiamen, but before they departed, they left convincing proof of the source and purpose of their persistent attacks. A packet of papers found on the dead body of one of Bowman's advance guards offered protection to all who would take the oath of allegiance to ". . . their rightful lord, King George III."

By Clark's statement, ". . . no people could be in a more

alarming situation . . . two hundred miles from the nearest
settlements . . . surrounded by numerous nations of the
Indians under the influence of the British government and
pointedly directed to destroy us. I was frequently afraid
the people would think of making their peace with Detroit.
Their distress may easily be conceived . . . but they yet
remained firm in hopes of relief." [3]

Many had rushed back east the previous summer. Within
a week after the capture of the Boonesborough girls, twenty
settlers had fled from a station on the Licking River. Ten had
joined them when they passed through Boonesborough. Seven
new stations had been abandoned, and by the end of 1776, not
more than 150 white men remained in the Kentucky wilderness.

Their reasons for staying varied. A few, perhaps, felt safer
in the wilderness than within reach of the law in the East. Young
daredevils like Simon Kenton loved the danger and excitement
of border warfare. The Boones, Callaway, Harrod, and other
family men had brought their all with them—wives and children,
livestock, household goods, tools and implements. The wilderness held whatever hopes they might cherish of future prosperity
and happiness.

Youthful leaders with vision and imagination, such as Benjamin Logan and George Rogers Clark, John Floyd and the Todd
brothers (John, Levi, and Robert), realized the strategic importance of the West. They sincerely believed that they could
serve their country in no better way than by holding the region
for it against the Indians and the British.

Others must have shared that motive for staying. John Floyd
stated it in a letter of July 21, 1776, addressed to Col. William
Preston. After describing the rescue of the Boonesborough girls,
he wrote:

I want as much to return as any person . . . but if I leave
the country now there is scarcely one single man hereabouts,
but what will follow the example. When I think of the de-

plorable condition a few helpless families are likely to be in, I conclude to sell my life as dear as I can, in their defense, rather than make an ignominious escape.[4]

From that, it seems reasonable to assume that the presence of a few families in the wilderness may have turned the scales in favor of holding the West for the United States. Without them, the men could, and in all probability would, have abandoned the region. However, with only a few of their horses left, they dared not make an attempt to return to the East on foot with slow-moving family groups.

In April, 1777, the settlers elected John Todd and Richard Callaway to represent them in the Virginia Assembly. After Colonel Bowman arrived at Harrodsburg in September, they held their first county court meeting.

Most of Clark's time was taken up in "the defense of our forts, the procuring of provisions, and when possible, surprising the Indians . . . burying the dead, and dressing the wounded."

Clark spent his few leisure hours in serious reflection on things in general, particularly Kentucky.

This led me to a long train of thinking, the result of which was to lay aside every private view and engage seriously in the war . . . until the fate of the continent should be known. . . . This . . . enabled me better to judge of the importance of Kentucky to the Union . . . and that nothing I could engage in would be of more general utility than its defense.[5]

On September 23 a message came from Boone with word that on the thirteenth Captain Smith had arrived at Boonesborough with forty-eight men— ". . . 150 more on the March for this also, with an account that General Washington had defeated Howe. Joyful News if true."

A corner of the Pioneer Memorial Fort at Harrodsburg. Unlike the buildings of the early years of settlement, the chimneys and foundations are stone. The "fire pole" was used to push the chimney away from the house if it caught on fire. Courtesy James J. Isenberg.

Colonel Bowman reached Harrodsburg on September 2 to take charge of military affairs as Kentucky's county lieutenant. Clark's spies had returned with all the information he ". . . could reasonably have expected." With the arrival of the latest reinforcements, Clark began preparations to leave Kentucky. On September 29 he bought a horse, ". . . price £12; swapped with I. Shelby, boot £10."

> Wednesday, October 1. I started for the settlement, twenty-two men; got to Logan's, twenty miles . . . 3d started on our journey, seventy-six in all, besides women and children.[6]

When George Rogers Clark again set out on the long trail he had traveled the year before with John Gabriel Jones as his sole companion, he told no one his purpose or his plans. His *Diary* records such items as places where he again swapped horses; where he lodged and what he paid for accommodations;

where he parted from his company; where he got a letter from Captain Bowman ". . . informing me that he had an order of court to carry salt to Kentucky."

On Saturday, November 1, he arrived at his father's house in Caroline County, Virginia, ". . . 620 miles from Harrodsburg." In Williamsburg on November 5, he ". . . had a confirmation of Burgoyne's surrender." There he bought ". . . two shirts and a book, 5/". Later he settled his militia accounts and ". . . bought a piece of cloth for a jackote, price 4.15; buttons and mohair 3/."

Clark had several interviews with Gov. Patrick Henry and ". . . private councils composed of select gentlemen," among them Thomas Jefferson, George Mason, and George Wythe. To no one else, apparently, did he confide the subject of those conversations. Nor did he record it in his Diary. He wrote later that ". . . to make it publick was a certain loss of it." [7]

George Rogers Clark had learned early in life the value of secrecy to the success of important plans and undertakings.

CHAPTER XI

The Siege of Boonesborough

God grants liberty only to those who love it,
and are always ready to guard and defend it.

—DANIEL WEBSTER

In the forts of Kentucky that winter the urgent need for salt soon became the greatest problem. By December, the supply was almost exhausted. Rather than risk the long, dangerous trip to the salt works on the Holston River, Colonel Bowman decided to send parties of men to make salt at the sulphur springs on the Licking River, almost sixty miles northeast of Boonesborough.

With Daniel Boone in charge, thirty men from the three forts left Boonesborough on New Year's Day, 1778. They took their axes, some corn meal, fodder for their horses, and several large iron kettles which the government of Virginia had sent to the Kentucky settlements.

Salt-making was a slow process even with water as briny as that at the Lower Blue Licks Springs.[1] The weather was so bitterly cold that hardly any game remained in the region and the men actually suffered from hunger. On February 7, while Daniel Boone was hunting miles away from the salt makers' camp and almost numb with cold, he was suddenly surrounded by a band of Shawnee warriors.

Knowing that resistance would be useless, he quietly allowed them to lead him to their camp. There he saw more than a hundred Indians under the command of two French Canadian officers, who told Boone that they wanted him to guide them to Boonesborough.

81

Sketch of Fort Boonesborough as it probably appeared at the time of the siege in September 1778. The river bank at the left is high enough to be easily tunneled to a point under the fort. From Boonesborough by George W. Ranck. Courtesy the Filson Club.

While professing his willingness to go along, Boone warned them that a large number of troops had recently arrived at the fort. He then offered to lead them to the salt-making party at the Blue Licks if they would guarantee fair treatment of the prisoners. On reaching the camp, he persuaded his party to surrender. The savages, delighted with this easy victory, started back the next morning to their village in Ohio.

In March, they took Boone and ten other men to Detroit, where the Indians accepted ransom money for all the prisoners except Boone. They refused to release him, although Sir Henry Hamilton, governor general of Canada, offered them five times the usual amount of ransom.[2]

The Shawnees left Detroit on April 10, taking Boone back with them to their village, old Chillicothe, on the Little Miami. There the old chief, Black Fish, told Daniel Boone that he intended to adopt him as his own son.

The old squaws prepared the veteran fighter for the ceremony of adoption. They pulled out all his hair, with the exception of a circle at the crown of this head. They scrubbed him vigorously in the creek, "to take out his white blood." Then they dressed him in Indian fashion, braided his scalplock with ribbons and feathers, and streaked his face with paint.

The chiefs and warriors then took him into their log council house, where Boone listened attentively, although without much understanding, to long speeches on the great honor of becoming a member of the Shawnee tribe. At the feast that followed, he had his first taste of roasted dogmeat, a choice Indian dish. He was now no longer Daniel Boone, an American citizen. He was "Sheltowee," or "Big Turtle," a fully-adopted Shawnee.

Big Turtle appeared happy and contented with his new mode of life. He took part in the games of his new brothers. He did well, but not too well, in the shooting matches.

After a while Black Fish allowed him to go hunting alone, only taking the precaution to count his bullets when he left and when he returned. Big Turtle, however, managed to keep the chief supplied with choice game by using only half a bullet and a small charge of powder each time he fired his rifle.[3]

On June 1, the Black Fish family took him to make salt at a spring near the Scioto River. Ten days later more than four hundred Indians, returning from an unsuccessful attack on the Greenbrier forts in Virginia, passed by their camp. The Black Fish party joined them on the way to Chillicothe.

Without appearing to listen, Boone learned that this large party, sullen and ill-tempered after its recent defeat, intended to make a surprise attack upon Boonesborough at once.

The next morning, Big Turtle leisurely oiled his gun and set off at his usual hour for hunting. Four days later, June 19, 1778, the guard at Boonesborough stared at a strange figure who held up his hands at the edge of the clearing and then staggered towards him. Could that ragged, bleeding creature with a bedraggled scalplock possibly be their lost leader?

Daniel Boone it was, more dead than alive, after his flight of 160 miles, during which he had stopped only once to kill game and broil meat.[4]

He found none of his family there to welcome him except his daughter Jemima, who had married Flanders Callaway. His wife, Rebecca, thinking him dead, had returned with Israel and her other children to her father's people in North Carolina.

When Col. Richard Callaway heard Boone's news of the coming Indian attack, he sent word immediately to the other forts and dispatched a messenger to Virginia for reinforcements. He hastened to repair the palisades and strengthen the gates. In ten days the fort was in battle order. The second stories of three of the corner blockhouses were finally completed after a wait of more than three years.

When August arrived and there was still no sign of the enemy, Boone organized a party of woodsmen and scouts to make an attack on one of the Shawnee towns. Four miles from Paint Creek Town on the Scioto, they overtook thirty Indians on their way to join the main army. In Boone's words, "A smart fight ensued betwixt us. . . . At length the savages gave way and fled. . . . We took from them three horses, and all their baggage." [5]

His scouts found the town deserted. Convinced that the entire army was headed for Boonesborough, the scouting party hurried homeward. They had no time to spare. At sunset, September 6, they galloped across the clearing and through the gates of the fort. That night the campfires of the Indians appeared on the hills on the other side of the Kentucky River.

Instead of making a surprise attack at dawn, the enemy appeared at ten o'clock the next morning in front of the fort. The red warriors, half-naked and vividly painted, numbered about 450. The chiefs included the most famous of the Shawnee tribe—Black Fish, Moluntha the Shawnee "King," Black Bird the Chippewa Chief, and the Kentucky-born veteran, Black Hoof.

Besides the Indians, there were a dozen green-clad French Canadians under the command of Lt. Dagneaux DeQuindre. To oppose this number, Boonesborough had at that time only about thirty men and twenty boys able to handle a gun.

While the astonished garrison watched through the portholes, a messenger carrying a white flag crossed the clearing and mounted a stump close to the nearest blockhouse. Putting his hand to his mouth, he gave the long, frontier signal, "Hallo-o-o!"

Again and again he called, "Hallo-o-o! Hallo-o-o!" At last, he heard an answering "Hallo-o-o!"

Then he called out, "I have letters from Governor Hamilton at Detroit for Captain Boone."

The fort officers, after talking this over, replied that they would receive the letters from three unarmed leaders. The messenger shortly returned with Black Fish, Moluntha, and DeQuindre. Captain Boone, Colonel Callaway, and Maj. William Bailey Smith went through the half-opened gates to meet them, carrying as a flag of truce a white handkerchief tied to the ramrod of a gun.

Hamilton's letters offered easy terms if the men in the fort would surrender and take the oath of allegiance to the king. Old Black Fish gently scolded his adopted son for leaving him, and explained, "I have brought along forty horses for the old folks and the women and children to ride." The Boonesborough officers played for time by asking for a truce of two days to give the people in the fort an opportunity to decide what they wanted to do.

However, the people, as they well knew, had already made their decision—"Better death than captivity." They spent those two days making greased patches, preparing flints, molding bullets, giving out powder, and cleaning rifles. The Indians could not fail to note that the women and boys made frequent trips to the spring, that the cows were not turned out again after they had been milked, that after dark, stooping forms stripped the gardens of everything that could be used for food.

When the messengers returned on the second day, Boone told them that the settlers were determined to defend their fort while a man was living. "We laugh at all your formidable preparations: But thank you for giving us notice and time to provide for our defense." [6]

To his defiant words DeQuindre replied, "Our orders are to take you captive and not destroy you. But if nine of you will come out and make a treaty with us, we shall withdraw from your fort and return home."

Suspecting treachery, but hoping for reinforcements at any hour, the garrison agreed to this strange request. While a sharp-shooter stood at every porthole in the nearest blockhouse, nine men from the fort met an equal number of the enemy near the spring. They feasted on Detroit's best and talked all day under the great sycamores. By evening they had agreed upon a treaty, to be signed the next day.

The peace commissioners from the fort noticed the following morning that young braves had taken the place of the older chiefs. After they had signed the agreement, "The Indians told us it was customary with them, on such occasions, for two Indians to shake hands with every white man in the treaty. . . . We agreed to this also. . . ." [7] Instantly, two young Indians grappled with each white man.

Climax of the Treaty

Callaway broke loose first and ran towards the fort, waving his hat as a signal to fire. Boone, too, jerked himself free and ran with the others, while bullets spatted about them in the dust.

That night the defenders heard the Indian leaders giving loud orders for packing and marching. DeQuindre's bugle notes grew fainter and fainter, but the fort gates remained closed the next morning. Although they could see no sign of their foes, those veteran frontiersmen felt certain that the enemy had not really gone.

When they realized that the people in the fort had not been fooled by their trick, the Indians began firing from behind trees. The frontiersmen returned their fire whenever a head or a body appeared at which to aim. One day during the siege, they noticed a muddy streak in the river. From a hastily built tower on the roof of a cabin they saw fresh earth being thrown into water. That could only mean that the enemy was digging a tunnel back from the riverbank to undermine the fort. The defenders at once began to dig a trench through several cabin floors to cut off the tunnel.

On Sunday night, September 13, the Indians began throwing lighted torches of cane and oily hickory bark against the stockade and shooting blazing arrows on the cabin roofs. The fort boys climbed up and put out the arrows amid a shower of bullets. They could not get to the torches outside the stockade, but the logs were damp from a long drizzling rain which still continued, and the torches burned out without igniting the walls of the fort.

On the eighth day of the siege, people inside the fort could plainly hear the sound of Indians digging in the tunnel. Only a few half-starved cattle were left for food. The defenders were exhausted with labor and heat and constant watching. They felt that they could not hold out through another day.

That night the rain became a downpour. Through the long hours the defenders waited, guns in hand, for whatever morning might bring.

Day came at last, bright, clear, and still. The men in the fort heard no sound from the tunnel, only distant voices across the river. No attacker could be seen. Scouts from the fort found that the enemy was actually in retreat.

The enemy had discovered the clay thrown out from the frontiersmen's tunnel and had decided that they could not blow up the fort. The savages, never very keen on manual labor, had departed in disgust.[8]

A week later, the long-looked-for relief party arrived, and Boone felt free to leave, but before he could get away, some of the militia officers brought charges of treason against him.

They were very human, those Kentucky pioneers. They had been under a constant strain for two years. The dreadful siege, through which they had come with only two of their number killed and four wounded, had sorely tried their nerves and tempers. Some of them had already sharply criticized Boone's conduct that year, and, after his return from captivity, one or two of his fellow officers resented his authority and leadership during the siege.

At the court-martial, held at Logan's Fort, Boone was called upon to answer charges that he had neglected his duty as a leader by surrendering the salt-makers without resistance; that, while a prisoner of the Indians, he had arranged with Hamilton at Detroit to surrender the people at Boonesborough; that he had weakened the garrison when they were daily expecting an attack by taking a large number on the Paint Creek expedition; that, before the attack on the fort, he had taken nine of its leaders outside to the Indian camp on the pretense of making a treaty of peace.

Boone explained that the surrender of the salt-makers and his friendly talks with Governor Hamilton were solely for the purpose of delaying an attack upon the fort. He declared that the Paint Creek trip was for scouting purposes, to learn the movements of the enemy. And the discussion of the make-believe treaty, which was held within rifle range of the fort, was to deceive the enemy and gain time for reinforcements to arrive.[9]

He was honorably acquitted of all the charges against him and shortly afterward was promoted to the rank of major. With his record and conscience clear, Daniel Boone once more started back, on the trail he had made, to join his wife and children in North Carolina.

The frontier settlement of Boonesborough was safe.

CHAPTER XII

In the Illinois Country

I am glad to take you by the hand,
and to make peace with your people.

GEORGE ROGERS CLARK

On the morning of May 27, 1778, a large fleet of flatboats rounded the last bend of the Ohio River above the Falls at what is now the city of Louisville. Before them the river widened out in a sweeping curve to the south. Just above the nearest and largest island, a tree-fringed creek, the Beargrass, flowed into the river on the Kentucky side.

The flatboat party, under the command of Maj. George Rogers Clark, landed on the southern bank between the creek and the island. Besides officers and soldiers, it included a dozen families who had traveled with them from Fort Redstone in Pennsylvania.

Clark observed that the large island opposite their camp would be an ideal place for training his soldiers and much safer than the mainland for the families. He moved to a small piece of ground detached from the mainland. The settlers called it Corn Island. Clark divided his army into four companies, commanded by Captains Joseph Bowman, Leonard Helm, William Harrod, and John Montgomery, all experienced frontier officers.

Recruiting had been slow on the Virginia frontier that winter. Clark had left Fort Redstone on the Monongahela on May 12, with less than one hundred and fifty men instead of the five hundred he wanted. He would accept only sixty of those who came from the Kentucky forts to join him, for fear of leaving those places too defenseless. A company from the Holston settlements, which he expected to join him at the Falls, failed to appear. He had a small army, indeed, for the venture on which he had determined.

After less than a month of intensive training, Clark called all the people on the island together to tell them for the first time what he intended to do.[1]

"We can never hope to win this war by staying in our forts," he said. "If we do the Indians will kill us all off, one by one. We must carry the war into the enemy's country.

"My spies tell me that the British forts in the Illinois country are weak. They could easily be captured by a surprise attack. The French people there do not like their British rulers. They would help us to drive them out.

"In addition to the usual pay, Virginia will give each man who goes with me three hundred acres of land. Look! Here is my new commission from Governor Henry, as lieutenant-colonel. Here are his secret instructions—to attack the British at Kaskaskia, and anywhere else I please.

"We start tomorrow for the Illinois!"

The soldiers stared at him, open-mouthed. They had enlisted, not too willingly, for only three months, to serve in Kentucky, a part of their own state of Virginia. They had had no thought of fighting in the Illinois, six hundred miles farther in the enemy's own country.

They looked at the guards standing near the boats, at sentries pacing the shore. They heard the roar of the rapids below the island. What could they do?

The next morning approximately 180 men boarded four large flatboats and rowed upstream for a mile to get into the main current of the river. As they headed downstream they noticed that the sky had darkened. A strange light, like a purple mist, quickly spread over the earth. It became so dark that the wild turkeys flew up into the trees to roost.

The boats shot over the Falls ". . . at the very moment of the sun being in a great eclipse, which caused various conjectures among the superstitious." [2]

"A bad sign," some of them muttered. But nothing short of an earthquake could have stopped George Rogers Clark that morning. The party went on, rowing in relays, two men at an oar day and night. The fourth evening they landed on an island near the mouth of the Tennessee River. While cooking food for their march overland, they saw a party of hunters in a boat.

Clark ordered them to land and closely questioned them about Kaskaskia, which they said they had left eight days before. After warning them not to talk to his men, he engaged one of them as a guide.

That night the soldiers hid their boats in a gully on the northern side of the island. The next morning they began the march of one hundred and twenty miles on foot towards Kaskaskia. They traveled light, in the Indian manner, with only their guns, knives, hatchets, and rations for four days.

For four days they had food; for the next two, they had none. In the evening of July 4, the soldiers halted on the east side of Kaskaskia River, three miles from the town. When darkness came, they found some boats at a farm nearly opposite the town. In two hours the entire army had crossed the river—unseen and unheard.

Monsieur Philip de Rochblave, the commandant of the British post at Kaskaskia, probably never knew what it was that wakened him that night and brought him to his door, half-dressed, to find a self-styled "colonel" on the other side.

Whatever it was, he awoke to the astounding reality that he and his garrison were prisoners of war. Kaskaskia, the little capital of the Illinois country since the time of La Salle, had surrendered in fifteen minutes to an army of less than two hundred weary, hungry Americans without the firing of a single gun.

George Rogers Clark knew that taking the front was only the first step in his enterprise. He must win the French inhabitants, who had been told by the British that Americans were more brutal and savage than Indians.

At first he gave the citizens of Kaskaskia little reason to question the truth of that statement. He had their militia officers arrested. He refused to talk to a committee that asked to see him. Then he ordered the leading men of the town to appear before him.

The old French gentlemen and the Catholic priest, Pierre Gibault, saw little to encourage them when they entered the room where Clark and his officers were seated. As Clark afterward described the scene, "We had left all our clothes at the river, we were almost naked, and torn by the river bushes and briers. They were shocked, and it was some time before they could venture to take seats, and longer before they would speak." [3]

When the priest at last found his voice, he asked, hesitantly, "May the people go to the church to take leave of each other, as they never expect to meet again?"

Clark replied that he had nothing to say about the church, but that the people must not go out of the town. They left him to take his message to the people, and then all of them went into the church. After remaining there for some time, the priest and the old men came back to thank Clark for the privilege. Then they humbly inquired if the people might keep some of their clothing, and food for the women and children.

This was too much for even Clark's assumed coldness. "Do you think," he asked, abruptly, "that you are speaking to savages? Can you suppose that we mean to strip women and children and take the bread out of their mouths? Or that we would stoop to make war on them, or on your church? We have come to prevent the loss of life, and not to plunder."

Then, very simply, he explained to them why America was at war with England. When he informed them that the king of France had become the ally of the United States, he observed that they were deeply impressed.[4]

"As for your church," he added, "we shall punish any one who dares to offer it an insult. You may return to your homes and go about your ordinary business without fear. Later, you may choose whether to become citizens of the United States and stay here or to remain subjects of Great Britain and leave the town." [5]

The Frenchmen could hardly believe their ears. They had come in hopeless despair. They left with joy in their eyes. Soon the streets were filled with happy, singing people, ". . . the bells ringing, the church crowded, returning thanks."

These new friends of the Americans soon had a chance to prove their gratitude. The next day a number of them offered to go with Captain Bowman to Cahokia and persuade their relatives and friends there to accept Clark's terms.

When Clark questioned Father Gibault about conditions in Vincennes, on the Wabash River, the priest told him that the British commander there had gone to Detroit. He then offered to go to Vincennes and explain the situation to the people there.

Clark, greatly pleased at this offer, promptly accepted it. On the first of August, Father Gibault returned with the joyful news that the people of Vincennes also had become citizens of the United States.

"They are telling the Indians," he added, "that their old Father, the King of France, is alive again and is a friend of the Big Knives; and that he is mad at them for fighting for the English."

Clark sent Captain Helm with only two American soldiers to take command at Fort Sackville in Vincennes. He could spare no more. Now that their term of enlistment was out, his troops were clamoring to go home.

By presents and promises, he induced about a hundred to re-enlist for eight months longer, but he had such a small force that he seriously doubted whether he would be able to hold what he had won. He instructed his soldiers to tell the townspeople that a large body of troops was located at the Falls, as ". . . an excuse for our marching into the Illinois with so small a force was necessary." [6]

Clark and his officers had visited the Spanish officials in Fort St. Louis, across the Mississippi from Cahokia, soon after they had taken possession of the British forts. He felt sure of their friendly interest in his cause. His next concern was to treat with the Indians. He knew that if he failed with them, all his previous success would amount to nothing.

The northwestern tribes were greatly puzzled and confused at the sudden turn of events. Their chiefs sought the advice of the French traders, who told them to go to Clark and sue for peace. Before he would agree to talk with them, Clark made a thorough study of the methods used by French and Spanish authorities in dealing with the natives. When he was ready he sent messages to all the tribes that he would hold a great council with them at Cahokia.

They came by the hundreds to hear what this young chief of the "Big Knives" would say to them. The night before the council began, some members of the Puan tribe tried to kidnap Clark. He promptly had their two leading chiefs arrested by the French militia and refused to see or speak to any member of the tribe.

"There was great counselling among the savages during the night," he recorded, "but to make them have a greater idea of my indifference, I assembled a number of gentlemen and ladies and danced nearly the whole night." [7]

The Grand Council of Cahokia the next morning was a colorful and dramatic spectacle. The flames of the great council fire glowed against a background of September-tinted trees. Hundreds of Indians squatted on the ground around it. Clark and his officers, in full uniform, were surrounded by their Virginia riflemen and French militia. Citizens of the Illinois towns and Spaniards from St. Louis stood near them. Beyond were the Puan captives and their guards.

Clark holds a council with the Indians. Courtesy Caulfield & Shook, Louisville.

After the Council was opened with the customary ceremonies, Clark addressed the assembled chiefs in one of the most remarkable speeches ever made by a white man to Indians.

"Men and Warriors!" he called in a loud, commanding voice. "Pay attention! I, too, am a warrior, not a councillor. I was sent by the great Council Fire of the Big Knives to take possession of this country and to watch the motions of the Red People. I will dispel the mist that is before your eyes, that you may see the cause of the war between the Big Knives and the English.

"The Big Knives are much like the Red People. They do not know how to make blankets and powder and cloth. . . . They buy from the English . . . as you and the French do. But their land got poor, and the women began to cry, to see their children naked . . . and began to make clothes for themselves . . . And the men learned to make guns and powder.

"This made the English mad, and they put soldiers in our country and would not let us make things nor trade with anybody else. They made us give two bucks for a blanket that we used to get for one. Our whole land was dark, and we hung our heads for shame.

"At last the Great Spirit took pity on us. He kindled a great council fire at a place called Philadelphia, stuck down a war post, left a tomahawk, and went away. The old men assembled at the fire, took up the hatchet and sharpened it, and put it into the hands of the young men.

"The young men struck the war post . . . They drove the English from place to place until they got so weak that they hired you Red People to fight for them.

"This made the Great Spirit so angry that he caused your old French Father and other nations to join with the Big Knives.

"You see, it is the Great Spirit against whom you are fighting. And if your women and children should cry, you must take the blame.

"I have told you who I am and why I am here. Look! Here is the bloody belt of war. Here is the white belt of peace. Take which you please. If you choose the belt of war, we shall see who can shed the most blood. If you take the belt of peace, you shall be brothers of the Big Knives and the French. But you must not say one thing and think the other. You may have time to council together, and give me your answer tomorrow." [8]

The Indians could not comprehend the political maneuvers of white nations, but they respected Clark's boldness and strength. They understood and admired his oratory, clothed in their own figurative language. The next day they again kindled the council fire, and the chiefs rose, one by one, and made their talks.

"The English are bad birds who have told us lies," they said. "We see now that the Americans are warriors, and we want to take them by the hand as brothers. We speak from our hearts, and not only from our lips. We are ready to take the white belt and smoke the pipe of peace."

After the peace pipe ceremony, Clark turned to the captive Puans. "You should be put to death," he said, sternly. "But I find that you are not men, only squaws. We shall have squaw clothes put on you and give you food to take home, as squaws do not know how to hunt."

The prisoners attempted to speak, but Clark turned away, saying that he would make no treaty with their tribe. The Indians became greatly excited, not knowing what to make of such strange behavior.

Suddenly two young Puan warriors came forward and knelt in front of Clark, covering their heads with their blankets. Two of their chiefs stood beside them. "We offer these two young men as a sacrifice," they said, "that you may spare our nation and smoke the pipe of peace with us."

Clark was amazed. After a tense, painful silence, he spoke gently to the young men, telling them to stand up.

"I am glad to find at least two real men in your nation," he said. "Only men like you should be the chiefs of a tribe.

"I am glad to take you by the hand, and make peace with your people." Then he presented them to his officers and to the French and Spanish gentlemen as the new chiefs of the Puan tribe.[9]

Clark spent five strenuous weeks at Cahokia, making treaties with the chiefs of the numerous Illinois tribes. Then, "having so far fixed matters as to have a moment's leisure," he returned to his headquarters in Kaskaskia.

His bloodless victories that summer removed for the time any threat of attack by the northwestern tribes upon the new settlement at the Falls. They gave the United States command of the Ohio River and an opportunity to get greatly needed supplies from the Spaniards down the Mississippi. To Virginia, Clark's native state, which had authorized and financed the expedition, they added a territory three times the size of Great Britain.

George Rogers Clark may have foreseen those immediate results during his long train of thinking in the fort at Harrodsburg the year before. But not even he could have imagined the far-reaching influence of his successful invasion of enemy country upon the fate of the continent and the development of freedom and democracy in the United States.

CHAPTER XIII

The Corn Island Settlement

The things courage can do!
—SIR JAMES BARRIE

Back in the Corn Island settlement at the Falls of the Ohio River, Capt. John Todd, Jr., summarized Kentucky news in June, 1778, in a letter to a friend in Virginia:

> Never did new Occurrences so crowd one another . . . Take the heads, thus: 1st. Col. Clark has arrived. 2. We have spared him about 60 men to make a stroke at Cascasky. A garrison of about 30 men and 12 families is settled at the Falls which I left last Tuesday. Our Corn and &c. is growing finely. Capt. Boone has run away from the Shawanese & arrived with abundance of News. &c. . . Indians appear frequently among us. . . We have killed 3 or 4 lately without loss except 2 wounded who will soon recover. . . My greatest pleasure here is thinking I shall make my Jack here if I can preserve my Nightcap.[1]

The "Nightcaps" on Corn Island were probably in less danger from the scalping knife than those anywhere else in Kentucky. Neither friend nor foe could cross the river by day without being seen. At night, the settlers slept securely behind the stout log stockade that Clark's army built across the island in front of their cabins.

99

That summer was probably as carefree as any that the people
on Corn Island had ever known. They did not have to stay cooped
up in a dirty, ill-smelling fort. They could attend to domestic
affairs and work in their gardens without the constant dread of a
surprise attack by Indians.

The children waded and fished in the river, hunted for turkey
eggs in the tall cane, climbed the trees, and swung on the grapevines that hung like thick ropes from the large sycamores and
cottonwoods.

The Falls, the dominating and most novel feature of their new
environment, was a source of wonder and interest to adults and
children alike.[2] They never tired of watching the swirling water or
of listening to tales about shooting the rapids and of portaging
around them.

The falls of the Ohio, looking upstream below Louisville.
This break in navigation made a portage of about two and
a half miles necessary except at certain stages of high water.
Courtesy Caulfield & Shook.

The latest was the story of Maj. William Linn's trip the previous
year. He had taken a party of soldiers in keelboats from Fort Pitt
to New Orleans to get a supply of gunpowder for the western
armies. On their return, they had to unload their cargo below the
Rapids and carry the boats as well as the kegs of powder more
than two miles through the woods to the mouth of Beargrass
Creek.

That was the time for the Indians to strike if any had been
around. Not until the powder was reloaded and the men again at

the oars in midstream did Linn's party feel safe from the danger of an attack.[3]

The Corn Island settlers had no word from the army that had gone down the river on the day of the great eclipse until Simon Kenton suddenly appeared one August morning.

"Clark has taken every fort in the Illinois," he told them. "Not a gun was fired nor a man wounded."

Before the astonished settlers could ask him half the questions on their tongues, Kenton slipped off to carry Clark's dispatches to Colonel Bowman at Harrodsburg.

Capt. John Montgomery arrived a few days later, with a squad of soldiers guarding Philip de Rochblave and other captured British officers. Their long journey would end at Williamsburg prison, a thousand miles from Kaskaskia.

In October, Major Linn and nearly half of the soldiers in the Illinois army returned. The islanders then heard the story of the Great Council at Cahokia. From their knowledge of Indians, it seemed almost unbelievable. They could not imagine Indian chiefs begging an American commander to smoke the pipe of peace with them!

Linn brought orders from Clark for the people at the Falls to build a fort on the mainland and leave the island before winter. A strong post there to protect river traffic and to keep the lines of communication open between the central Kentucky settlements and the Illinois towns was a military essential to the success of Clark's plans.

He had not selected the place as his advanced base by accident. No locality on the western waters was better known. It had been accurately mapped in 1766 by a British officer, and ten years later John Williams, secretary of the Transylvania Company, expressed the general opinion of its future destiny: ". . . the Falls, it is certain, must be the most considerable mart in this part of the world; the lands around it . . . rich and fertile, and most agreeably situated; which had occasioned many people to fix their affections on that place." [4]

However, the coveted area had been granted and surveyed before John Williams ever saw it. Lord Dunmore, royal governor

of Virginia, had bestowed tracts of two thousand acres each upon
several officers, according to the terms of the Royal Proclamation
of 1763, "in consideration of military services performed" in the
French and Indian War.

The choicest tract went to Dr. John Connolly, "late a Surgeon's
Mate." As surveyed for him in 1773 and 1774, it began ". . . at
a hoop Ash and Buckeye . . . Thirty-five poles above the mouth
of Beargrass Creek," which entered the Ohio at the foot of what
is now Third Street. The tract extended along the south bank of
the Ohio for about two miles. Connolly and Col. John Campbell,
as equal partners, bought for themselves two thousand river front
acres adjoining this grant.[5]

*The settlement on Corn Island opposite Louisville. The rows of trees
on the right border Beargrass Creek where all boats tied up above the
falls. Courtesy the Filson Club.*

At the outbreak of the Revolutionary War, Campbell had sided
with the Americans. Connolly stayed with the British. From Fort
Pitt, he busied himself organizing Indian raids against the frontier
rebels. If American troops had not captured him and kept him in

prison until the war was over, the first West would have had a very different history.

The Kentuckians assumed that Connolly, as an active enemy, had forfeited his title to the land. Accordingly, Col. Richard Chenoweth, who was in charge of building the fort, proceeded to run his lines as if no previous survey had been made.

He selected a place on the riverbank at the top of a steep ravine nearly opposite the cabins on Corn Island, near the present junction of Twelfth and Rowan Streets. After the slope was cleared, this site would command a view up and down the river for a mile or more. A clear, cold spring at the foot of the ravine provided an abundant supply of water.[6]

Building a fort in the wilderness goes slowly, at best. As the mellow days of autumn passed and chilly winds began to blow, the island settlers grew impatient to move. They were uncomfortably crowded, trying to make room for other settlers who had recently arrived. Hunters found it increasingly difficult to go back and forth from the island to the mainland for game. Heavy autumn rains made the people uneasy about the possibility of high water and floods. The holiday on Corn Island was over.

In December, some families moved across to their new cabins before the rest of the fort was finished. They immediately began to plan for a combined housewarming and Christmas party.

No frontier community had better reason to rejoice than those first families of the future metropolis of Kentucky. They had suffered no actual want, no attack by British or Indians, and no loss in battle. The new fort would shelter them through the coming winter. The war, they confidently believed, would be over by spring; then they could lay out their town and build permanent homes on their own lots.

In happy ignorance of conditions elsewhere, they went briskly ahead with preparations for their party. They invited every one in the settlement as a matter of course; and all the people came, including some traders who had stopped at the island to mend their leaky boat.

The frontiersmen held their party in the large northeast corner room that would become a blockhouse when the fort was com-

pleted. For a table, the men laid boards on poles supported on
forked sticks driven into the ground. The housewives set this with
all the table service the settlement possessed—wooden bowls, trays
and plates, pewter spoons and horn-handled knives and two-
pronged iron forks, some tin cups and Delft cups and saucers. The
centerpiece was a roasted opossum, hanging by its tail on a stick
of wood.

The menu included barbecued deer, bear, and buffalo; roasted
fish, raccoon, rabbit, wild goose, pigeon, turkey, corn pone, hoecake, battercakes; lye hominy, both boiled and fried; pumpkin
pie sweetened with wild honey, and nuts which the children had
gathered.[7]

Guests and hosts sat down at noon and did not rise from the
table until none could eat another mouthful.

According to pioneer custom, dancing should follow the feast,
but the Negro fiddler, Cato Watts, who had played on summer eve-
nings on the island, had worn out all his fiddle strings. The party
might have ended without any music at all if one of the traders, a
young Frenchman named Jean Nickle, had not chanced to mention
his fiddle to Miss Ann Tuell.

"A fiddle!" she exclaimed. "He has a fiddle!" The other young
people quickly gathered around them.

"Won't you play for us?" they begged.

No young Frenchman could possibly refuse such coaxing. By
the time he had returned from the boat with his fiddle under his
arm, the young men had taken down the tables and cleared the
center of the room. Older people sat against the walls, holding the
small children on their laps.

"I will teach you the *Branle,*" Monsieur Nickle said, standing on
a stool in front of the big fireplace and waving his fiddle bow.
"This is a brand new dance, just come from France."

After arranging the young people in a circle, he began to play
the music, directing the young men to leap in circles. Instead, they
"leapfrogged" over each others' heads.

Jean Nickle shook his head. "Perhaps the minuet will go better," he suggested. "The lady must curtsy low with outspread
skirts; the gentleman must bow from the waist, with his right hand

over his heart, like this." He showed them the bow and began to play the slow music of a minuet.

Instead of gliding, the young men romped and ducked their heads like geese when they should have bowed slowly and gracefully.

"No, no!" Nickle exclaimed, waving his fiddle and bow for them to stop. "We shall try the *Pavane*. In this, you must fold your arms and strut like peacocks, the ladies first passing the gentlemen and then the gentlemen strutting past the ladies."

This gave the young, vigorous backwoodsmen a chance they could not resist. They not only strutted, but gave the peacock's call, and the dance ended abruptly in a roar of laughter.

At this point old Cato appeared at the door, his white teeth gleaming, fiddle in his hand. Where he had found new strings, and how many beaver skins they had cost, only Jean Nickle and Cato knew.

"Mought I play now, while the gen'leman restes?" he asked, bowing low.

At the first scrape of his bow across the strings, everyone able to "shake a leg" had lined up for a Virginia reel. They needed no prompting to dance to his music. The head couple led off with shuffles, jigs, pigeon-wings, and other capers. Then the next couple had its chance to do as well, or better. They kept it up until midnight, when old Cato could play no more.[8]

Long before that hour arrived, Jean Nickle, unnoticed, had returned to his boat, shrugging his shoulders at the wilderness folk and their ways, with no thought that several years later he would return to teach dancing in that very settlement. Cato Watts had carried off the honors at the first Christmas party at the Falls of the Ohio.

CHAPTER XIV

The Forlorn Hope

Never in the field of human conflict
have so many owed so much to so few.
—WINSTON CHURCHILL

At that first Christmas party at the Falls of the Ohio, the Kaskaskians feasted and danced as merrily as the settlers. None among them seemed gayer than their young commander, but George Rogers Clark was far from carefree.

The French outnumbered his American troops ten to one and the Indians, a hundred to one. Clark knew that both would desert him if the British attempted to recapture the fort.

He had heard rumors that Sir Henry Hamilton, the lieutenant governor of Canada, was in the vicinity with a large force of British soldiers and Indian allies. Clark had sent out spies, and not one had returned.

Daily, Clark hoped and watched for the arrival of some messenger with news from the world beyond the flooded lowlands that surrounded the town. It might be news of the Revolutionary War, if, indeed there was still a war! Or it might be news from his base at the Falls, from the other Kentucky forts, or from Detroit. Most of all, Clark wanted news from Detroit!

He had not heard from Virginia in nearly a year, nor had he received a message from Captain Helm at Vincennes for several weeks.

The first news from the outside came on January 29, 1779, brought by Francis Vigo, a St. Louis merchant whom Clark had sent to Vincennes in December to arrange for supplies for the garrison there. It could hardly have been worse.

"Hamilton retook Vincennes in December," Vigo told Clark gravely. "I was in the fort at the time. Captain Helm, with only four men on whom he could depend, demanded and received honorable terms of surrender. Hamilton had thirty British regulars, fifty French volunteers, Indian agents and interpreters, and about four hundred Indians.

"He has sent the Indians away, to watch the Ohio and to make war on the frontiers, especially in Kentucky. He has settled down for the winter, with his regulars and a few volunteers. In the spring, when the Indians return, he intends to sweep the country clean of rebels."

In his mind Clark saw it all just as Hamilton was planning it—Illinois first, then Kentucky. "And well if the desolation would end there."

Why wait for spring, Clark reasoned. He sprang from his chair and sent for his officers. They discussed their situation. They could retreat to Kentucky, take refuge in the Spanish fort at St. Louis; or stay and fight it out with Hamilton.

"Gentlemen!" Clark declared, "I can see no alternative. We must either quit this country or attack Mr. Hamilton at Vincennes. As he cannot suppose we should be so mad as to attempt to march eighty leagues through a drowned country in the depth of winter, we may surprise him." [1]

A chorus of approval greeted his words. Not retreat, not inaction, but attack—swift, sudden, secret—that was their decision.

Clark's letters and other writings and Joseph Bowman's *Journal* give the details of the hurried but careful preparations. Clark arranged for credit with the local merchants, for which he mortgaged his own land. He recalled the Cahokia Volunteers. The party loaded a large rowboat with provisions and ammunition and assembled horses and packsaddles. A new company was recruited and the entire army outfitted with winter clothing.

When all was ready, Clark wrote a letter to Gov. Patrick Henry, to be sent to Virginia by special messenger. "I am Resolved," he wrote, "to Risque the whole on a Single Battle. . . I know the Case is Desperate . . . We have this Consolation; that our Cause is Just and that our Cuntrey will be greatful and not [condemn] our Conduct in Case we fail." [2]

Their war boat, *The Willing,* left Kaskaskia on February 4 with Lt. John Rogers in command of its crew of forty-six men. His orders were to go down the Mississippi to the mouth of the Ohio, then up that river and the Wabash to a point ten leagues below Vincennes. There they were to await further directions.

The army of seventy American soldiers and sixty French volunteers crossed the Kaskaskia River on the afternoon of February 5, 1779, accompanied by the entire population of the town. They knelt bareheaded in a drizzling rain to receive Father Gibault's blessing. Then, followed by the prayers and cheers of the people, the men wheeled into line to march, wade, or swim across the drowned lands of Illinois to Vincennes.

Crossing the "Drowned Lands" of Illinois between Kaskaskia and Vincennes, February 1779. A panel in the mural painting in the Seelbach Hotel, Louisville. Courtesy Caulfield & Shook.

The first week passed pleasantly, almost gaily. Each morning one company mounted the horses and hunted, while the others marched ahead on foot. At night the hunters entertained their comrades around campfires, feasting on buffalo meat, telling stories, dancing and singing until the day's trials were forgotten and they almost imagined they were in possession of Vincennes.

In six days they had marched 174 miles and had reached the banks of the Little Wabash. It was the first of four flood-swollen rivers whose muddy waters mingled in one unbroken inland lake between them and their objective, still about sixty miles away. If they traversed those miles, they must do it without game or fire. They must wade through icy swamps by day and shiver under a winter sky by night. The first real test of the quality of their leadership and of their loyalty had come.

How the Illinois Regiment met that challenge can be told best in Clark's and Bowman's own words. Acting, when he viewed the Little Wabash, ". . . as though crossing the water would be only a piece of diversion," Clark ordered Captain McCarty's company to make a dugout canoe in which to explore the drowned land and mark the trees to the next high spot of ground. "Our horses swam across, . . . and we began our march, our vessell loaded with those that was sickly."

In that way the army crossed two of the four rivers. "In the evening of the 17th we got to the lowlands of the river Embarass. . . it being nine miles to St. Vincents, . . . every foot of the way covered with deep water . . . and not a mouthful of provisions." [3]

Clark detailed a squad to stay with the horses, which they could take no further. The other men, loaded with heavy packs, must continue on foot or in canoes. When he overheard some men talking of returning to Kaskaskia, he laughed at them and told them to go hunt for deer. The next day he put more men to work making canoes. He knew, however, that he dared not risk the loss of a day and night in ferrying so many starving men to the next half-dry spot of land.

With every eye fixed on him, Clark whispered to those nearest him to do as he did. "I took some water in my hand, poured on Powder, Blacked my face, gave the war whoop, and marched into the water." The men stared at him, then followed. "I ordered those that was near me to begin a favorite song of theirs." [4]

The song passed down the zigzag line as the men sloshed on with rifles held high, stopping to wait for a canoe only when the water was chin deep. Another sound kept time with the song—

the merry "R-r-r-rat-a-tat-tat! R-r-r-rat-a-tat-tat!" from the drum of a fourteen-year-old boy sitting astride the shoulders of the tallest sergeant.

They lodged that night at the Sugar Camp on about half an acre of high ground. Before them the next morning lay the Horse Shoe plain, four miles wide, covered with water breast high. There, Bowman states, ". . . we expected some of our brave men must certainly perish, having froze in the night, and so long fasting." [5]

Clark, evidently feeling that the supreme test of their endurance had come, spoke to his troops in words of praise and affection that warmed their hearts and fired their courage. "When we reach those woods," he concluded, pointing across the flooded plain, "you will have a sight of Vincennes, your long-wished-for object."

With a cheer, they followed him into the water. As they waded past him, Clark noticed three or four men looking about furtively.

"Major Bowman!" he called, loudly. "Fall back to the rear with twenty-five men and shoot every man that refuses to march on."

After that, the men marched on as best they could. "All the Low men and Weekly Hung on the Trees and floated on the old logs untill they weare taken off by the canoes." [6]

The tallest and strongest among them, after reaching dry ground, kindled fires, pulled the weaker men from the water's edge and walked them up and down until the icy numbness left their limbs. Some of them had overtaken an Indian canoe filled with squaws and children, who had a half-quarter of buffalo meat, some corn, tallow, and kettles on board. They quickly made broth and doled it out first to the weaker men, a little at a time.

That afternoon the army crossed the lake in canoes and camped on Warrior's Island, in full view of the fort. While waiting for night, Clark wrote a note to the inhabitants of Vincennes and sent it in by a duck hunter whom some of his young Frenchmen had captured.

"Being now within Two Miles," he wrote, "I. . . request of such of you as are true citizens. . . to remain Still in your houses, and that those (if any there be) that are friends to the King of England will instantly repair to the Fort and Join his troops and Fight like men." [7]

Through their spyglasses, the officers saw the hunter enter the
town and men gather about him. Apparently, no one went to the
fort to warn Hamilton. The American army found every street
deserted and every house dark when it reached the high ground
back of the town. In darkness the troops received their last whispered orders, then silently found hiding places behind houses and
trees and the riverbank.

Inside the Vincennes fort a soldier heard something.

"Sst! What was that?" he called to his nearest mate.

"Just another party of drunken Indians saluting as they pass. Go
to sleep."

"Look!" the soldier shouted. "A guard has fallen! Shot down
through the porthole! Rebels must be attacking us! Sound the
alarm!"

The fort drums began to roll. Within a minute or two the cannon blazed and roared through the portholes, doing no damage
except to houses across the street.

Every time a porthole was opened, some rebel bullets found
their mark within the fort. "Fine sport for the sons of Liberty, if
only our ammunition holds out until *The Willing* arrives!"

Several citizens of the town gave Clark powder and lead which
they had hidden when Hamilton retook Vincennes in December.
With this timely help, he determined to bring Hamilton to terms
before the Indians could gather.

At nine o'clock the next morning, February 24, he sent a letter
with a flag of truce to General Hamilton, demanding the surrender
of the fort. "The firing then ceased during which time our men
was provided with a Breakfast it being the only meal of Victuals
since the 18th inst."

When General Hamilton replied that he and his garrison were
". . . not to be awed into an action unworthy of British subjects,"
Clark ordered the firing to begin again. To Hamilton's request
later in the day for a truce of three days, Clark replied that he
would not ". . . agree to any other terms than that of Mr. Hamilton's surrendering himself and Garrison prisoners at discretion." [8]

By that time one-sixth of Hamilton's British regulars had been
wounded. His French volunteers refused to fight against their rela-

tives with Clark. Having no means of knowing the size of the American army, Hamilton accepted Clark's terms.

His white flag appeared at the gate of the fort. Before the day closed he had signed articles of surrender in which he agreed to deliver up Fort Sackville, with all of its supplies and ammunition, and the garrison with its arms, as prisoners of war. He gave his reasons—"the remoteness from succour, the state and quantity of provisions, the unanimity of officers & men on its expediency, the honorable terms allowed, and lastly, the confidence in a generous enemy." [9]

An old print of Fort Sackville at Vincennes. The National Memorial to George Rogers Clark has been erected on this site. Courtesy the Filson Club.

At ten o'clock, February 25, 1779, Captain Helm for the second time hoisted the American colors over Fort Sackville, while the cannon boomed a salute of thirteen guns. Sir Henry Hamilton, lieutenant governor of Canada, and his well-dressed officers and redcoated garrison marched out and surrendered their swords and weapons ". . . to a set of uncivilized Virginia woodsmen armed with rifles."

Hamilton, the man who intended to wait for spring, left Vincennes on March 7 with about twenty-five other prisoners of war. Before him lay the long, hard trail to Williamsburg through the country he had planned to "sweep clean of rebels."

He found the people ". . . in eternal apprehension from the Indians," the Kentucky forts ". . . in a wretched state, obliged to enclose the cattle every night within the fort, and carry their rifle . . . to plough or cut wood."

The Kentucky officers were cold but courteous. However, throughout the journey, Hamilton's guards had to protect him from the fury of the settlers, who held him chiefly responsible for the misery and suffering inflicted upon them by the Indians.

Events crowded fast upon Clark after the capture of Vincennes. *The Willing* arrived a few days later. It had picked up his messenger, William Myers, who bore dispatches from Virginia, expressing the thanks and gratitude of the governor and the legislature for the bloodless victory of the previous summer.

The assembly, acting more promptly than it had in the case of Kentucky, had immediately created the "County of Illinois" and appointed Clark's personal friend Capt. John Todd, Jr., of Harrodsburg, as its civil governor and county lieutenant. It had also promoted Clark to the full rank of colonel and his able second-in-command, Joseph Bowman, to that of major.

On March 5, Captain Helm returned from a tour up the Wabash with seven captured boats loaded with British soldiers, provisions, and supplies for Hamilton's garrison. Clark now had food and clothing to spare for his ragged army.

The capture of Hamilton, their "Great White Chief," brought dismay to the Indians of the Northwest. Their leaders came to Clark, begging him to renew the chain of friendship and smoke the sacred pipe of peace with them. Their seemingly genuine desire for peace promised to be one of the most valuable results of his victory.

On March 20, Colonel Clark again left Captain Helm in charge at Vincennes. He started back to Kaskaskia on board his war boat, *The Willing,* attended by five other armed boats and seventy men.

As the little town came into view, they saw people gathered at the wharf with drums and fifes and waving banners. Laughing and weeping, the Kaskaskians embraced and kissed their returning friends and relatives. Half-wild with joy, they hailed and welcomed their young commander, the Conqueror of the Northwest who had come back victorious without the loss of a man.

One can hardly read the vivid records of that "late uncommon march" through the drowned lands of Illinois without in some measure sharing the emotion of those citizens of old Kaskaskia.

Tales of failures and of successes, of tensions and of courage marked the trail to the settlement of the first West.

CHAPTER XV

Tug of War

*We derived strength from our falls
and numbers from our losses.*
—KENTUCKY ADDRESS TO CONGRESS,
NOVEMBER 10, 1788

The capture of Vincennes did not mark the end of Colonel Clark's campaign. To march to Detroit before the enemy could rally his forces was the next step in his plan of conquest. He set the date and place of the rendezvous for the expedition—June 20, in Vincennes. "In case I was not disappointed in the number of troops I expected, I even counted Detroit my own." [1]

But the number he expected never came. Virginia, hard pressed for soldiers for the eastern armies, sent only 170 poorly equipped men instead of the promised five hundred. Col. John Bowman had promised to send three hundred men from Kentucky, ". . . if it lay in his power." [2] Only thirty arrived.

Several members of Clark's gallant Illinois Regiment had died; many were ill from the hardships and exposure of the march to Vincennes. Clark could barely muster enough active soldiers to man the places he had taken and to garrison the new fort at the Falls.

Detroit, that "nest of vipers," remained in the hands of the British. From it they continued to send out the Indians to raid the frontier settlements, hoping that ". . . the terror and losses of the inhabitants will operate powerfully in our favor."

The Kentucky settlers did not rely on or encourage such a hope. In the early spring, Colonel Bowman ordered the militia ". . . to plant their corn, and be in readiness to rendezvous in May at the

117

mouth of the Licking." He directed those at the Falls to come up the river in boats for the army to use in crossing the Ohio River.

About seventy men under Capt. William Harrod, returning from the Falls to the Redstone region in Pennsylvania, joined Bowman's forces. Companies under Benjamin Logan and William Whitley met him at the Licking. In Capt. John Holder's company from Boonesborough was Maj. George M. Bedinger, whom Bowman made his adjutant.

Instead of leading this volunteer army to join Clark in Vincennes, Bowman decided to attack the Shawnees in Ohio first. He named George Clark and William Whitley, who had twice invaded the region north of the Ohio River to recapture stolen horses, as pilots or guides for the expedition.[3]

Each man "found" himself, which meant that he rode his own horse, brought his own package of jerked meat and parched corn, his camp outfit and rifle. At the Licking rendezvous, the officers distributed powder and lead. Crossing the Ohio on May 28, 1779, the troops followed their pilots single file up the valley of the Little Miami. Before midnight of the next day they had reached a clearing a short distance below Chillicothe, the most southern of the Shawnee villages.

There, Bowman gave orders for the attack. Logan's men moved to the left, between the town and the Little Miami; Harrod's to the right. The two forces would meet north of the village. Holder's troops hid on the south to intercept the Indians if they attempted to escape in that direction.

It was a good "Indian" plan, but the village dogs began to bark and an Indian man came out to see what the commotion was about. He stumbled into Holder's troops, and a soldier shot at him. He called out loudly as he fell. Instantly, the squaws cried, "Kentuck! Kentuck!"

The Indians ran out of their homes, some into Holder's waiting company, some heading for the river into Logan's. Most of them took refuge in a two-story council house and several large cabins near it.

There they waited for the customary daylight attack, but the invaders did not venture within range of the rifles inside the council house. Some began to ransack the cabins and set fire to them; others rounded up the horses outside the town.

Bedinger and several other men had hidden behind a large log about forty paces from the council house. They could hear the

The name of Benjamin Logan appears throughout the pioneer history of Kentucky. As the solitary founder of St. Asaph's (Logan's Station), he commanded one of the three most important places in the early years. Courtesy the Filson Club.

loud voice of a Shawnee leader calling to his people: "Remember, you are men and warriors! Your enemies are only Kentucky squaws. Fight! And be strong!"

The attackers were sure that Indian runners had escaped through their lines and gone for help from neighboring villages. About nine o'clock, Bowman gave the order to retreat. He called out to the men behind the log, "Make your escape!"

"Put your hats on sticks to draw their fire," Bedinger ordered his comrades. "Then run! One, two, three! Now!" He himself started first, dodging the bullets fired at him. Before the Indians could reload, most of the others behind the log had followed their leader to safety.

As the Kentucky troops reformed their lines in the woods, a Negro woman ran towards them from the village. She called out that Simon Girty was only a few miles away with a hundred Mingo warriors. The number grew as the word spread among the invaders.

About fifteen miles south of Chillicothe the Indians overtook the troops at the ford of a creek. According to plan, the white troops formed a hollow square with the plunder and the horses inside. Every man, white and red, slid off his horse and got behind a tree or fallen timber.

The contest lasted for three hours with no advantage on either side, but the red force was increasing and the white men were falling from weariness and hunger. Bowman ordered some of his troops to mount and charge the enemy.

"Come, boys! Let's rush them!" Bedinger called to those near him. "Get your tomahawks ready and reserve your fire!"

Forty or fifty followed him. A chief fell, mortally wounded. As soon as the Indians near him had lifted him on a horse and hurried away, the others fell back beyond firing range.

The white army quickly mounted and rode from the scene of battle. They rested a short time at night, but at dawn they were off again. On June 1, the broad Ohio rolled between them and the enemy.[4]

The campaign ended where it had begun, a few miles from the mouth of the Licking River. There Bowman auctioned off the

spoils of war—furs, hides, blankets, ornaments, horses. Then
the Pennsylvanians headed for their homes up the Ohio, the Kentuckians for their forts.

All told, they thought they had done a good job. They had
burned half of the cabins in Chillicothe. They had destroyed
large quantities of corn, ammunition, and other supplies. They
had carried off nearly two hundred horses. Yet, many people, then
and later, considered the campaign a failure. What George Rogers
Clark thought of it can readily be imagined. "Never was a person
more mortified than I was at this time . . . Detroit lost for want of
a few men."[5]

How the British regarded it is revealed in a letter Capt. Henry
Bird wrote on June 9, 1779, to his superior officer in Detroit.

We had collected at the Mingo town near 200 savages, . . .
When low! a runner arrived with accounts of the Shawanese
towns being attack'd by a body from Kentuck. . . . News
flew that all the Towns were to be attack'd & our little body
separated in an Instant past reassembling. . . . The unsteady
Rogues put me out of all Patience![6]

The Shawnees made no more large attacks that year. Bowman's
campaign may have done more for the Kentuckians than they
realized at the time.

A foe that spared neither white man nor red appeared in the
West before the year ended. This common enemy, known as the
Hard Winter of 1779-80, began its attacks in November. It
covered the ground with snow and ice that remained until nearly
March. It froze the streams solid. It sent snow and sleet down
the wide chimneys and through cracks between the logs of cabin
walls.

At night wild beasts fought with the settlers' stock to get near
the cabin chimneys for warmth. "Go through the cane and see
cattle laying with their heads to their side," said one pioneer, ". . .
Just literally frozen to death . . . A great country for turkeys,
and they had like to have starved."[7]

The settlers also suffered greatly from lack of food. At Bryan's Station, five miles from Lexington, George Bryan gave five hundred acres of his land for a horse with which to hunt buffalo and bring in meat for the starving people in the fort.[8]

Before the snows had melted, the rush of new settlers into Kentucky began. Bands of immigrants, released from their icebound camps by the coming of spring, staggered into the settlements. And, alas! Summer brought a rush from the other side of the Ohio.

Captain Bird had once more got his "unsteady Rogues" together. With 150 white soldiers and several cannon, he left Detroit on May 25, 1780, gathering up his red allies as he moved south. By the time he reached the Ohio he had nearly one thousand Indians under the command of four white leaders—George and Simon Girty, Alexander McKee, and Matthew Elliott.

Bird had planned to attack the fort at the Falls while Clark was away in Illinois, but his Indians flatly refused to go so far from home or to fight against Clark's cannon. Bird had to yield to their demand to attack the nearest Kentucky forts. His troops rowed their keelboats up the Licking to its forks, then cut a road and dragged their cannon through the woods.

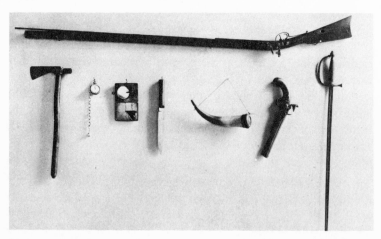

Pioneer equipment for hunting or fighting. Flintlock rifle, tomahawk, watch, pocket compass and sun dial, hunting knife, powder horn, officer's pistol and sword. Courtesy the Filson Club.

The season was so wet and rainy that few settlers were working their lands. Bird's army appeared in front of Ruddle's Fort on South Licking on the morning of June 24, before any person in Kentucky had seen or heard of it.

In spite of the size of the invading force, Capt. Isaac Ruddle and his company refused Bird's call to surrender and stoutly defended their fort until nearly noon. Then Bird moved his small cannon into place. It barked sharply: once! twice! But its small lead balls stuck in the logs and did little damage.

When Bird moved his six-pounder into position to fire, Ruddle realized that he could resist no further. Before surrendering, he demanded and obtained from the British officers a written promise of safety and fair treatment of the prisoners.

Bird's own official report tells what occurred when the gates were opened:

> Whilst Captain McKee and myself were in the fort settling these matters with the Poor People, they [the Indians] rush'd in, tore the children from their mothers' breasts, killed a wounded man, and every one of the cattle.[9]

Each savage claimed as his prisoner the first white person he could lay his hands on. The Indians tomahawked mothers clinging to their children. They rolled the babies down the bank of the creek, killing those that cried. When Ruddle appealed to the British commander to restrain the savages, he answered, truthfully, that he could not.

After throwing the bodies of the murdered settlers in a pile and covering them with stones, the enemy moved on to repeat its easy victory at Martin's Station on Stoner Creek, five miles away. There Bird took the precaution to put the prisoners in charge of his Canadian soldiers and allowed the Indians only to plunder the cabins.[10]

With his cannon, Captain Bird could have taken every fort in central Kentucky, but the Indians had destroyed the settlers' cattle, with which he had expected to feed his army. He had nearly three hundred prisoners and not one pound of meat. His savage allies, satisfied for once with blood and plunder and prisoners, had already begun to leave. A prisoner, whom they had captured as they crossed the Ohio, had spread a rumor that Clark was on his way up from the Falls.

Bird's one wish now was to get his cannon and his prisoners beyond the reach of pursuit.

> We had brought no food with us & were now reduced to great distress, & the poor Prisoners in danger of being starved . . . The Indians almost all left us within a day's march of the enemy. It was with difficulty I procured a guide thro' the woods . . . I marched the poor women & children 20 miles in one day over very high mountains, frightening them with frequent alarms to push them forward, in short, Sir, by water & land we came with all our cannon & c 90 miles in 4 days . . . rowing 50 miles the last day . . . I could Sir, by all accounts have gone through the whole country without any opposition, had the Indians preserved the cattle. Everything is safe so far, but we are not yet out of reach of pursuit, as a very smart fellow escaped from me within 26 miles of the enemy.[11]

Captain Bird reached Detroit on August 4, 1780, with about 150 prisoners, ". . . mostly Germans who speak English." Many were Tories who had fled to the wilderness of Kentucky to escape persecution by rebels in the East. Including those in the hands of the Indians, ". . . the whole will amount to about three hundred and fifty."[12]

CHAPTER XVI

In Shawneeland

Though we had peace, yet 'twill be a great while ere
things be settled: though the wind lie, yet after a storm
the sea will work a great while.

—SELDEN

War continued. All of Captain Bird's prisoners who survived that terrible march from Vincennes would, in time, be exchanged or paroled. History has told us little of the fate of most of those carried off by the Indians.

Occasionally the savages would take a few captives to Detroit to get money for rum or powder. Some paroled prisoners eventually returned to their former homes, but most of them were never heard of or seen again in Kentucky.

John Hinkston, the "very smart fellow" mentioned in Captain Bird's report, escaped before the Indians reached the Ohio River. The second night after Ruddle's surrender was very wet and dark. While the Indians were trying to make a fire, Hinkston sprang between the guards, ran into woods, and hid in a deep shadow beside a log.

After the Indians had given up the search in the darkness, he steered his course by the feel of the west wind on his wet hand until he thought he would be safe from pursuit.

The next morning the fog was so dense that he could not see a tree twenty yards away. He heard the howls and cries of what seemed to be wild animals. Carefully avoiding the direction of the sounds, which he knew were made by the Indians, he escaped through fog. That night he arrived at Lexington, one of the many new settlements that had sprung up in 1779, after Clark's capture of Vincennes.[1]

Robert Patterson, James Morrison, and other settlers there gasped with astonishment when they heard Hinkston's story. Indians in the country for nearly two weeks, and gone, unseen, with hundreds of prisoners!

They sent riders to notify the other stations, an express to the Falls, and one to Colonel Clark in Illinois, to ask him to lead them against the enemy.

Clark had already learned of Bird's plans from a prisoner who had escaped from the Indians before the invaders entered Kentucky. At that time he was at Fort Jefferson, which he had built in the spring just below the mouth of the Ohio. He promptly sent the troops with him there up the Ohio and set out on foot with two companions, all disguised as Indians, hoping to beat Bird to the Falls.

Clark learned on the way that Bird had gone up the Licking instead. He changed his own plans and hurried on to Harrodsburg.

There he found the little wilderness capital buzzing with excitement. A messenger had arrived that very morning with the news of Bird's raid.

Joining the crowd, Clark heard hardly a mention of the tragic fate of several hundred people. The one word on every man's tongue, seemingly the one thought in every man's mind, was "Land! Land! Land!"

This deplorable situation had its roots in the haphazard way in which Virginia had permitted settlers to choose almost any location and shape of a tract of land. Scores of squatters, who would be difficult to oust, had settled on land to which they had no other claim than that of possession.

The country, in all likelihood, could hardly have been settled under any formal method, but the result of such haphazard choices was a crazy-quilt pattern of overlapping "shingle" claims that led to quarrels and lawsuits.

Legal red tape added to the difficulty of securing a valid title to a genuine claim. The holder of any kind of warrant—cabin right, military, treasury—must have his survey registered at the land office in Richmond.[2]

Few of the early settlers had even paid their original purchase fee. Fewer still had found the money, time, or opporunity to have their claims registered.

In its 1779-1780 session, the Virginia Assembly made a belated attempt to bring some kind of order out of the confusion, by passing a new Land Law. It sent four commissioners out to Kentucky to administer this law and to issue certificates on claims that were accepted as valid.

The commissioners held their first court at Logan's Fort in October, 1779. The first certificate they issued was in the name of Isaac Shelby, for making a crop of corn in 1776, on land "on a branch that heads at the Knob Lick & about a mile and a half or two miles from the said Lick a southeastwardly course."[3]

Clark found the land office in full swing in Harrodsburg when he arrived. He opened recruiting headquarters across the road from it, but the crowd stayed on the other side, haggling, bargaining, quarreling, while speculators and agents played up the Indian raids to scare claim owners into selling cheaply.

Clark realized at once that he must put an end to that competition. He elbowed his way through the crowd to the register's desk.

"Will you close this office at once, and keep it closed until the present emergency has passed?" he requested.

"I must keep it open," the official replied. "I have no legal right to close it."

"Then I'll order it closed as a military necessity," Clark replied. "And I enlist you in the army."

Turning to the crowd, he announced, "The land register's office is closed. Now will you volunteer to help us whip the Shawnees?"

"Let them back east that hold warrants to thousands of acres come out and fight," a man sneered.

"Send for your State troops from the Falls," another spoke up. "They're paid to fight. As soon as we get a few more to join us, we're startin' back east."

"Then you will go on foot," Clark announced. "I have sent soldiers to Crab Orchard to take horses, arms, and ammunition from every man who tries to leave the country."[4]

By such bold, high-handed methods he succeeded in raising an army of one thousand men. They rendezvoused on August 1,

1780, at the Licking—militia companies from the several stations, regulars from the fort at the Falls. These brought some Kaskaskia artillery—"a double fortified six-pounder, a fortified piece"—up the Ohio with them.

"When we got there, mouth of Licking," one soldier said later, "we got just six quarts of corn. Might parch, pound, bake, or do as we pleased with it, but that was what we were to get. . . . We were like a parcel of young pigs just learning to crack corn; went crack! crack! all through the tents."[5]

They camped on the northern shore of the Ohio only long enough to build a blockhouse at the site of Cincinnati. There they left some surplus supplies and the sick and wounded men, with forty soldiers to guard them and the boats. Then the invaders from Kentucky swung up the Miami valley on foot, with only enough horses to carry supplies and drag the artillery.

In spite of the skill and secrecy with which Simon Kenton and William Whitley piloted the troops under Clark and Logan, the Indians got word of their coming. "A man ran off and gave the Indians information. We marched hard after finding he was gone," said Whitley.

When they reached Old Chillicothe, the scene of Boone's captivity, they found the town deserted.

We went there in a mighty hurry . . . Traveled nearly all night the last night . . . When we came to Old Chillicothe the Indians had burned it down, all to some two or three cabins that were full of fur and deer skins," said William Clinkenbeard.

. . . Plenty of corn, roasting ears. We let it be there till we came back. Every man then, that had a sword or big knife, had to work . . . Some standing sentry; others at work round the big corn field.[6]

Clark had learned years before in Dunmore's War that the Indians carried no food on their long, swift raids except a pouch of parched corn, depending for meat upon any game that crossed their paths. The Shawnee warriors would have no corn for raids in Kentucky the following summer if he could prevent it.[7]

"We . . . had to cross a little prairie before we came to the second town [Piqua, on Mad River]," said William Clinkenbeard. ". . . I was pioneer to cut a road for the cannon that day. While we went through that prairie the Indians fired upon us from their cabins . . . Held their guns too high. Could hear them biz! biz! over us.

"Clark had two cannons. We just had them filled with grape [shot] and fired at them. We saw nor heard more of them [there]. They then met us at the woods.

"The battle lasted about two hours. The Indians then gave way. We never found one of their dead . . . We couldn't pack roasting ears and we had no provision to pack, and so we . . . had to return.

". . . They never built up old Chillicothe or Pickaway towns again." [8]

At Piqua, as the Kentuckians fired their last volley, a man in Indian dress threw away his gun and ran towards them. "Don't shoot!" he called out. "I am a white man! I am a white man!"

They heard him too late. When they reached him, he could just whisper his name, "Joseph Rogers!"

He was George Rogers Clark's young cousin who had helped to guard the gunpowder brought down the Ohio in 1776. The Indians had captured him in their attack upon the party carrying the powder to Harrodsburg.

In his moment of victory, Clark knelt beside his boyhood companion and comrade and held him in his arms until he died. Rogers was buried there, with others who had fallen in the battle.[9]

Then, "having no provisions . . . and having done the Shawnees all the mischief in our power," Clark led his men back home.

They had taken no prisoners, but they had destroyed eight hundred acres of corn and vegetables, the main food supply for scores of Indian families.[10]

CHAPTER XVII

Along the Packhorse Trail

Some to endure and many to fail,
Some to conquer and many to quail,
Toiling over the Wilderness Trail.

—ANONYMOUS

In June, 1778, George Rogers Clark had dared take no more than sixty men from the Kentucky forts for his invasion of the Northwest. Four years later, August, 1780, he led an army of one thousand men from Kentucky into the Shawnee country. Those numbers bear witness to the rapid increase in population south of the Ohio within a short time after his victory at Vincennes.

General McIntosh, at Pittsburgh, several weeks after hearing of the Vincennes victory, wrote to General Washington that ". . . the immigration down the Ohio from this quarter I fear will depopulate it altogether. . . It is thought that near one half of what remain here will go down to Kentucky, the Falls, or the Illinois." [1]

"Everybody coming to Kentucky," said one old pioneer later. "Could hardly get along the road for them; and all grand Tories, pretty nigh. All from Carolina Tories. Had been treated so bad there, they had to run off or do worse." [2]

Such were the fortunes of war. When the Americans got the upper hand, the Tories fled to the wilderness. When the British were winning, the rebels emigrated.

In Sheperdstown, Virginia, Maj. George M. Bedinger had received a letter in March, 1779, from Colonel Bowman in Kentucky. "Clark has taken all the Illinois and Wabash forts," the letter said. "Let's go out in the spring, boys. There will be plenty of surveying for us to do."

Within a month, Bedinger and nine other white men and two Negroes were on their way to the Kentucky wilderness.[3]

Not all who so emigrated to the West were young, vigorous frontiersmen. Thousands of men, women, and children went ". . . in successive caravans, forming continuous streams of human beings, horses, cattle and other domestic animals all moving onward along a lonely and houseless path to a wild and cheerless land." [4]

America owes much to those pioneer men and women. They went for personal reasons, staking their all on the hope that Clark's conquest in the west would hold. But, as members of a very real army of occupation, they helped to make that hope a reality and to strengthen America's chances of winning the war and the peace.

In one company of several hundred people who made that journey "through privations incredible and perils thick" was a group from eastern Virginia known as "The Traveling Church." After young Capt. William Ellis had returned from a long stay in the West, his fellow members in the Upper Spotsylvania Baptist Church near Fredericksburg discussed the idea of moving to Kentucky as a body.

"We shall be eaten up with taxes if we stay in this war-wasted and debt-ridden country."

"Ellis says land is richer out there. And cheaper."

"We would not be taxed to support a State church."

"We would be free to worship as we please."

"It is wild and dangerous. Think of the risk for our wives and children."

"Our children would have a better chance than here."

"We could go as a group and build a fort to protect ourselves."

Finally, a majority of the congregation voted to emigrate with their pastor, Lewis Craig. This group disposed of their homes and other property; arranged for tracts of land in Kentucky; assembled necessary supplies for the journey. In September, 1781, they were ready to start.[5]

The departing congregation spent their last Sunday at the old church with friends and relatives who had come to bid them farewell. Lewis Craig, in his sermon, recalled their long struggle for religious freedom and civil rights. In his congregation sat Elijah Craig and several other preachers who had, like himself, been in Fredericksburg prison on bread and water "for conscience' sake."

At a distance, Captain Ellis, the only white man there who knew what lay ahead of them, carefully inspected the arms and ammunition of the men he had selected to guard the company. Farther off, in the midst of a group of black men watching the stock, Peter Craig, who had gone out with Ellis two years before, exhorted his brethren. That night the Spotsylvania pilgrims slept in the church, in their wagons, or on the ground under the trees.

At dawn, "The Traveling Church" broke camp and set forth, with its Bible and communion service, its books and records. Captain Ellis and Peter Craig led the way. Behind them stretched a long procession of packhorses and wagons, people and livestock.

Looking back at the bend of the road for a last glimpse of the old church, the pilgrims saw the rays of the rising sun flash on its windows and gleam on the white headstones in the churchyard. Quickly they turned and looked straight ahead.

A week later they were toiling over the Blue Ridge at Buford's Gap. Behind them lay the little villages and rolling farms of the Piedmont. Before them, as far as the eye could see, the forest-covered mountains rose in gloomy silence.

The women burst into tears at that first glimpse of the wilderness. At a whispered word from Captain Ellis, one of the Negro men twanged his banjo and started singing a lively song. Others quickly picked it up, keeping step to the tune. The children clapped their hands and laughed. Smiles broke through the tears, and the line again moved forward.

By the second Sunday the group had reached Fort Chiswell, a busy frontier station nine miles east of Wytheville, where the Shenandoah route from the north met the Blue Ridge road from the east. State troops guarded the nearby lead mines. Traders were busy buying and selling, pioneer parties going and coming, or waiting for others to join them.

The travelers appeared different when they left that refuge. They had traded their wagons and other treasured possessions for pack-saddles and powder, salt and bacon, flour and meal. Instead of kneebreeches and ruffled shirts, full-skirted dresses and gay bonnets, they wore the latest in pioneer fashion—buckskin and stout linsey-woolsey.

Captain Ellis had changed the order of march, placing some of the armed men and older boys in front to watch for danger signs, hunt for game, and select camping places at night. Behind them came the families, straggling out in a single line along the dim, narrow trail. Only a few women were riding. Nearly every one carried a heavy pack, a bag or a basket.

On they passed, family after family. The cattle and sheep followed, with men, boys, and dogs running along the trail to keep them from straying into the forest. Last came the rear guard.

Back in Fort Chiswell, the tinkle of bells grew fainter. The thin line of dust settled, and one more company of the westward-bound army of homemakers had disappeared into the wilderness.

Before dark the advance guard had found a place for the night's encampment. They had cut branches and strips of bark and leaned them against trees or cliffs for shelter. After the evening meal and prayers, the women and children crawled into these makeshift tents. The men unloaded the burdened packhorses, fed, watered, and tied the stock to graze, and stoppered their bells with a chip or twig. Then they lay down between the shelters and the smoldering embers of the fires, while the sentinels kept watch over the sleeping camp.

A week later, "The Traveling Church" met another company of emigrants at Black's Fort, near Abingdon, Virginia. While there, they learned of the surrender of Cornwallis at Yorktown.

"But that will make no difference in the wilderness, friends," warned the Black's Fort party. "Captain Billy Bush says the Indians are thick along the trail and in Kentucky. And the Tories on the Holston are as dangerous as the Indians. You should not try to go on. We have been waiting here nearly a year."

That was bitter news to the Spotsylvania travelers, who had hoped to reach their destinations in Kentucky before winter came. It seemed to them like a year instead of only three weeks since they had left their old homes. But there was good grazing for their stock around Black's Fort, and the pilgrims sorely needed a rest. They settled down in temporary huts and spent the time preparing for the two hundred and fifty miles they had yet to travel.

In the meantime Lewis Craig helped to organize the Baptists in Captain Bush's company into a new church.[6] Then, early in November, they resumed their journey. "It is better to risk the weather now than the Indians in the spring," they reasoned.

The travelers would see no more towns or farmhouses; only deserted cabins and a few stockaded forts along the trail. Up to that time, they had made their way over dry roads and forded shallow streams. From now on, the trail would be wet and slippery, and the creeks and rivers swollen with heavy autumn rains.

In shivering little groups the people stood one morning on a bank of the first broad, swift river on their route, wondering how they could ever get to the other side. However, Ellis and his men had learned the Appalachian way of crossing a stream. They made rafts by tying and lacing logs together with grapevines and strips of bark.

Unloading the first horses, they placed the packs and bundles on the rafts. Then while two men held the horses by their bridles on the downstream side, others paddled, using long poles to guide the raft towards the opposite bank.

The horses scrambled up the steep slope. The ferrymen emptied the raft and steered it back for another load, and by nightfall families and their possessions were on the other side of the river.

It was snowing hard when they gathered around the campfires at the foot of Clinch Mountain for evening prayer. The musical voice of Lewis Craig repeated the old promises: "The Lord is my strength . . . Of whom then shall I be afraid?" (Psalm 27). "Yea, though I walk through the valley of the shadow of death, I will fear no evil" (Psalm 23).

Fervently he prayed for guidance, for deliverance. Deep-toned "Amens" echoed from the mountain wall. Then the women and children crept under the sheltering boughs and the comforting fires were put out.

"Halt! Who goes there?" A guard called out in the dark.

Captain Ellis knew what that meant.

"Quick! The Indians! The Indians!" he shouted, leading the way. Riflemen followed him to investigate. "All here?" Captain Ellis asked the guards when they returned.

"No. One picket is missing."

Men found the picket's body, stripped and scalped, beside the trail the next day. The travelers halted for another wayside funeral, and another sorrowing family trudged along the bloodstained trail to Kentucky.

They made only thirty miles in three weeks, barely more than a mile and a half a day, reaching the foot of Cumberland Gap on the first day of December. An icy wind moaned and whistled through the bare branches of the trees, and snow and wet leaves covered the ground. The riflemen in front moved cautiously up the winding trail. Trembling with dread, the shawled and bonneted women followed, clasping whimpering babies in their arms. The burdened packhorses scrambled for a footing on the slippery rocks.

Bruised and shaken, but safe on the other side of the mountains, the travelers forded Cumberland River in icy water waist deep, then pushed on faster through the rough plateau country. Where the trail forked, some of the company continued northward on Boone's Trace to Boonesborough. William Ellis, Lewis Craig and other Spotsylvania pilgrims followed Logan's route northwest.

Beyond Rockcastle River, milder weather and sunshine lifted their spirits. The Negroes again burst into song and even the grimmest face relaxed into a smile. A night or two later they camped at the head of Dick's River, again drying rain-soaked packs and clothing by the campfires. They were cheerful in spite of the weather, for that would be their last night in an open camp.

But again the dread cry rang out: "Indians! Indians!"

This time Captain Ellis and his men chased them off without loss of life, although the savages stole some of their horses and cattle. No one slept again that night. The pilgrims ate their breakfast of jerk and hoecake before sunup. They were determined to reach English's Station before dark. It was the first of a chain of new forts, and stood eight miles ahead; they succeeded in reaching it.

The next morning the travelers passed the palisaded cabins beyond the gap at the Crab Orchard. That night they arrived at St. Asaph's, Logan's Fort, and were welcomed with a volley of guns.

Friends and relatives ran to meet each other. They laughed and cried as weary bodies relaxed in the comfort of cabin fires, hot food and the protection of stout log walls.[7]

The pilgrim women and children remained in Logan's Fort until a new settlement was built on Gilbert's Creek, a few miles away. It was named Craig's Station. One morning a group loaded their packhorses once more. Captain Ellis blew his horn and "The Traveling Church" swung into line for its last march.

On a Sunday morning a few weeks later, the Craig's Station settlers gathered for service in the Gilbert's Creek Baptist Church, the first building to be erected for Christian worship on Kentucky soil. It stood on a steep, cleared hill within sight of their fort. Its walls had loopholes instead of windows, and outside, sentries stood guard at every corner.[8]

Within that building were the same Bible and books the congregation had used in Virginia. The same pastor, Lewis Craig, stood behind the rough log pulpit. On the puncheon benches before him sat many of the people to whom he had preached the year before on that farewell Sunday in Transylvania County.

They were the same in name and outward form, but they were Tidewater Virginians no longer. The old church and the old homes were six hundred miles away; the old plantation life belonged to the past. Tense, alert, tempered and sharpened by the hardships and sufferings of their long journey, the Spotsylvania pilgrims had become Kentucky settlers, facing a perilous future in the first West.

CHAPTER XVIII

The Western Front

*Not stones, nor timber, not the art of building
constitute a state; but wherever men are who know
how to defend themselves, there is a city and a fortress.*
—ALCAEUS

Settlements in the first West were becoming organized.

Under the laws of Virginia, the inhabitants in any place could set aside 640 acres for a town site, choose trustees, and petition the legislature for permission to establish it.

Boonesborough was legally established as a town in October, 1779.

In April of that same year, in the settlement on Corn Island, seven trustees were chosen "by the intended citizens of *the town of Louisville* at the Falls of the Ohio." [1]

George Rogers Clark had probably selected the name in honor of Louis XVI, king of France. The town, laid out in half-acre lots along Main Street, according to a plan which he drew, was established on May 1, 1780.

Maysville, at the mouth of Limestone Creek, Harrodsburg, and Washington (Simon Kenton's station a few miles from Maysville) soon followed the example set by Boonesborough and Louisville.

The Louisville settlers at the Falls, however, were very uneasy about the title to their lots on the Connolly survey. To clear up the uncertainty about that and other tracts granted to Tories, the Virginia Assembly passed an act in 1780 for the escheat and sale of any land in Kentucky claimed by British subjects. The act specified that money received from the sale of eight thousand acres of

139

such lands should be used "for the purpose of a public school, or seminary of learning." [2]

The first court of escheat was held in Lexington on July 1, 1780. The jury decided that Alexander McKee and John Connolly were enemies of the United States and declared that their lands belonged to Virginia.

The settlement of Lexington provides an interesting example of pioneer democracy and initiative in action. A band of hunters, camping at the site in June, 1775, had named it in honor of the battle of Lexington in Massachusetts. In April, 1779, Capt. Robert Patterson and twenty-four other men from Harrodsburg built a blockhouse near what was later known as the "Public Spring." The following January, about fifty settlers entered into "Articles of Agreement between the Citizens of Lexington," under which public affairs were conducted. They elected trustees, drew lots, and petitioned Virginia to establish their town.[3]

The General Assembly set aside 640 acres of "unappropriated land" for that purpose in 1782, but plans for building were disrupted by war conditions. The trustees made a new plan the following year, reissued deeds for the new lots, and demolished the fort. Although it had a later start than some other settlements, the location of Lexington was so desirable that it quickly became the largest town in Kentucky.

The heavy immigration in 1779 and 1780 soon brought forth petitions for new county organizations. Settlers north and west of the Kentucky River complained about the risks and hardships of having to go to Harrodsburg on various kinds of legal business. To meet their requests, the assembly voted on November 1, 1780, to divide Kentucky County into three.

Fayette County took in the settlements north and east of the Kentucky River. Lexington became its county seat and John Todd its county lieutenant. Lincoln County, south of the Kentucky, included the three earliest settlements, with Harrodsburg as its county seat and Benjamin Logan in charge of its affairs.

Jefferson County included all the rest of Kentucky. Its population was so scattered that the magistrates went from station to station to hold court. Not until 1784 did Louisville become the county seat. At first, John Floyd, its county lieutenant, probably used his own station on the Middle Fork of Beargrass Creek as headquarters.

The Kentucky settlers were still not satisfied with their political status, however. From the beginning, they had protested against the injustice of having to take all important court cases to the capital of Virginia for trial. To relieve them of the heavy expense and legal handicaps of that requirement, the assembly passed an act in 1782 to make Kentucky a judicial district. This gave the three counties a Supreme Court of their own with power to try serious offenses and even cases of treason.

John Floyd and Samuel McDowell were the first judges of the new court. At Harrodsburg, where they held the first meeting in 1783, they instructed the attorney general, Walker Daniel, and John May, the clerk of the court, to select a suitable place for the capital of the new district, and to build a courthouse and a jail ". . . of hewed or sawed logs nine inches thick." [4]

Daniel and May chose a site near Crow's Station, ten miles southeast of Harrodsburg. The new settlement there, named Danville, became the political capital and center of the District of Kentucky for the next ten years.

Virginia could readily grant its western citizens' requests when they did not call for men or money, but the frontier leaders knew that both would be needed as soon as the Indians had recovered from Clark's expedition into the Shawnee country. An old settler said that ". . . the Indians used to say the whites were like hogs. You might rouse them up a while, but they would soon lie down again." [5]

George Rogers Clark had determined that they should not lie down again if he could prevent it. In the autumn of 1780, soon after his Shawnee campaign, he went to Richmond, Virginia, to ask again for an expedition against Detroit.

Gov. Thomas Jefferson and the assembly made Clark a brigadier general and promised him both men and money. General Washington ordered the commander at Fort Pitt to furnish him with cannon and a regiment of continental soldiers stationed at that place.

At Pittsburgh, Clark found it harder to recruit soldiers than it had been the summer before in Kentucky. The place was full of Tories and agents for the old land companies that were still scheming to get possession of the West. The Pennsylvanians would not enlist under a Virginia commander. The general at Fort Pitt refused to honor Washington's order. As the last straw, the Virginia Assembly voted in June, 1781, ". . . to put a stop to the Expedition."

Clark had no choice but to return to his base at the Falls with the few men who had enlisted. He left orders for other troops under Col. Archibald Lochry to follow him. Colonel Lochry's group was attacked by a party of Indians, who killed or captured every man in the company with the exception of one. That disaster was the final blow to Clark's hopes of taking Detroit.

Still he would not give up his long-cherished dream. Back at the Falls, he called a meeting of the militia officers of the three Kentucky counties to ask their help in raising an army. "Nothing will put a stop to the War in this region," he told them, "but the Reduction of the British Indian posts and possession of Lake Erie." [6]

The Kentucky officers could not see their way to ordering their militia so far from their homes. Instead, they wrote a joint letter to the Virginia Assembly, asking it to undertake the expedition with state troops. At the same time, they requested Virginia to build forts at the mouths of the Kentucky and the Licking Rivers and Limestone Creek. The assembly refused to reconsider its previous decision, and Clark's last effort at a venture against Detroit had failed.

The Indians concluded that the "Big Knives" had lain down again. Rumors spread through the settlements that the Indians were gathering a large army in the Northwest, and on April 16, 1781, John Floyd wrote to the governor of Virginia, "We are all obliged to live in our forts in this country, . . . forty-seven . . . have been killed or taken prisoner by the savages, besides a number wounded, since January." [7]

In February, the garrison at Kaskaskia abandoned that post, leaving Virginia's French citizens in Illinois without military protection. The garrison in Vincennes was on half rations, with no money or credit. The troops and settlers at Fort Jefferson on the Mississippi sank their cannon and went up the Ohio to the Falls. They found the garrison there in the same destitute condition as themselves. "Not a mouthful for the troops to eat, nor money to purchase it with; . . . the credit of the government is worn bare. . . unless supplies soon arrive . . . I fear the consequences will be fatal." [8]

The western front was crumbling at every point, but Virginia seemed powerless to send even the most necessary supplies to its posts in the West. By the summer of 1781, its back was to the wall. Benedict Arnold, at the head of a British army, was within a few miles of Richmond. Thousands of Virginian soldiers under General Lincoln had surrendered to Cornwallis in the Carolinas. The Country seemed to be going to pieces, not only on the western front, but everywhere else.

One of the principal reasons for the desperate conditions in America was the refusal of the states to grant the Continental Congress sufficient power to deal with its problems on a national scale. Early in the War a committee had drawn up a plan of union, the "Articles of Confederation," which would give the Continental Congress greater authority and would enable it to make foreign treaties and alliances. Many leaders thought that the one hope of saving the nation lay in the prompt adoption of that new form of government for the United States. [9]

The Articles of Confederation, however, required the approval of all thirteen states before that document could become the law of the land. Several of the smaller states—Maryland, New Jersey, Delaware, Rhode Island—had refused to sign. They demanded that all states must surrender any western land claims before they would agree to accept the proposed plan of union.

Virginia and a few other states with land claims in the West vigorously objected to such a sacrifice. Either by charter rights or conquest, they held those lands, their delegates asserted. In that same way, Maryland and other states held the territory they claimed.

After repeated appeals from the Continental Congress, every

state except Maryland had signed the Articles by February 22, 1779. A few days later, Clark's victory at Vincennes vastly increased the area claimed by Virginia. Maryland promptly declared that it would never sign until Virginia ceded the newly acquired territory to the Continental Congress, to become the common property of all the states. There the matter stood for more than a year, while conditions throughout the country rapidly grew worse.

Finally, as a last desperate hope of saving the United States, and for its own survival as well, Virginia reluctantly agreed to surrender the Northwest on three conditions. These were that Congress should guarantee to Virginia the title and possession of its western lands south of the Ohio River; that the Northwest should be a "common fund"; and that all other claims to any part of it should be declared void.

The Maryland delegates, accepting that hard-won victory in good faith, signed the Articles of Confederation on March 1, 1781. Then, to the utter amazement of many of its members, the Congress voted not to accept Virginia's deed to the Northwest Territory!

The reasons for that astonishing action lay behind the scenes in the cutthroat political struggle carried on by various land companies to get possession of the land "on the western waters." That struggle had started long before the Revolution began. During the war, the promoters and agents of these companies had continued such efforts in the Continental Congress, in the state legislatures, in the western settlements, and in England.

Some companies, claiming that they held grants from the Iroquois tribes, attempted to get the Congress to set up a new state, to be called "Vandalia," south of the Ohio. They had enough influence to delay the acceptance of Virginia's cession of the Northwest and to get a special committee appointed to study the whole subject of western land claims.

The biased attitude of Virginia's packed committee can be judged from the main points in its report. Virginia, it said, had no claim to any land beyond the mountains. The Iroquois tribes had owned it and had transferred it to New York and the Vandalia

Land Company. The report claimed that the Congress should accept New York's offer to transfer its claim to such land, and, finally, that Congress should repay the Vandalia Company for its expense in buying the Iroquois claims—in land south of the Ohio! [10]

The report brought a flood of protests from all parts of Virginia. In Kentucky, the people swore that they would never submit to be handed over to a scheming land company; that they would not pay again for land they had won at the cost of so much sacrifice and suffering.

These people had written many petitions to Virginia in the troubled years of the western settlements, but never had they sent anything like the impassioned appeal in which they implored Virginia to save them from the fate that threatened them if the Congress accepted that report.

In their Memorial, signed by more than seventy leading citizens, the Kentuckians stated their political attitude in no uncertain terms. Their arguments said ". . . if the country they possess does not of right belong to Virginia, the property of course must be vested in themselves, and that Congress has no right to any part thereof . . . Justice is what they claim . . . They view themselves as Virginians . . . it is through them . . . that the greater part of the western waters is not now in the possession of their most inveterate enemies, and could easily prove the importance they have been to the United States." [11]

That spirited protest did not go unheeded. Virginia had no supplies, no money, no soldiers to send to its frontier citizens, but it did have capable and courageous leaders who would stand up for the rights of those citizens. When the committee's report came up for consideration in the Continental Congress, a Virginia delegate, Arthur Lee, demanded the right to speak before any action was taken.

"I offer the following resolution," he said, "that before any vote is taken about the cession of Western lands, the secretary shall call the name of each member present; and that each member do declare upon his honor whether he is, or is not, personally interested directly or indirectly in the claims of any company or companies

which have petitioned against the territorial rights of any one of
the states . . . and that such declaration be entered on the
journals." [12]
The Continental Congress never voted on that resolution. Too
many of its members were unwilling to face the searching test of
honor that it imposed, and, until it was disposed of, no vote could
be taken on the report of the committee. Arthur Lee's alertness
and his skillful use of a parliamentary maneuver had saved the
first West for Virginia, and, possibly, for the United States of
America.

The battle for the new West was shifting from physical combat
to engagements between the minds of men; yet both kinds of fighting would continue for some time.

CHAPTER XIX

The Dark and Bloody Ground

The battle, sir, is not to the strong alone;
it is to the vigilant, the active, the brave.

—PATRICK HENRY

The Revolutionary War ended in October, 1781 with the surrender of Lord Cornwallis at Yorktown. That is what people in the East generally thought. Newcomers in the West the following winter and even some earlier settlers at first shared that idea. Peace, they believed, was just around the corner.

That corner proved to be a long way off. England had not struck her final blow to confine the American Rebels to the region east of the mountains. The Indians had not made their last raid to drive the hated whites out of their ancient hunting grounds.

The Americans themselves provided the spark that set the border aflame. In the spring of 1782 a company of Pennsylvanians under Col. David Williamson captured a band of peaceable, unarmed Christian Indians at the Moravian Mission near Sandusky. In cold blood they murdered every captive—forty men, twenty women, and thirty-four children.

The warriors of the Lake Erie tribes, in a fury of hate and revenge over that brutal massacre, killed or captured and tortured nearly every man in a second expedition from Fort Pitt, commanded by Col. William Crawford.

The British leaders—Captains William Caldwell, Alexander McKee, Matthew Elliott, and the infamous Girty brothers—were greatly encouraged with that victory, their most complete in years. With the help of the chief of every tribe between the Alleghenies

147

and the Wabash, they revived the old league of Pontiac with the purpose of driving the Americans out of the West.

They laid their plans with masterly skill. During the winter and spring small bands of Indians prowled through Kentucky, stealing and killing stock, attacking settlers in their fields or lonely cabins.

Virginia had authorized Colonel Clark to build the three forts on the Ohio for which the Kentucky militia officers had asked. But no money or supplies had been sent to carry out the order. Clark did succeed in getting one war boat built to guard the main river crossings. With two hundred miles to patrol, its crew never sighted an Indian canoe.

The militia officers tried to send help where needed. But they found it ". . . no easy matter to order a married man from a fort where his family was to defend another when his own was in imminent danger." [1]

Late in March a band of twenty-five Indians attacked Estill's Station, south of Boonesborough, shortly after Capt. James Estill had started with all of his men except one to the relief of another place. Two boys from his station, Samuel South and Peter Hackett, ran until they caught up with him.

"Injuns," they gasped. "At our fort! Killed Cap'n Innes' daughter! Scalped her! Took your man Monk!"

Estill's party overtook the raiders near Mount Sterling. There the well-trained Wyandots surprised the pioneers with a new technique in Indian fighting. Instead of running behind a tree to reload after the first fire, they threw down their rifles and rushed upon the whites with uplifted tomahawks. Both leaders and nearly all of their followers fell in that bloody battle which history knows as "Estill's Defeat." [2]

By August, the savages seemed to be everywhere at once. On the tenth, a party of them captured two boys at Hoy's Station, south of the Kentucky River. Capt. John Holder hastily assembled seventeen men from three stations to pursue the enemy. Near the Upper Blue Licks he ran into an ambush of a much larger force and had to withdraw after the loss of four men.

On August 15, news of that encounter reached the settlement of Bryan's Station, five miles northeast of Lexington. The fort

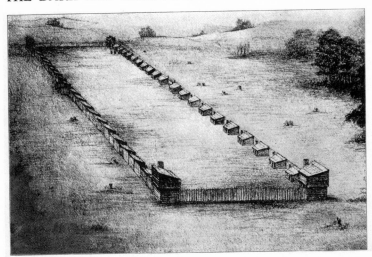

Bryan's Station Fort, built in 1779 by the Bryans of North Carolina, relatives of Rebecca Bryan Boone. Courtesy the Filson Club.

there was occupied by forty-four men and a dozen families, many of them former members of the "Traveling Church" group from Spotsylvania. The garrison, preparing to go to the relief of Hoy's Station, decided to pursue the Indians at the Blue Licks instead. Cabin fires glowed throughout the hot night while the men ground corn and ran bullets, and the women baked bread.

At sunrise on August 16, the pursuers were mounted and ready to gallop out when they heard the sound of rifle fire. It came in the nick of time. Five minutes later only women, children and old men would have remained in Bryan's Station.

The riders swung off their horses and gathered around Capt. John Craig to plan for the defense of their own fort. The Indians, they reasoned, probably thought that the men had already gone in pursuit of the enemy. The defenders must try to keep them guessing. They must send word to the nearest stations. They must contrive in some way to draw the Indians out of the forest into the open.

Two messengers, Thomas Bell and Nicholas Tomlinson, rode swiftly out the road towards Lexington. The Indians gave no sign of their presence. The women went outside and milked their cows. Still no sound came from the forest.

The large fort stood on a hill above Elkhorn Creek, surrounded by several hundred acres of cleared land, much of it in growing crops. Its twelve-foot high stockade and two-story blockhouses were in order. It was the only one of the sixty stations then in Kentucky in which every cabin roof sloped inward. Like most of the other stations, it had no well or cistern within the enclosure. Water for drinking and domestic purposes was brought up from an unprotected spring at the foot of the hill.[3]

The ruddy faces of the women and girls whitened as Captain Craig explained why there must be no change in the routine of fort life that could be observed by the Indians. They must go for water that morning as usual.

There was a moment of shocked silence, followed by a murmur of protest. Then Mrs. Jemima Suggett Johnson picked up her wooden yoke with a cedar bucket swinging from each end.

"Come, Betsy," she called to her ten-year-old daughter, and started toward the gate.

The others—eleven matrons and fifteen young girls—followed them down the narrow, stump-filled path. They glanced up at the nearest blockhouse, where sharpshooters with two or three guns apiece manned every porthole. They tried to chat and joke as usual, not daring to look too closely at the thick growth of dogwood and pawpaw saplings around the spring. All waited until the last bucket was almost full. Then they hurried up the hill, spilling some of the water in their haste.[4]

When they were safe inside, Jerry Craig led a decoy party of a dozen men a short way out the Lexington road. As they circled to return to the fort through the opposite gate, riding fast to raise a cloud of dust, the savages began firing at them.

This was evidently the signal for the main body of Indians to rush toward the fort on the other side. A heavy volley from the portholes quickly drove them back to the shelter of the forest.

Realizing their mistake about the presence of the garrison, the enemy's next move was to set fire to several cabins outside the fort. They would have succeeded in burning the fort had not a light breeze blown the flames in the opposite direction, but some blazing arrows lodged on cabin roofs and fell inside the stockade. While Parson David Suggett, eighty years old, prayed with all his might, the small boys of the fort were boosted up to the roofs by their mothers to put out the fires with piggins of water and gourd dippers. Betsy Johnson, snatching a blazing arrow from the sugar-trough cradle of her baby brother, Richard Mentor, probably saved the life of a future vice-president of the United States.[5]

The fort was still safe as the long, hot day drew to a close. The casualties within it were few, but outside, a scene of utter destruction met the eyes of the hard-riding settlers from the nearest stations who fought their way into the fort by nightfall. They saw cabins in smoldering ruins, hundreds of cattle and sheep and hogs killed, flax and hemp fields burned, potatoes and other vegetables pulled up by the roots, one hundred acres of young corn destroyed.

By ten o'clock the next morning, when more reinforcements arrived, the Indians had gone, but they went slowly, leaving a plainly-marked trail as if daring the pioneers to follow.

The men assembled in Bryan's Station that morning had no intention of disappointing them. The only question was when the pursuit should begin. They discussed it with a freedom known only among frontier militia, where officers and privates were friends and neighbors.

"After them at once!" urged some.

"They may be twice our number," others warned. "Remember Estill last March. And Holder at the Blue Licks last week. Let us wait until Logan comes with his men from Lincoln."

"If we wait they will reach the Ohio and escape. We should go tomorrow."

By dark their preparations were complete—bullets molded and filed smooth, gunlocks oiled and cloth patches greased, flints picked sharp. The decision to start the next morning was almost unanimous.[6]

At dawn on Sunday, August 18, 182 men, almost one-third of them commissioned officers, left Bryan's Station under the command of Col. John Todd of Fayette County. The trail led past the ruins of Ruddle's Station where the Indians had evidently camped the night before. From the number and location of their campfires, Daniel Boone thought that the enemy had a much larger force than their own.

The pursuers rested between midnight and dawn. At sunup they were only four miles from the north fork of the Licking River, and from that point they advanced more cautiously along the wide buffalo trace that led to the narrow ford near the Blue Licks Springs. As the high, almost bare ridge on the other side of the U-shaped bend of the river came into view, the vanguard saw a few Indians slowly disappearing over the top.[7]

At Boone's suggestion two scouts were sent to reconnoiter. When they reported that they had seen no sign of the enemy, Colonel Todd called a council of war. Each officer had his say, but all looked to Boone for the final word.

He had good reason to know the region. Not far distant was the scene of his capture by the Indians in 1778. The Blue Licks Springs, where his salt-making party had surrendered, were almost within sight. Every sign that his keen eyes had observed during the forty-mile march called for the utmost caution. Yet he spoke with his usual calmness as he counseled delay.

"The Indians have shown themselves on the hill beyond the river, loitering as if to invite pursuit," he said. "There are two ravines there filled with bush and timber for their protection; it is not wise for us to run heedlessly into the trap set for us. Now I propose taking a party and reconnoitering in their rear by going around for the purpose." [8]

Hugh McGary, it appears, opposed this sober advice. He had been among the few who counseled delay before the army left Bryan's Station. Now, while the council of war was still on, he spurred his horse into the stream and cried out, "All who are not cowards, follow me!" [9]

The others accepted his challenge, but after a headlong rush across the Licking they re-formed their lines at Todd's command. The plan of battle was for Major Harlan's company to ride hard upon the enemy and for the others to follow on foot at close range—Colonel Trigg commanding on the right, Major McGary in the center, and Colonel Boone on the left.

The three lines moved forward in good order along the trace up the narrow ridge. When they were within forty yards of the ravines, a furious volley of rifle fire burst upon them from the front and both sides, almost instantly followed by a deadly hand-to-hand conflict. The unequal contest lasted not more than fifteen minutes. Then ". . . he that could mount a Horse was well off, and he that could not, saw no Time for delay." [10]

Some did delay, however, in the frantic retreat towards the ford. Daniel Boone looked for the last time upon his dying son, Israel, before leading his men to a lower crossing of the Licking.

Anthony Sowdusky heard a wounded man cry, "For God's sake, don't leave me!" He stopped to lift him up in front of his saddle before riding off. Aaron Reynolds, seeing his lame captain, Robert Patterson, on foot, quickly dismounted and put him on his own horse.

At the river, wounded Abraham Scholl said to Andrew Morgan, "I'm afraid I can't get over the river with my rifle; I can't part with it." Morgan replied, "Hold to my shoulder . . . and we will mutually support each other."

On the other bank of the river a tall man on a fine horse looked back a moment and saw mounted Indians tomahawking his comrades as they struggled in water breast high. Quickly jumping off his horse, he called upon the other riders to halt. Nearly a score rallied around him and opened fire on the savages. To the courage and humanity of that hero, Benjamin Netherland, many of those on foot owed their escape.[11]

Colonel Logan and several hundred men from Lincoln County reached Bryan's Station on the nineteenth and followed the route taken by Todd's army twenty hours earlier. They met the first returning horseman, William Pittman, about one o'clock. From his parched lips they heard the sickening details of the battle at the Blue Licks.[12]

The appearance of Jacob Stucker as he crossed the clearing of Bryan's Station at nightfall told the anxious women the tragic story of defeat. Amid tears and prayers they answered the calls and ministered to the needs of exhausted men who straggled in during the night.

*Large forest trees have grown on the burial site of the fallen heroes
of the battle of Blue Licks. Courtesy Lafayette Studio, Lexington.*

Of the gallant band that had left Bryan's the day before, at
least seventy had been killed, wounded or captured. Nearly
every ranking officer had fallen: Colonels Todd and Trigg, Ma-
jors Bulger and Harlan, Captains Bulger, Gordon, Kincaid, Mc-
Bride, Overton, a host of others. No station in Fayette or Lincoln but mourned the death of one or more members. "There
was scarcely a home in Harrodsburg that had not lost a father,
brother, or husband."[13]

On August 24, Colonel Logan led more than four hundred
men to the scene of the tragedy. They collected all the bodies
they could find on the battleground, in the river, in the woods.
Among the dead, friend looked for friend, kin for kin. "They
were all stript naked, scalped & mangled in such a manner that
it was hard to know one from another." [14]

The men scraped away the thin earth on the top of the ridge and enclosed a bare space on the hillside with walls of loose stones forty feet long and four feet high. In this common tomb they laid the bodies of their fallen comrades and covered them with rocks and logs and brush—the customary form of burial under such circumstances.

Weary, hungry, heartsick ". . . and somewhat dubious that the enemy might not have gone off quite," Logan's army re-crossed the Licking and started back on the long ride to their home stations, leaving the heroic dead at rest.

CHAPTER XX

The Turning Point in the West

When Virginia needed a sword I found her one.
—GEORGE ROGERS CLARK

History, in search of a scapegoat, has usually laid upon headstrong Hugh McGary the blame for the disastrous defeat at the Battle of the Blue Licks; yet no military leader in Kentucky escaped criticism. According to some, Logan was too slow; others said Todd would not wait because Logan outranked him. General Clark believed that the Indians had stolen into the country unseen because the officers of Fayette County had neglected to keep spies and scouts on duty along the Ohio River.[1]

The severest criticism of all was directed against Clark himself. The militia officers of Fayette and Lincoln, in their reports to Gov. Benjamin Harrison, complained bitterly of the manner in which Clark conducted the military affairs of the district. He kept troops at the Falls, they charged, to build a new fort, ". . . to protect Jefferson County, or rather, Louisville, a town without inhabitants," leaving their own frontier unguarded.[2]

The governor, as ready as anyone to shift blame from his own shoulders, immediately censured Clark for not building the three forts on the Ohio, as he had been directed to do the previous December. Clark's spirited reply was that it took men, money and materials to build forts, none of which either Virginia or the Kentucky counties had supplied.

But neither blame nor defense could alter the facts or bring back the dead. The people in Kentucky would have to face the immediate, serious problem of the effects of the defeat at the Blue Licks upon their own future.

"Such was the panic this tragedy cast over the community," said Mrs. Sarah Graham later, "Lawrence offered my father the whole 400 acres of his preemption, . . . for one little black horse to carry his family back to Virginia; exclaiming, that after all their toil, they had to lose the whole country." [3]

Daniel Boone, not one to take alarm lightly, wrote to the governor on August 30: "I have Encouraged the people in this County all that I could; but I can no longer Encourage my neighbors or myself to risque our Lives here at such Extraordinary hazzards." [4]

In September, Andrew Steele wrote, "If some mode of preservation is not speedily adopted, the wealthy will emigrate to the interior and the poor to the Spaniards. Dreadful alternative! Nature recoils at the thought!" [5]

Concern over the success of the British and Indians at the Blue Licks was not confined to the Kentucky counties. "What if it should be the policy of the British Ministry to drive in from the other side of the Appalachian mountain before the signing of the preliminaries of peace?" inquired Col. Arthur Campbell. "How much more harm than good can one fool do." [6]

"If no succour is sent to Kentucky," Col. William Christian wrote to Governor Harrison, "and the War with the British continues another year, it is more than Probable the whole of the Inhabitants will be killed, taken to Detroit, or driven aways. And when that is no longer a Barrier, [other counties] . . . must suffer.

"In the meantime, Sir, I . . . offer myself . . . to aim at raising five hundred volunteers to hasten out on horseback . . . to be joined by what Force that Country could spare . . . to make an Excursion throughout the Shawney Country." [7]

To add point to their fears, a band of Indians that had remained in the region to spy on Clark's movements attacked Kincheloe's Station in Jefferson County on September 1. They carried off thirty-seven prisoners. John Floyd reported to Clark that he dared not pursue the Indians, since his men had hardly any powder or lead.

Urgent appeals for help piled up on the governor's desk: Are we to be wholly forgotten? Send five hundred men! Two hundred!

Send a few pieces of artillery! Powder! Lead! At least, send county surveyors, promised for two years past, to encourage new settlers, to keep land claimants from leaving!

To all requests for aid to Kentucky and to Colonel Christian's generous offer, the governor gave the same reply. The "deranged state of our Finances" made it impossible for Virginia to send help of any kind. Nor could he sanction an invasion of the enemy's country, as ". . . the Assembly have not taken off their restrictions on offensive Operations against the Indians." [8]

The Kentuckians at last pulled themselves together and faced the bitter truth. They had nearly lost their country; they might yet lose it, partly through their own neglect of duty and lack of unity. If they held it, the Indians must be punished. These frontiersmen could expect no aid from a bankrupt Virginia or an impotent Congress; their only hope was in themselves, in their own resources, material and spiritual.

Forgetting for the time their political and military jealousies, the officers of Fayette and Lincoln Counties again turned to Clark to lead them. In council with him at the Falls they planned an expedition against the Indians. They would draft men, if not enough volunteered. They would impress provisions and horses, if necessary.

Such drastic measures were not needed. More than a thousand men responded to Clark's call for volunteers. Many, unable to join, gave beeves, packhorses and other supplies, accepting certificates of value as promises of very doubtful future repayment by Virginia. Clark personally mortgaged thirty-two hundred acres of his own land to provide flour for the army.[9]

This would be no half-baked, impetuous undertaking. Never had George Rogers Clark planned every detail of an expedition more carefully. Never had frontier militia submitted to drill and discipline so willingly. When the troops met at the old Licking rallying place on November 4, 1782, every company and every squad knew its task, its place.

Clark issued strict orders to the officers. They must permit no man to quit his rank, no firing except on the enemy, no prisoners to be put to death lest the Indians retaliate by killing their white captives. All plunder taken must be delivered to the quarter-master.[10]

Col. Benjamin Logan, always Clark's second in command on such expeditions, had charge of the central Kentucky division; Col. John Floyd of the one from Jefferson County. Parties for scouting, flanking, and making roads for the light artillery went ahead up the Miami valley.

No white army of that size could hope to take the red man entirely by surprise. A few minutes before Floyd's division reached the first Shawnee village, an Indian spy saw them and ran ahead, giving the loud alarm cry. Another caught it up and passed it on. Not an Indian could be found when the white army arrived at the place.

However, the Indians had a narrow escape. "When we got to the town," said one soldier, "I went into a cabin and saw some dumplins they had been boiling, taken off in a tray, warm yet, smoking. I thought now I would have my belly full, but couldn't eat them. They were made of corn and beans with enough of meal in them to make them stick together, and without any salt." [11]

Again, as in the invasion in 1780, the "Big Knives" burned and destroyed everything except what the white troops could use. Two-thirds of the Shawnee towns were in ashes in a few hours. Lorimer's big British trading post at the head of the Miami met the same fate at the hands of Logan's division.

"The Quantity of provisions burnt surpast any Idea we had of their stores of that kind. The loss of the enemy was ten scalps, seven prisoners, and two whites retaken, ours one killed, one wounded," wrote Clark in his official report to the governor on this unauthorized expedition.

He ended it with this tribute to his command: "I must beg leave to Recomment to your Excellency, the Militia of Kentuck, whose behaviour on the Occation do them Honour, particularly their desire of saving prisoners." [12]

This was a different story from that of the Blue Licks, and the avengers had punished only the nearest tribe. Only Shawnee villagers were made homeless, left without food or shelter on the verge of winter. The crafty and cruel Wyandots and other tribes further north, who had been the chief offenders in Kentucky that year, went untouched, but no tribe would fail to understand the meaning of that display of strength so soon after the battle of the Blue Licks.

The way to Detroit lay open before the invaders. Clark had one thousand men, eager to do his bidding, but he dared not go farther, against the orders of the Virginia Assembly. Peace negotiations had already begun in Paris. The Revolutionary War had ended in the West.

When the war had begun in 1775, the West was an almost unknown wilderness. James Harrod and his hardy followers had built a few log cabins in the Salt River valley. Daniel Boone and his pathmakers had blazed a trail to the banks of the Kentucky. Richard Henderson had led his company of adventurers over it to found a new colony "on the western waters."

When the war ended in 1782, the first West had become a settled region with more than ten thousand inhabitants. These people, for the most part, had come into the wilderness seeking homes and better living conditions. Necessity had forced them to become fighters and to play a unique part in the war and in the development of the country.

In defending themselves, they had held back the savages from the frontiers of the eastern states. By planting themselves firmly in an uninhabited region, they had provided Virginia with a far better title to it than any ancient royal charter could give.

While the East fought a defensive war on its own soil, the Revolution in the West became a war of conquest under the matchless leadership of George Rogers Clark. Boone's trail and Henderson's ambitious attempt at colonization gave him the lever with which he forced Virginia to assert its authority and to erect a new county in the wilderness.

With less than two hundred soldiers, Clark had made the only successful invasion of the enemy's country during the war. He swept the British from the Illinois and the Wabash and carried the boundary of the United States to the banks of the Mississippi River.

To accomplish what he had set out to do, Clark had burdened himself with debts that neither his native state nor his nation ever repaid; ". . . but a cuntry was at stake," he wrote, "and if it was imprudence, I suppose I should do the same should I again have a similar Field to pass through." [13]

When he led his army back to Kentucky late in November, no one had any further doubt that the West could be held. The United States might still lose it through internal dissensions in the Congress or by inept diplomacy at the peace conference, but they would not lose it through the failure of the western settlers to maintain their own rights and to defend themselves against the British and the Indians.

Part Three

THE PIONEER STATE
OF THE WEST

CHAPTER XXI

The Treaty of Paris

Peace hath her victories
No less renowned than war.

—MILTON

Not many people in the East were tall enough mentally during the Revolutionary War to see over the mountains and understand what was taking place on the other side of them. Fortunately for America, three men did understand—Benjamin Franklin, John Adams, and John Jay—and these three had the task of negotiating the terms of peace in Paris.

Franklin, the elder statesman of his day, was better known in Europe than any other American. Before the outbreak of the war, he had spent nearly a dozen years in London as agent for Pennsylvania and several other colonies. After the signing of the Declaration of Independence in 1776, the Continental Congress had sent him as its representative to France to try to get recognition and material aid for America.

The Parisians feasted and flattered the witty old philosopher, but King Louis XVI and his ministers of state knew that open acknowledgment of the independence of the United States would mean war with England. They secretly gave just enough aid to keep the struggling states from collapsing altogether, while they waited to see if these Americans had more than an even chance of winning the war.

America's brilliant victory at Saratoga in October, 1777, apparently turned the scales in its favor. Early in 1778 the French government recognized the independence of the United States and made a Treaty of Alliance with the Continental Congress.[1]

165

The Congress sent John Adams to Paris in 1778 to arrange
terms of peace with Great Britain. It instructed him to do nothing
without the knowledge and consent ". . . of the ministers of our
generous ally, the King of France."

*Portrait of John Jay by Gilbert Stuart. Courtesy of Frick Art Reference
Library.*

However, the honest, outspoken New Englander found it impossible to work with Count Vergennes, the crafty prime minister of France. He left Paris in disgust and spent most of his time abroad at the Hague in The Netherlands. There he succeeded in securing recognition of his country and a loan from the thrifty Dutch government.[2]

John Jay, the third member of the American peace commission, was a young New York lawyer who had represented his state in several sessions of the Congress. In 1779, he was sent as minister from the United States to the court of Charles III of Spain.

His mission, like that of Franklin, was to obtain recognition and financial aid for his country. He met with little success during the three painful years he spent in Spain, but he learned some valuable lessons in European diplomacy. The prime minister, Count de Florida Blanca, kept him waiting month after month, ". . . like a beggar asking for alms," before he would condescend to talk with him on the subject. There were questions.

What consideration was Jay prepared to offer?

The consideration that every nation gives—repayment with interest.

Security?

What security could the struggling United States offer mighty Spain, whose New World possessions reached from western Canada to the southern tip of South America?

The Continental Congress could solemnly pledge the United States to surrender all claim to the use of the Mississippi and to any land in its valley,[3] he learned. Would Congress do that?

John Jay, without friends in a strange country, and ". . . unpracticed in the ways of courts," knew only too well the desperate plight of his nation. Yet he stood like a rock against the demands of Spain and even the advice of some members of the Congress.

"We need assistance and you must procure it," wrote one of them, urging him to accept Spain's terms. "We ask a territory and a navigation. The territory we cannot occupy, the navigation we cannot enjoy, . . . the rapidity of the current will forever prevent ships from sailing up. . . ."[4]

John Jay had a broader vision of the West and its future. "The Americans," he replied to de Blanca, "almost to a man, believe that God Almighty had made that river a highway for the people of the upper country to go to the sea by." [5]

From Franklin, in Paris, to whom he appealed for advice and support, came these encouraging words: "Poor as we are, yet as I know we shall be rich, I would rather agree with them to buy at a great price the whole of their right on the Mississippi than sell a drop of its waters. A neighbor might as well ask me to sell my street door." [6]

The long war had eventually become much more than a two-sided struggle between thirteen English Colonies in North America and their mother country. First France, then Spain, and later, the Netherlands, entered it, each with the hope of paying off old scores against England.

The autocratic governments of France and Spain feared, even more than did England, the democratic ideas and ideals that had brought on the American Revolution. A victorious America, with its radical doctrines of human rights, of freedom of conscience, speech, and press, would need to be held in check.

Spain and France would give just enough grudging help to enable the States to win their independence from England. But France, with a long-range view of the past and the future, was determined to keep the States dependent after the war was over.

The war-weary British would gladly have made peace with America in order to give their full attention to their ancient foes in Europe, but France and the Continental Congress, in their Treaty of Alliance in 1778, had agreed not to make peace separately with England until that nation had acknowledged the independence of the United States.

In addition, the Congress, too trustful of its allies, had directed its commissioners to discuss everything fully with Count Vergennes in Paris and to follow his advice. That wily politician held them to their instructions. Every nation taking part in the war, he insisted, should have a share in making the peace that would end it.

Vergennes had won Spain over as an ally by promising to help it either to get Gibraltar back from England or to obtain full con-

trol over the Mississippi Valley and the coast of the Gulf of
Mexico. Yet France, in its treaty with the United States, had defi-
nitely agreed to guarantee to them all their possessions and any territory ". . . that they might obtain during the war from any of
the dominions . . . possessed by Great Britain in North America." [7]

The subject of independence naturally came first with the Americans. John Adams positively refused to take part in the negotiations
until his country's representatives could meet with those of other
nations on equal terms. However, England, its nominal enemy,
and France and Spain, presumably its friends, all had other views.

"Independence? Yes, of course. But later, along with other
important matters."

Those matters, as the Americans well knew, had to do chiefly
with the boundaries of the new nation; yet the discussions dragged
on for several months before that subject was directly mentioned.

Lord Shelburne, directing peace negotiations for England from
London, had a better understanding of the strategic value and the
potential natural resources of the western country than did most
Americans. He instructed Richard Oswald, his agent in Paris,
to avoid any mention of land, but to bring up the subject of
"compensation" at every meeting. "America must pay the de-
spoiled loyalists whose land and other property has been taken
from them." [8]

To that, Benjamin Franklin had a ready reply: "Many houses
and villages of the Americans have been burned by the British
and their Indian allies. Let England draw up a bill of what we
have destroyed, and we shall do the same for her. Perhaps a
part of Canada would settle the difference." [9]

"Canada? Preposterous! We must have the same lands that
we had before the war. That is the only condition on which we
will discuss the question of independence. Your western boundary will run along the crest of the Appalachians, *here.*"

The American commissioners knew what had taken place west
of the Appalachians during the war. "America would never consent to that," they replied firmly. "Our citizens beyond the mountains outnumber the British ten to one. Our boundary must be the
Mississippi River, *here.*"

"But your settlements are all south of the Ohio," the British spokesman countered quickly. "We must have an establishment north of it, to repay the loyalists whose lands you have taken."

"We have three thousand citizens north of the Ohio," the Americans replied. "We hold every fort in the Illinois country. The Northwest is ours, not only by charter rights but by conquest and settlement." [10]

France and Spain, while agreeing that the United States must have no western territory, had no intention of permitting England to grab it all. Spain had retaken East Florida during the war. Vergennes demanded for Spain, as their price for peace, all western land south of the Cumberland River and the sole right to navigation on the Mississippi.

John Jay, after his humiliating experiences in Spain, was convinced that Vergennes had a deep-laid scheme for regaining ultimate control of the entire Mississippi Valley for France. Without consulting his associates, he determined upon a bold move to break the deadlock. He knew that its failure would certainly bring upon him disgrace and ruin, possibly death as a traitor, but Jay, possessing high moral courage, took the risk.

He secretly sent a messenger to Lord Shelburne in London to inform him of his own suspicions regarding the designs of Vergennes. He pointed out how it would be to England's interest to acknowledge at once the independence of the United States. That action would release the Continental Congress from its bargain with France. Then England and America, as equals, could discuss the terms of a separate peace between themselves.

Shelburne promptly acted upon Jay's suggestion by sending a new order to the British agents in Paris to negotiate peace terms with the commissioners of the "Thirteen United States of America." [11]

That agreement did not end the arguments over territories and boundaries. The British held out for western lands to compensate their loyalists. In Franklin's words, "They wanted to bring their boundary down to the Ohio and to settle their loyalists in the Illinois country. We did not choose such neighbors." [12]

To their persistent demands, John Adams, as stubborn and contentious as any Britisher, replied, "We have no notion of cheating anybody. Paying our debts and compensating the Tories are two separate questions. British creditors can present their claims against Americans through our State courts and get judgment for what is rightfully due them." [13]

The American commissioners would not budge an inch from that stand. George Rogers Clark and the armies of settlers and homemakers had won the West and held it against the British and their Indian allies in the wilderness. To keep that West, Franklin and Adams and Jay successfully fought the battles of diplomacy in Paris against the combined efforts of four great nations in Europe.

The British finally had to yield, since they could not continue the war against all four of their enemies.

On the last day of November, 1782, the commissioners of England and the United States signed the preliminary treaty which Jay had drawn up. After England and France had settled their differences, the final draft of the Treaty of Paris was signed on September 3, 1783, by the representatives of Great Britain, France, Spain, the Netherlands, and the United States of America.

That historic document began with these words: "His Britannic Majesty acknowledges the said United States [naming the thirteen separately] to be free, sovereign and independent States." The second article described the boundaries of the said United States as extending westward to ". . . a line to be drawn along the middle of the said river Mississippi until it shall intersect the northernmost part of the thirty-first degree of north latitude."

One article dealt entirely with the fishing rights granted to Americans off the shores of Newfoundland and Canada. Others contained agreements about the collection of debts, the release of prisoners of war, and the disposal of confiscated property.

Two other parts of the Treaty of Paris deeply concerned the West. In one, England agreed that ". . . his Britannic Majesty shall, with all convenient speed, . . . withdraw all his armies, garrisons, and fleets from the said United States, and from every port, place and harbour within the same." That would include Detroit and other centers of Indian plots on the Great Lakes.

The other, Article VIII, stated that the ". . . navigation of the river Mississippi, from its source to the ocean, shall forever remain free and open to the subjects of Great Britain and the citizens of the United States." [14]

Benjamin Franklin, John Adams and John Jay had good reason to feel gratified at the successful outcome of their diplomatic mission. They had won far more than a mere acknowledgment of the independence of their country. That alone might have proved to be only a temporary victory.

These men had also secured England's full surrender of any British claim to the western lands of the several States and to the Northwest Territory. Both France and Spain had admitted that the Mississippi River, instead of the crest of the Appalachian Mountains, was the western boundary of the new nation. Those pledges might insure its permanence.

The peace commissioners had kept faith with their countrymen, living and dead, with those who had pledged their lives and their sacred honor when they signed the Declaration of Independence, with those who had hammered out the policies and the destiny of the United States in the Continental Congress, with those who had fought on Bunker Hill and King's Mountain, with those who had starved at Valley Forge and waded through the icy swamps of the Illinois, with those who had fallen at the battles of Concord Bridge and the Blue Licks.

They had done surprisingly well for the "Thirteen United States of America."

CHAPTER XXII

The Beckoning West

*"Something hidden. Go and find it. Go
and look behind the Ranges —
Something lost behind the Ranges. Lost
and waiting for you. Go!"**

"United!" "Independent!" The words seemed like a mockery in the light of actual conditions in the early 1780s in America.

Hundreds of ships lay at anchor in the harbors. Thousands of idle sailors roamed the streets of the towns. Men who could not pay their debts filled the jails. Bands of unpaid soldiers spread terror through the countryside.

The United States of America had rid itself of the detested British Navigation Acts, and thereby put itself outside the British commercial system. When John Adams, first minister to Great Britain, tried to secure better trading arrangements, he was asked, "Do you want thirteen treaties, or one?"

The Continental Congress pleaded with the states for power to levy taxes and import duties, to regulate commerce among the states and with foreign nations. But the thirteen jealous little republics were united in one thing, at least—their determination not to give the Congress any more power than it already possessed.

Nature in some parts of the country contrived to make bad matters worse. "Such a drought was never known here before," wrote Jesse Benton in North Carolina to Thomas Hart in Maryland.

"I have often heard talk of Famine, but never thought of seeing

---

*From: "The Explorer" from THE FIVE NATIONS, by Rudyard Kipling. Copyright by Rudyard Kipling, reprinted by permission of Mrs. George Bambridge and Doubleday & Company, Inc.

anything so much like it as the present times in this part of the country. . . .

"The winter has been very hard upon the livestock and I am convinced that abundance of Hogs and Cattle will die this Spring for want of Food . . . Cash is scarcer here than it ever was before . . . there are many Mobbs and commotions among the People." [1]

Conditions were no better in the other states. Everywhere, people were debt-ridden and distressed, out of work, restless, longing to be anywhere other than where they were.

In one direction only did they see a ray of hope—the direction in which dissatisfied people have been moving since the dawn of history—west, always west, following the sun.

The West has borne many names in different ages and countries. At that period in the New World its name was "Kentucky." There it lay, on the far side of the mountains, waiting, beckoning, offering a new chance to the discouraged, a safety valve to the discontented.

Among those who heeded its call in 1782 was John Filson of Pennsylvania, a well-educated, keenly observant man in his middle thirties. Very little is known of his earlier life. He had taught school in Wilmington, Delaware. On his first visit to Kentucky he surveyed much land in Fayette and Jefferson counties.

But he spent most of his time visiting in the cabins of the earliest settlers—Daniel Boone, James Harrod, Levi Todd, Christopher Greenup, William Kennedy, John Cowan and many others. One of them said of him afterwards that he ". . . could ask more questions and answer fewer than any man of his day."

Filson's life ended, like that of countless others, in a forest mystery. In 1788, while surveying a tract in the region of the site of Cincinnati, he ventured too far from his companions and was never seen again. [2]

He had returned to the East in 1784, after his first visit to the West. A few months later he had published a book of 118 pages at Wilmington: "The Discovery, Settlement and Present State of Kentucke. . . The whole illustrated by a new and accurate MAP of Kentucke, drawn from actual surveys."

The map itself was a treasure house of information about the first West, ". . . a masterly work to have been produced more from conversation with the pioneers than from the use of the compass and chain." [3]

". . . the wonder is not that it lacks this or that, but that it presents so much that was absolutely essential to the rapid development of the region at the time. Trails, watercourses, stations, towns, mineral deposits, and relief features are shown . . . in their proper relation and each separately and correctly named." [4]

Of greatest interest now are the names and locations of its approximately fifty fortified stations and towns. These were most numerous in the region northeast of the Kentucky from Boonesborough through Lexington to Lee's Town below Frankfort. A row of them was strung out along the Wilderness Road from English's Station near the Crab Orchard, through Whitley's and Logan's, to another group around Danville and Harrodsburg between Dick's and Salt Rivers.

Farther west stood Squire Boone's Station (near Shelbyville) and Bardstown. A dotted line traced the Wilderness Road from Bardstown to Bullitt's Lick on Salt River; from there through Floyd's and other stations on the Middle Fork of Beargrass Creek to Louisville at the Falls.

Beyond the Falls on the west and Captain Johnston's on the north, beyond Strode's on the east and Shelby's on the south were "Fine Cane Lands," "Abundance of Iron Ore," "Salt Springs," "Green River Plains . . . most Fertile and cover'd with excellent Grass and Herbage." In short, the unbroken wilderness, as it all had been only ten years earlier. [5]

Filson's book, the first ever published about the western wilderness, became one of the best sellers of its day. Before the end of the year Filson wrote to General Washington (to whom he had dedicated the map) that ". . . the impression of 1500 have in the Course of a few weeks met with a rapid sale, which encourages me to offer the publick a second edition of this book, which I intend in the Course of this winter." [6] By another year, English, French, and German editions had been published in Europe.

Its contents were a strange collection of biography, geography,

natural history, and personal observations and comments. The best
known section is Filson's "quaintly philosophical" account of Daniel Boone's adventures in Kentucky, which he had ". . . from his
own mouth." He freely admitted his debt to the pioneers, especially
to Boone. In return, his book assured that frontier leader a permanent place among the immortals of American history.[7]

Filson stated in his *Preface* that he had written his book ". . .
solely to inform the world of the happy clime, and plentiful soil
of this favored region." It should be noted, however, that this first
press agent of the West was personally interested in land development and speculation!

His style, in places, was as dry as a catalog, but his readers
were looking for facts, not fine writing, and Filson gave them facts,
vouched for by those experts on the geography of central Kentucky
—Boone, Harrod, and Todd.

"The country, in some parts, is nearly level," he wrote, "in
others again hilly, . . . The country in general may be considered
as well timbered, producing large trees of many kinds, and to be
exceeded by no country in variety. Those which are peculiar to
Kentucke are the sugar tree, . . . the honey-locust, . . . The coffee
tree greatly resembles the black oak. . . .

"The pappa-tree . . . bears a fine fruit, much like a cucumber
in shape and size, and tastes sweet. The cucumber tree is small and
soft, with remarkable leaves. . . . Black mulberry trees are in
abundance. The wild cherry tree . . . the buckeye . . . the tulip-
bearing laurel tree, or magnolia, which has an exquisite smell.

"Here is great plenty of fine cane, on which the cattle feed and
grow fat. . . . Where no cane grows there is abundance of wild rye,
clover, and buffalo grass, covering vast tracts of country. . . . The
fields are covered with abundance of wild herbage not common to
other countries. The Shawenese sallad, wild lettuce, and pepper
grass, and many more . . . .

"This country is richest on the higher lands, exceeding the
finest low grounds in the settled parts of the continent. When cultivated it produces in common fifty and sixty bushels per acre; . . .
The first rate land is too rich for wheat till it has been reduced by
four or five years cultivation." [8]

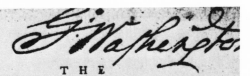

THE
DISCOVERY, SETTLEMENT
And prefent State of
K E N T U C K E:
A N D
An ESSAY towards the TOPOGRAPHY, and NATURAL HISTORY of that important Country:

To which is added,

An A P P E N D I X,
CONTAINING,

I. The ADVENTURES of Col. *Daniel Boon*, one of the firft Settlers, comprehending every important Occurrence in the political Hiftory of that Province.

II The MINUTES of the *Piankafhaw* council, held at *Poft St. Vincents*, April 15, 1784.

III. An ACCOUNT of the *Indian* Nations inhabiting within the Limits of the Thirteen United States, their Manners and Cuftoms, and Reflections on their Origin.

V. The STAGES and DISTANCES between *Philadelphia* and the Falls of the *Ohio*; from *Pittfburg* to *Penfacola* and feveral other Places. —The Whole illuftrated by a new and accurate MAP of *Kentucke* and the Country adjoining, drawn from actual Surveys.

By *JOHN FILSON.*

The title page of Filson's Kentucke. This copy belonged to General Washington and bears his signature. Courtesy Library of the Boston Athenaeum.

"The western waters produce plenty of fish and fowl. The buffalo-fish . . . the catfish, sometimes exceeding one hundred weight. Salmons have been taken in Kentucke weighing thirty weight. The mullet, rock, perch, garfish, and eel, are here in plenty. . . . On these waters, and especially on the Ohio, the geese and ducks are amazingly numerous.

"The land fowls are turkeys . . . pheasants, partridges, and ravens: The perraquet, a bird in every way resembling a parrot, but much smaller; the ivory-bill woodcock, of a whitish colour with a white plume, flies screaming exceeding sharp. . . .

"Among the native animals . . . the buffalo, which resembles a large bull . . . I have heard a hunter assert, he saw above one thousand buffaloes at the Blue Licks at once. . . . They feed upon cane and grass, as other cattle, and are innocent, harmless creatures.

"There are still to be found many deer, elks and bears, within the settlement. . . . There are also panthers, wildcats and wolves.

"The waters have plenty of beavers, otters, minks, and muskrats: Nor are the animals common to other parts wanting, such as foxes, rabbits, squirrels, racoons, groundhogs, polecats, and oppossums." [9]

"The reader, by casting his eye upon the map, and viewing round the heads of Licking, from the Ohio, and round the heads of Kentucke, Dick's River, and down the Green River to the Ohio, may view, in that great compass of above one hundred miles square, the most extraordinary country that the sun enlightens with his celestial beams." [10]

"This fertile region, . . . stored with all the principal materials for art and industry . . . where afflicted humanity raises her drooping head, where springs a harvest for the poor; . . . an asylum in the wilderness for the distressed of mankind . . . a land of brooks of water, of fountains and depths . . . of wheat and barley, and all kind of fruits." [11]

The reader, long before he had reached that burst of rhetoric, was seeing, through the magic of the printed page, what young Boone had visioned as he listened to John Finley's tale in the Pennsylvania woods twenty years earlier. The words rang in his ears. He heard them in his dreams: "Soil too rich for wheat . . .

well-watered . . . trees of great variety. . . . cane, clover . . . springs and wells . . . fish . . . wild turkeys . . buffaloes . . . game . . ."

In his mind's eye, he contrasted Filson's glowing picture of the fabulous West with the distressing conditions about him. He began to think of going—sometime. He pictured himself on the way—out West, to Filson's "Kentucke."

Twelve thousand people were living there in 1783 before the news of peace had filtered through the wilderness. By the next summer that number had doubled. Virginia became alarmed at the rapid loss of its population. That did not concern those who had caught the western land fever. They were free men, in a free country. No state could bid them stay or go.

They went from every class and rank. Businessmen formed companies to buy up warrants, as the safest and most promising investment at the time, sending agents and surveyors to locate their land. Rich men, after making their wills, set out with thick packets of warrants in their saddlebags. Planters whose farms had been ruined by war went with their soldier sons.

Young doctors went, hoping to find patients who could pay their bills; young lawyers, to seek their fortunes in the happy hunting ground of disputed land titles. Poor men, with nothing more than an ax or a rifle, went to find work.

They went from seacoast towns, from villages, from Tidewater and Piedmont farms, from mountain valleys. They went from every region—north, middle, south. One and all, they turned their backs on the past and the sea and the East, and set out to find the "pot of gold at the end of the rainbow," out where their West began, in Kentucky.[12]

CHAPTER XXIII

The Flatboat Route to the West

On no other river in the world has such a
remarkable social movement ever spent its force.

—HULBERT

The westbound emigrant had a choice of two routes to his desired haven. He could travel on foot or horseback over the difficult trail through the mountains that had made the first burst of immigration possible. The other route seemed designed by nature itself as a highway to the West. The Indians called it the Ohio, "River of many white caps." French explorers knew it as "La Belle Riviere."

Sketch showing different kinds of river craft on the Ohio in pioneer times. From "Keelboat Age on Western Waters" by Leland D. Baldwin. Courtesy University of Pittsburgh Press.

John Filson described it and its many tributary streams in his book: "The beautiful river Ohio, bounds Kentucke in its whole length, being a mile and sometimes less in breadth, and is sufficient to carry boats of great burthen. . . . The only disadvantage this fine river has, is a rapid . . . called the Falls of Ohio. . . . Excepting this place, there is not a finer river in the world for navigation by boats." [1]

Filson had also logged both routes from Philadelphia to the Falls. The land route passed through Maryland, then up the Shenandoah Valley in Virginia, joining the Wilderness Road near Roanoke. The total distance was 826 miles.

The other route crossed Pennsylvania by 320 miles of wagon roads over the mountains to Pittsburgh. From that point, the voyagers floated down the river 592 miles to the Falls. [2]

Filson could have added to his directions for both routes: "Travel at your own risk." The land route had its advantages for those who traveled light, either from choice or necessity. On the other hand, the emigrant who journeyed by water could load all his possessions—food, household goods, implements, livestock, supplies of every kind—on board and float downstream with the current.

It was almost always a mistake to land on the northern or "Indian" shore. The fate of Col. Archibald Lochry's party in August, 1782, was a tragic example of that error. Coming down from Fort Pitt to join Clark at the Falls, they had landed on the northern side ". . . to cook provisions and cut grass for the horses, when we were fired on by a party of Indians from the bank. We took to our boats, expecting to cross the river, and were fired on by another party in a number of canoes, and soon we became a prey to them." Forty men lost their lives, and sixty-four more were captured in that attack. [3]

When armed forces met with such disaster, family groups might well hesitate to embark on the Ohio. Yet some early emigrants did take the risks of the more dangerous route.

In 1781, fifty families from a Low Dutch Reformed Church in eastern Pennsylvania had decided to move out West. Crossing the state in wagons as far as Pittsburgh, they floated down the

Ohio in flatboats to Limestone Creek, then followed the wide buffalo trace to Boonesborough, without any serious mishap. Providence must have looked after them, for they knew nothing of wilderness conditions or the ways of Indians.[4]

The river route became more popular after the Revolutionary War had ended and the danger presumably would be less. In 1782, William Rowan, ex-soldier, ex-sheriff of York County, Pennsylvania, brought his own and four other families down the Ohio in a flatboat. His nine-year-old son John, who became a United States Senator, later wrote his recollections of that voyage.

The party left Pittsburgh in October with provisions enough to last nine days. They expected to reach the Falls in six or seven days. At that time ". . . there were no persons residing on the Ohio, on either side from Wheeling to the Falls . . . The whole distance was one entire unbroken wilderness, inhabited only by savages."

The travelers tied up at the mouth of the Little Kanawha to cut firewood. They led the cattle ashore to graze on the tall cane. Andrew Rowan, then twelve years of age, borrowed a gun and sneaked off into the woods to kill a deer.

He had never shot anything, but he aimed at a buck and wounded it. He kept it in sight in the snow until nearly night before he realized that he was lost. Then he followed a creek downstream, hoping it would lead him back to the river. When he could no longer see to travel, Andrew went to sleep under a fallen tree, putting his hat over his feet to keep them from freezing.

Late on the third day he found the camp of his distracted family. He had not seen a fire or tasted food during all that time. His frostbitten feet and legs ". . . were immersed at the suggestion of mother, to the knees in a tub full of whiskey for some hours. He lost the first joint of both big toes."

The Rowan party spent a long, cold winter on the boat, icebound at the mouth of the Great Kanawha. For two months they had no bread. Frequently they had no meat, for game was scarce and none of the men was an experienced hunter. They would never forget Andrew's first hunting trip. Nor would they forget another harrowing experience on the Ohio. It occurred a year later when they were nearing the Yellow Banks (now Owensboro) on their way to Green River. Late at night the lookout saw a row of campfires on the Indian shore. The men fastened the cattle boat and the family boat together and silently rowed closer to the Kentucky side, hoping to pass the Indians without being seen.

Suddenly, war whoops and yells broke the silence. Repeated calls by the Indians brought no response from the boats. Then the Indians rushed to their canoes.

"At this moment," wrote John Rowan, "my mother arose from her seat. . . collected all the axes and placed one by the side of each man . . . and then sat down in silent composure, retaining an ax for herself. The other women of the boat had lain down in despair and pulled their beds over their faces and heads.

"Having hovered in our rear and sides . . . for nearly two miles, they [the Indians] gave up and returned. We continued sail during the night and the forepart of the next day, when we arrived at the Yellow Banks." [5]

Another story of a flatboat voyage down the Ohio was related by the late Mrs. Norvin Green of Louisville, who heard it from her grandmother, Mrs. Martha Nuttall Demint.

Martha's parents, Elijah and Polly Price Nuttall, lived on the east shore of Maryland. In 1784 they decided to move to Kentucky. They traveled in wagons across Pennsylvania, with their eleven children and ten slaves, and all the livestock and household goods that they could bring along. [6]

When they arrived at Pittsburgh that autumn, they found that the river was too low to afford any protection from the Indians. Mr. Nuttall tried in vain to find living quarters in the bustling frontier town. Every tavern and house was overflowing with people, many of whom, like himself, were waiting for a rise in the river. He finally succeeded in renting a farmhouse for the winter.

After getting his family settled, Elijah Nuttall went to the river front to buy a boat. He found feverish activity on both banks of the Ohio and its tributaries, the Allegheny and the Monongahela. The air rang with the sounds of busily-plied axes and saws and hammers.

One day in early spring, after a week of rain, Elijah Nuttall told his family that they could start on their voyage. When they went on board the next day, they saw canoes, dugouts pirogues, keel-boats, barges, flatboats, even rafts.

Nuttall's own boat had a flat-bottomed frame about seventy-five feet long and fifteen feet wide. The cabin in front was divided off for living quarters, with two rows of bunks alongside the walls, one above the other. The rear of the boat was boxed off for stalls for the stock.

A swinging oar about seventy feet long was fastened on top of the cabin roof, for steering the boat. Two other heavy oars or sweeps forty feet long swung through an opening on each side. A high plank wall pierced with loopholes ran all the way around the upper deck.

When everyone was on board, the pilot gave a signal for the ropes to be untied from the trees on shore, and the clumsy craft moved slowly into the current of the river. The boat headed down-stream.

Night had come by the time they had eaten the hot supper which Mrs. Nuttall and her helpers prepared on the deck fireplace. Then they hung quilts in front of the bunks and put the children to bed. At night the boat was tied up to trees on the shore, and every-one slept.

During the long days the voyagers watched the ever-changing scene of alternating hills and valleys. To measure their progress they counted the rivers and creeks that entered the Ohio. They fished by trailing their lines over the high wall.

When the boat reached Limestone Creek, the pilot tied it up for the night, and everybody went ashore. The settlement there had only a blockhouse and a few cabins. With the best harbor on the Ohio, it was so exposed to attack that no one stayed any longer than was absolutely necessary.

The most dangerous part of the voyage was along the great northern loop of the Ohio near the mouth of Licking River, where the Shawnees and other Ohio tribes of Indians most frequently crossed the river to attack the settlers. Whenever Indians appeared or the lookout saw smoke rising among the trees, the crew double-manned the sweeps to pull the boat out of range of their guns.

At last the boat reached the quiet waters of Beargrass Creek above the Falls at Louisville. It had made its first and last trip,[7] for forty men could not row such a vessel upstream. The lumber in it could be sold "for almost its weight in salt."

Early records are full of accounts of desperate midnight battles on the river, of whole boatloads of white people carried off as prisoners by the Indians, of boats drifting aimlessly, charred to the water's edge, with only dead bodies on board.[8]

Before 1786 there was no fort on the Ohio between Wheeling and the Falls to protect voyagers from the Indians and gangs of white outlaws. That year the Congress ordered Fort Harmar built at the mouth of the Scioto, opposite the lookout rock on the Kentucky shore. In 1789 Fort Washington was built (of flatboat lumber) where a new settlement had been laid out at the site of Cincinnati, to keep watch over the Indians' invasion point at the mouth of the Licking.

Sketch of Fort Washington, erected by the Federal government in 1789 on the site of Cincinnati, Ohio, to guard against the Indians. Courtesy the Filson Club.

For about fourteen months, Lt. Ebenezer Denny, stationed at Fort Harmar, kept a record of river traffic that passed that place. Between October 10, 1786, and May 12, 1787, he counted 177 boats bound for Limestone and the Falls, carrying ". . . 2,689 persons, 1,333 horses, 766 cattle, and 102 wagons."

From June 1 to December, 1787, the count was ". . . 146 boats, 3,196 souls, 1,371 horses, 165 wagons, 191 cattle, 245 sheep, and 24 hogs." [9]

That was just a good start for 1788, when the flatboat tide really set in. Before it ebbed, thirty to forty years later, more than a million people had floated down the broad Ohio to seek new homes in Kentucky and the later West.

CHAPTER XXIV

Homespun

If ever we are a great and happy people, it must arise from our industry and attention to manufactures.
—JUDGE HARRY INNES

"If the Ohio had run upstream instead of down, I should have gone back the next day after I arrived at the Falls," Col. Armistead Churchill admitted in his later years.[1]

Thousands of other immigrants, especially those from towns and villages, must have felt the same way when they first came into contact with actual frontier conditions. Many, disillusioned or fainthearted, returned to the East, not by the Ohio River, but over the toilsome Wilderness Road.

No settlement had enough log taverns to shelter all who came. None had vacant cabins for rent or sale. Those newcomers were fortunate who had friends or relatives to take them in until their own homes could be built, but a settler rarely refused a stranger a place at his hearth and his table.

His frontier hospitality had a very practical side. Any guest brought some news from the world beyond the mountains, perhaps from his host's old home back east. If he stayed, he would be another recruit for the local militia company. He might want to buy land or have his own surveyed. At the least, he could carry a surveyor's chain or swing an ax or a hoe.

Bands of immigrants often came together and built their stations near the earlier forts for mutual help and protection. John Floyd mentions that six new stations were founded in the spring of 1780 on the Middle Fork of Beargrass Creek.

189

That same year, Capt. Thomas Helm, Col. Andrew Hynes, and Samuel Haycraft, Sr., ventured to locate forty miles south of the Falls in Severn's Valley (near Elizabethtown). They built their forts in a triangle on three hills, close enough to hear the firing of a gun or the falling of a tree. In less than two years, more than twenty other families had joined them in that region.

A number of other stations sprang up near the early one founded by Col. Isaac Cox, halfway between the Falls and Harrodsburg. Salem, later Bairdstown, then Bardstown, became the center of that group. Sometimes adventurers went to new real estate developments, such as the Transylvania Company had started at Boonesborough. The town of Vienna, now Calhoun, began in that way.

Church groups came out in a body, as the "Low Dutchers" and the "Traveling Church" had done. In 1785, a large colony of Roman Catholics from Maryland located on Pottinger's Creek several miles from Bardstown. By the spring of 1787, fifty Catholic families had settled in the valley of Rolling Fork of Salt River, near what is now New Haven and Lebanon.

Thousands arrived with no more worldly goods than a bundle slung over their shoulders. A few brought boatloads of supplies and furnishings. Their polished dressers and tables and fine china and silver looked strangely out of place in log cabins with rough puncheon floors.

Whether they came with much or little, nearly all immigrants began life in the West in the same way the first families had. "If equality ever existed in a civilized society, it was in those early periods of the settlement of Kentucky—when danger, mode of living, and other circumstances, common to all—had placed all, on a common level."[2]

"We were saving of lead," said William Clinkenbeard. "I shot a buffalo, got the bullet and then shot a deer, after chewing the bullet round. . . . The first dishes we had were trenchers made by one Terry in the Station—a turner. . . . A parcel of those dishes out of buckeye, new and shining, and set on some clapboards in the corner of the cabin, I felt prouder of in those times than I could be of any dishes to be had now."

Until they could raise their own flax and hemp, other pioneers followed Mrs. Poague's example in spinning and weaving nettle fiber and buffalo wool. "Made the buffalo wool into hats, too," said Clinkenbeard. "The first hemp seed I got was while I was in the Station after I married. Saved the stocks and broke it and my wife made me a shirt out of it. Raised a right smart patch next year."[3]

"They used to spin more hemp in those times than they did flax," Jeptha Kemper recalled. "Every family had to wear their own make. They had no stores, and if they had, they had no money to take to them."[4]

Mrs. Sarah Graham's mother brought four pounds of un-seeded cotton from Virginia and shared it with two other women. The first year they raised fourteen pounds of cleaned cotton. "Mother gave seven yards of cotton for one shoat; with nine yards she got some salt from Beargrass [Creek]; and a little money besides," [5] a daughter wrote.

John Sanders set up the first "store" in Louisville in a large flatboat that the spring flood of 1780 had left stranded at what is now the corner of Third and Main Streets. He tied the boat to a tree, added a roof and some doors and windows, and used it as a warehouse or "keep" for furs and skins. In a region prac-tically without money, his receipts passed from hand to hand as freely as banknotes or currency.

Daniel Brodhead of Pittsburgh opened Louisville's first general store in 1783 on Main Street in a double log cabin almost in the shadow of Fort Nelson. Over the same counter he sold "nails and calico, axes and broadcloth, delfware and silks, furniture and bonnets, lumber and hats, sugar and medicine, whiskey and books."[6]

Ephraim January had the only store in Lexington when Jeptha Kemper went there. "You could have put it all in one waggon. If there had been much buying, two or three families would have bought it out. But it was so hard to get the goods there, and they cost so much at first, that there were but few purchasers." [7]

One of Washington's officers, the handsome, affable Gen. James Wilkinson, came to Lexington in 1784 and opened the first

dry goods store in that town. Like Brodhead, he ". . . took in pay
for what he sold the produce of the country, such as peltry, tobacco, corn, whiskey, linen, and linsey." [8] For small change they cut
Spanish silver dollars with a hammer and chisel into halves, quarters, "bits, and picayunes."

When a pioneer merchant had cleaned out his stock, he leased
his stand to another, loaded the goods he had taken in exchange
on flatboats, and went down the rivers to the Spanish towns on
the lower Mississippi.

After selling out for cash, he took ship in New Orleans for
Philadelphia. In a few months he was back with a fresh stock
which had come by wagon to Pittsburgh, thence down the Ohio
to Limestone or the Falls. His profits were enormous, if his boats
and cargo escaped the triple risks of shipwreck, Indians, and
white pirates.

*Sketch of an early tavern in Louisville. The glass panes in its windows
must have aroused great interest when it was built. Courtesy the Filson
Club.*

The high cost of transporting goods from the East (about $65 a ton) soon turned the thoughts of some pioneers to making their own products. They imported millstones at an early date to grind their corn and wheat. They quickly discovered the superior virtues of the water in the clear limestone springs of central Kentucky for making good whiskey. In 1783, commercial plants were built at Louisville and south of the Kentucky River ". . . for distilling spirits from Indian corn."

Settlers had often risked their lives to make or buy salt. This pioneer necessity was one of the first Kentucky products to find a market beyond the limits of the district. By 1786 the works at Mann's and Bullitt's Licks in Jefferson County and at the Blue Lick Springs had an output more than ample for local needs.

The enterprising General Wilkinson soon managed to get much of that profitable trade into his capable hands. In a letter dated December 19, 1786, he directed his agent to go to Bullitt's Lick for a supply of salt. "You will make the best of your way to Nashville, and there dispose of it for cotton, beaver furs, raccoon skins, otter, &c." [9]

Not all of the progress in the West was of a material nature. During those strenuous early years the settlers had to fight and live much as the savages did in order to survive. Yet they had not taken leave entirely of the civilization of which they were a part, although many had few outward signs of it in their homes.

Other forts besides Harrodsburg had residents like Mrs. Jane Coomes who made A B C paddles and set the copy by which little fingers were taught to write. "Schools were kept in all the forts," according to Nathaniel Hart, Jr., who had gone to school to Malcolm Worley. Mr. Worley kept a Latin school in Harrod's tract, within sight of the station. In 1786 or 1787, Nathaniel and his brother John went four and a half miles to school at Strode's Station, carrying their guns. [10]

Male teachers usually combined "school keeping" with surveying and clearing. Lexington's first teacher, John McKinney, is famous in pioneer history for his battle with a wildcat that invaded his schoolroom. His pupils may have seen John Filson's map in the making. Some fort "scholars" may have used the manuscript arithmetic that William Calk brought with him to Boonesborough. After 1785, Georgetown, Bardstown, and several other places had private boarding schools for boys. Transylvania Seminary, the first school for higher education west of the Alleghenies, owed its beginning to the vision and initiative of Col. John Todd, who was killed at the battle of the Blue Licks.

In 1780 Todd had persuaded the General Assembly of Virginia to set aside a part of the escheated Tory lands in Kentucky for a school fund. The seminary opened as a grammar school in May, 1785, in a log schoolhouse at Crow's Station (later, Danville) with James Mitchell as the principal. Four years later its trustees transferred it to ". . . the neighborhood of Lexington, adjacent to the Presbyterial Meeting House." [11]

Religious services or "preachings" were held in forts and stations from the start. The first church group constituted in Kentucky met under a sugar maple in June, 1781, at Hynes' Fort (Elizabethtown). That, like many other early churches, was a Baptist congregation.

By 1783 the Baptists had three associations with a total of forty-two congregations in Kentucky. In that year, the Reverend David Rice of Danville organized the scattered Presbyterians in the district into several regular congregations.

Methodist and Catholic organizations soon followed those two pioneer denominations. Francis Clark brought together the first Methodist "class" in 1783 near Danville. In 1787, the Bishop of Baltimore sent the Reverend Father M. Whelan to minister to the Catholic families on Pottinger's Creek.[12]

What some of those early preachers may have lacked in learning they more than made up for in zeal and devotion. Danger and tragedy stalked their lonely rides through the forest. It was said of one of them, Benjamin Linn, that wherever a settlement was made on Green River, "he was an early visitor . . . swimming rivers, passing through the most perilous dangers. . . . He counted not his life dear unto him, that he might preach the unsearchable riches of Christ, instruct and sometimes confirm and comfort the suffering forefathers of Kentucky." [13]

Later immigrants had their share of losses and tragedies caused by the Indians. The savages never again invaded Kentucky in force after Clark's second expedition into the Shawnee country, but bands of them continued to prowl around the stations and lonely cabins, keeping the settlers in constant fear.

At Strode's, "Old Mr. Kennedy had lost his wife, and the women in the Station had turned in and made him thirty yards of hemp-linen, and washed it up and hung it out. Women's wash day in the fort; hung it all out, and the Indians we failed to report got it all." [14]

The pioneer's most necessary and valued possession was his horse, and *nothing* did the Indians covet more. When young Clinkenbeard's father came out in 1782, ". . . he brought five head of horses. One mare with foal. . . . The colt he kept, but the Indians got all the others. . . . They took a mare from Old John Constant for which he had given 700 acres of land—a racing animal . . . . Constant bought another mare of his sister. The Indians took both of these at once." [15]

Fort Nelson, built by General Clark in 1782, guarded the Ohio at the unloading place above the falls. Courtesy the Filson Club.

The savages continued to take heavy toll of human life. Among their many victims in 1783 was Col. John Floyd, one of early Kentucky's finest citizens, shot down near his own station in Jefferson County. The next year, Daniel Walker, the district's

talented attorney general, lost his life in the same way between
Bullitt's Lick and the Falls.

The time had passed, however, when the Indians could hope to
check the stream of settlers pouring into the West. By 1785, the
population had increased so much that Virginia organized four
new counties to meet the demands of its western citizens for local
government. Jefferson County lost three-fourths of its area to form
Nelson County; northern Fayette became Bourbon County; Mercer and Madison were carved from the northern part of Lincoln.
Three years later Mason County was organized from the part of
Bourbon bordering the Ohio River, and western Fayette became
Woodford County.

Most of the inhabitants of those nine counties in the District
of Kentucky still lived in or near the stations or in log cabins on
their own farms. Nearly all of them wore homespun clothing. Many
were "land poor," or burdened with debt. Few, indeed, had found
the elusive pot of gold.

*"Constitution Square" in the Weisinger Memorial State Park in Dan-
ville. Replicas of the original buildings that stood on this site are the
District Courthouse (left) in which the statehood conventions met, the
Gaol, and the Meeting House. Courtesy the Studio Shop, Danville*

In his old age, Nathaniel Hart, Jr., gave this as his opinion of
the possibilities open to all: "In every case, settlers, who have
come here, however poor, if they have been sober (and indus-
trious), have become wealthy. And there are many such." [16]

Whatever their worldly state, all those settlers had found a new outlook, a wider horizon. In spite of hardships, privations, dangers of every kind, they had a deeper sense of personal freedom and an optimistic hope in the future of their region.

CHAPTER XXV

Blazing a New Trail

*They were on a ground which human footstep had
never trod, and had an election—of dangers only.*

—WILLIAM LITTELL

The hardy pioneers and homemakers in Kentucky had established themselves in the wilderness and held back the British and their Indian allies during the war. A few months after the treaty of peace was signed in Paris, they began to blaze a new uncharted trail to win their own independence as a state.

They set out in November, 1784, at the close of the meeting of the general court in Danville, and the Indians, as might be expected, were the immediate cause.

Colonel Logan had received word that the Cherokees and the Chickamaugas were getting ready to invade Kentucky. Remembering their unpreparedness and the tragedies of 1782, he called a meeting of the militia officers then in Danville to discuss plans for protecting the settlements.

They could do nothing legally to head off an invasion. No man in Kentucky had authority to call out the militia. The government of Virginia had no ammunition in the district, and no public money on hand with which to buy any. Even if the militia had had everything necessary to carry on a campaign, the governor had ordered the officers not to lead their troops out of the district without his direct permission.

"We are supposed to wait until the Indians have actually crossed our borders. Then inform the County Lieutenant, who must send a formal notice to an officer sixty or even a hundred miles away," was one officer's bitter comment on the situation.

"And before he came back with the Governor's permission, the tomahawk and the scalping knife would be on our heads," another added.[1]

"We must find some way out of this predicament," said another officer. "If the Indians don't come this time, they will later. They know as well as we that the Congress has forbidden us to invade their country and will do nothing to keep them out of ours."

"What can we do?" asked a young officer.

"Tell our people how unprotected they are," an older man replied. "When we get home, ask each militia company to elect delegates to meet here next month. By that time we may think of some plan to defend ourselves."

The delegates at that next meeting (December, 1784-January, 1785) discussed the problem of defense for ten days, without finding a solution. They decided that Virginia could help a great deal if it would only change some of its laws.

"But no law can shorten the distance between us and Richmond," one man remarked. "For Virginia to try to govern this District is like England's trying to govern the Colonies, with mountains between us in place of an ocean."

"The remedy for that is the same that the Colonies used," stated another decidedly. "Kentucky should separate from Virginia and become an independent state."

The other delegates stared at the speaker. What did he mean? They all knew of various plots by "new state" agitators to get the Congress to set aside Virginia's claim to Kentucky. For a moment the sinister idea of seizing control of the government by military force hung in the air.

"When we get home, let us urge the people to elect delegates during the county court days in April, to meet here in May," the last speaker continued, as if answering an unspoken question. "That will give all of us time to think about separation."

His hearers relaxed. They were militia officers, but they were civilians first, with deeply rooted regard for law and order.

"How many should they elect?" a member asked, "the same number from each county, as we do now?"

"I don't think that way is fair," a Lincoln County officer replied. "People, not land, ought to be represented. My county has nearly twice as many people as either Fayette or Jefferson. We ought to have more delegates. I move that each man we elect shall represent about the same number of people."

His proposal, which probably set a world precedent for equal representation, seemed reasonable to his fellow members. They later resolved ". . . that 12 delegates from Lincoln, 8 from Fayette, and 8 from Jefferson should be chosen, basing the number upon the freehold population." [2]

Separation was not a new idea in 1784. As early as May 15, 1780, several hundred inhabitants of Kentucky and Illinois Counties had petitioned the Continental Congress to organize them into a state. Virginia had, in fact, provided in its constitution for new states to be formed in due time out of its western territory. The turn of political events in 1784 had only served to bring the subject into sharper focus.

That first year of peace, while not the darkest in the western settlements, had been one of the most trying. The Continental Congress, after finally accepting Virginia's cession of the Northwest Territory, had failed to restrain the Indians or to force England to give up posts on the Great Lakes.

In Kentucky itself, the heavy immigration, the unpaid military claims, the plots and counterplots of various groups had brought about a condition almost bordering on anarchy. The confusion over land titles had reached a tragic climax in Louisville when Col. John Campbell returned there in 1783 after long years in a Canadian prison.

He had a valid claim, as everyone in the West knew, to a large tract of land below the Falls. Few of them knew, however, that the notorious Tory, Dr. John Connolly, had sold and conveyed ". . . to the said John Campbell" in 1773 the half of his original tract on which the town was laid out.

The settlers at the Falls faced the total loss of the lots they had cleared and the homes they had built if Campbell could prove his ownership. They began a long legal battle to retain their titles in the Virginia legislature, of which Campbell himself was a member, where all the odds and the decisions were in his favor.[3]

It was against that background of local, national, and international tensions that the twenty-eight delegates to the next convention met in May, 1785, at Danville.

They chose Col. Samuel McDowell of Danville, war veteran, lawyer, and judge of their highest court, as president, and Thomas Todd of Lexington as clerk. After a week's debate on the subject, they resolved unanimously ". . . . that a petition be presented to the Assembly, praying that this District may be established into a state, separate from Virginia"; and, when that was done, that it ". . . ought to be taken into the Union with the United States of America, and enjoy privileges in common with the said States."[4]

They drew up their petition in proper legal form, and then, the delegates decided not to send it to Virginia!

Such a move was unheard of. Never, to their knowledge, had a sovereign state been asked to divide itself voluntarily to form another independent one.

Yet this was not the reason the delegates decided not to present their petition. Neither did they hesitate from timidity or fear of reprisal. These men knew what they wanted, as individuals. They were not so certain as to what the people wished. Did those who had elected them understand the issues? Did a majority of the people really desire separation from Virginia?

To reassure themselves on those points, the delegates prepared an address to the people of the district, probably one of the earliest examples of a referendum. They gave as their reason for the delay in sending the petition to Virginia that ". . . they were unwilling to proceed in a matter of such magnitude without a repeated appeal to your opinion." [5]

They recommended that the people should hold another election during the county court days in July, on the principle of equal representation; and that the delegates should meet in Danville ". . . on the second Monday of August next, to take further into consideration the state of the District."

Copies of the petition to Virginia and of the address to the people, handwritten, as there was no printing press then in the district, were sent to the clerk of each county, to be posted on the door of the courthouse.

The returns from the July election proved unmistakably that the desire for statehood was not ". . . the ill-directed or inconsiderate zeal of a few." In every county, the majority had elected candidates who stood squarely for separation.

Of the twenty-eight members of the August convention, Benjamin Logan was the sole representative of the first group of adventurers who had broken the wilderness trails ten years earlier. Among his fellow members were four judges of the District of Kentucky, George Muter, Harry Innes, Samuel McDowell, and Caleb Wallace. Most of the others were Virginia lawyers or Revolutionary officers.

Judged by the standards of any place or age, the people of Kentucky had chosen a notable group to lead their migration into new political territory.[6]

With its clear mandate from the people, the August convention unanimously voted to ask Virginia for an "act of separation." To emphasize its importance, the delegates chose Judges Muter and Innes to present their petition to the Assembly at Richmond."[7]

Virginia's response was prompt and favorable. On January 10, 1786, the assembly passed an Enabling Act, granting the request of the Kentuckians for separation, under certain conditions.

The District of Kentucky must elect delegates in August, five from each of the seven counties. They must convene in September, 1786, to make certain that the inhabitants of Kentucky really wanted to separate from Virginia.

If that proved to be their wish, they could choose any date before September, 1787, on which to establish their independent government. However, before that could take place, the Continental Congress must agree to admit Kentucky into the union of States.

In the meantime, Virginia and Kentucky would have many other things—debts, taxes, land titles, boundaries—to discuss and arrange between themselves.[8]

These were all very reasonable, very sensible conditions and were accepted by the people, for the most part, with patience and good will. Kentucky had won its main point—Virginia was willing. Almost too willing, some thought. Did the mother state welcome the chance to rid itself of the burden of providing for and defending its western district?

Overly cautious, said some. Why keep Kentucky waiting nearly two more years for its independence? Why require the consent of a helpless and indifferent Congress?

Public opinion divided sharply on those and other questions during the lively preelection campaign. The issues were hotly debated in Fayette by General Wilkinson, the popular leader of those who desired immediate separation, and Humphrey Marshall, a conservative young lawyer. Wilkinson won the election and his opponent's lasting enmity by what many considered to be a sharp political trick.

Elsewhere, the voting was quiet. The people, confident of a favorable outcome, felt that they were already far on the way towards their goal. The time would pass quickly, with so much to be done. Before they realized it, they would be planning to celebrate their own independence. Kentucky was on its way to statehood.

CHAPTER XXVI

The Tangled Web of Politics

*The sum of all we strive at is that every
man may enjoy the same rights that are granted
to others.*

—JOHN LOCKE

Indian trouble had been brewing in the Northwest ever since England had surrendered that region to the United States. The Illinois tribes, joined by the Shawnees in Ohio, had formed a powerful union for the avowed purpose of destroying all white people in the Ohio River Valley.

The danger of an invasion of Kentucky appeared so imminent in 1785 that at the August convention, delegates had urged the militia officers to do whatever they could to head it off. On September 10, 1786, George Rogers Clark personally led an army of twelve hundred men towards the Wabash. Benjamin Logan with the Lincoln County troops invaded the Shawnee country.

On the fourth Monday in September, 1786, the date set for the meeting of the next convention of Kentucky delegates, ". . . a number sufficient to proceed to business could not be had." [1] Many of its members-elect were either with Clark or Logan, and the convention had to mark time until they could return.

In January, 1787, the absent delegates reported for duty in Danville. The convention quickly declared by unanimous vote that it ". . . was expedient for and the will of the good people of the District that the same should become a state separate from and independent of Virginia, upon the terms of the act." [2]

"That ought to convince the Assembly that the people of Kentucky know what they want," a member remarked, as the presiding

officer, Judge McDowell, signed his name to the petition for separation.

As some members were preparing to leave for their homes, an
express rode up with a package of mail for McDowell.

"Wait!" he called. "Here is a message from the Assembly."

"What is it?" they asked, gathering around him.

"The Assembly has passed a new Enabling Act," he replied,
reading quickly.

"Why? What does it say?"

"Our meeting delayed so long . . . feared we could not meet the
conditions of the first Act. Thinks the Congress needs more time
to consider such an important matter. . . . Assembly has been told
that many people in Kentucky do not want a separate state.

"We must hold another convention in September. The Congress
must give its consent to separation before July 4, 1788. Then the
new state can begin its separate government by January 1, 1789."

Instantly the room was filled with exclamations of disapproval
and frustration.

"They knew why we couldn't meet earlier," said one member.

"That puts us back to where we were a year ago," said another
as they left the room. "Our people won't like this delay." [3]

The people of Kentucky, however, soon had something far
more disturbing to think about than this latest setback in their
quest for statehood. They learned from correspondents in Pittsburgh the terms of a proposed trading treaty that John Jay, then
the Secretary for Foreign Affairs, was trying to arrange with Don
Diego Gardoqui, Spanish minister to the United States.

Both France and Spain had failed to get what they wanted in
America at the peace conference in Paris in 1782. Four years later
the situation seemed favorable for another attempt. Economic conditions had steadily worsened in the United States. Rebellions such
as that led by Capt. Daniel Shays in Massachusetts threatened
to overthrow the governments of the states and the nation.

Spain had permitted Americans to use the Mississippi River
and its harbors during and after the Revolutionary War. Suddenly, in 1786, it ordered its agents at Natchez and New Orleans
to stop all American boats and confiscate their cargoes.

Then, on instructions from Madrid, Gardoqui offered the United States the coveted privilege of trading with the Spanish colonies in the West Indies. In exchange for this favor, the Continental Congress must agree to give up all use of the Mississippi by American citizens for twenty-five years.

In the East and in the North, many people believed that the profitable trade of the West Indies might save the tottering republic from bankruptcy or disunion. The distressed merchants and shipowners fairly jumped at the tempting bait that Spain dangled before their trade-hungry eyes.

But a storm of protest, such as the West had not known since Arthur Lee delivered it from the clutches of scheming land companies, swept through Kentucky.

"Not use the Mississippi for twenty-five years! What chance would we have for trade? It is our only outlet to a market. We need it, now. We demand the right to use it."

A Kentucky committee, appointed by the Supreme Court at Danville, declared that ". . . the inhabitants of the Western country . . . will not tamely submit to an act of oppression which would tend to a deprivation of their just rights and privileges." [4]

In this stand, the West had the support not only of Virginia, but also that of the Carolinas and Georgia. They agreed with Virginia that ". . . the free use and navigation . . . of the waters leading into the sea . . . ought to be considered as guaranteed to them by the laws of God & nature, as well as compact." [5]

Those four states instructed their congressional delegates never to vote for such an unjust arrangement. Maryland, although it claimed no western lands, stood with its southern neighbors. The Articles of Confederation required the vote of at least nine states to ratify a treaty. With five of the thirteen against it, the proposal stood little chance of being passed.

However, the effects of the attempt to make such a treaty were almost as disastrous as if it had been ratified. The bitter discussions over its terms produced the first great rift between East and West, North and South. No section understood the peculiar problems and difficulties of the others or made any noticeable effort to do so.

The Kentuckians, especially, felt neglected and misunderstood.

The proposal to close the Mississippi to their trade came at a time when their cup of resentment against the Virginia Assembly and the Continental Congress was already running over, and unscrupulous schemers were quick to take advantage of the situation.

They stirred up the people with dismal prophecies of the results that would follow such a treaty with Spain. Immigration into the West would cease, they said. Many already there would leave. Those who remained would fall prey to the Indians or the Spaniards.

"What will the Congress ever do for us?" they demanded. "It has not yet made the British give up Detroit and the other lake ports after three years of peace. It has withdrawn the Continental troops and left us exposed to Indian raids. It has publicly censured our leaders when we tried to protect ourselves. Now it is ready to sell us out for the benefit of the northern shipowners and merchants."

"Why should we wait any longer? Why should we stay tied to Virginia? What right has it to hold us back?"

"Let us declare our independence at the next convention," the most radical suggested. "Then the Congress will have to take us in and we shall have the same rights as any other state."

The growing unrest in the West alarmed every thoughtful person in the country. General Washington expressed his anxiety in a letter to Henry Lee in July, 1786. "There are many ambitious and turbulent spirits among its inhabitants," he wrote, "who . . . have turned their eyes to New Orleans, and may become riotous and ungovernable, if the hope of traffic with it is cut off by treaty." [6]

The leader of those who were demanding immediate separation from Virginia was Washington's former officer, Gen. James Wilkinson. He saw in the proposed treaty a unique opportunity to further his own personal fortune and ambition. While the West and the South were in an uproar over the closing of the Mississippi to American trade, he sent a boatload of Kentucky products to New Orleans, in open defiance of Spanish orders.

Following it in another boat, he demanded a personal interview with Don Estaban Miro, the governor general of the Spanish province of Louisiana. He told the astonished official that the western settlements were determined to obtain the use of the Mississippi; that General Clark was gathering an army and supplies at Vincennes to invade Louisiana.

Miro was too far from the western settlements to know much about the sentiments of their inhabitants. He must have heard of Wilkinson by reputation. He certainly was acquainted with Clark's military achievements. His lively fears of an American invasion made him more than half willing to believe that Wilkinson spoke the truth.

The American general assured the Spanish governor that he had sufficient influence in Kentucky to persuade the people to declare their independence and to join Spain as an ally, in order to get the use of the Mississippi. For himself, he asked only a private trading privilege to send goods down the river and sell it in New Orleans, and a "concession" to furnish the Spanish government with tobacco at ten cents a pound.

The governor of Louisiana saw nothing unusual in that proposition. Other Americans had obtained trading privileges by bribing Spanish officials. It was no secret that merchants in Natchez smuggled goods up and down the river at charges varying from 15 to 25 percent.

No one before Wilkinson, however, had offered to deliver the West—lock, stock, and barrel—into the hands of Spain. Miro was skeptical. To convince him of his sincerity, Wilkinson secretly renounced his American citizenship and took the oath of allegiance to the king of Spain.[7]

His sole purpose in that infamous bargain was to advance his own interests. He gave Miro a list of prominent Kentuckians, with the amount of "persuasive gold" he would need to win each of them over to Spain.

In that matter, Wilkinson double-crossed Miro. The bribe money, with only one or two exceptions, remained in his own possession. Yet the results of the intrigue were far-reaching. Many honest men in Kentucky whose names were on Wilkinson's list found their honor and their loyalty under suspicion.[8] His insinuations and libelous letters about George Rogers Clark helped ruin that brilliant leader's public career.

While Wilkinson was weaving his web of deceit and treachery, other Kentuckians were making sincere efforts to solve the problems of the West with fairness and justice. In the winter of 1786-87 a group of thirty leading citizens living in or near Danville organized a debating club for the purpose of discussing political and social questions and issues.

They met on Saturdays at the home of a member or at the courthouse or a tavern. Many of them, as delegates to the different conventions, helped to shape the course of those meetings.

Naturally, they discussed the navigation of the Mississippi, deciding that its immediate use would not benefit Kentucky. They debated the question of separation from Virginia. They agreed that representation in the legislature, when Kentucky did become a state, should be by population and not by counties. In an early meeting they appointed a committee to ". . . prepare a Bill of Rights and a Constitution" for the future state.

At that time the laws of Virginia inflicted the death penalty for twenty-seven different crimes, those of Massachusetts for ten. The Danville Political Club members took a more advanced view and agreed that only two crimes—murder and treason—should be punished by death.

In discussing the rights of the Indians to the lands that they occupied, the members put aside all personal feeling over the loss of relatives and friends. They concluded that ". . . the Indian tribes cannot . . . be deprived without their own consent, of the exclusive right to the territory claimed by them." [9]

While these men were considering the important issues of the time in the remote District of Kentucky, delegates from every state except Rhode Island assembled in May, 1787, in Independence Hall in Philadelphia. With General Washington presiding, this group of outstanding leaders held its meetings in such secrecy that the secretary kept no minutes of what was said or done.

They had been elected for the avowed purpose of amending the Articles of Confederation. But, like the militia officers in Danville in 1784, they soon found themselves treading on new political ground. By the time they adjourned their meeting on September

17, 1787, they had drawn up and signed a constitution for an entirely new form of government for the nation.[10]

The purposes of that "untried and novel experiment" in political relationships were stated in its opening paragraph: ". . . to form a more perfect union, establish justice, insure domestic tranquility, provide for the common defense, promote the general welfare, and secure the blessings of liberty to ourselves and our posterity."

From stately Independence Hall in Philadelphia to the log courthouse in Danville in the District of Kentucky, from the oldest to the youngest settlements, honorable and patriotic citizens, north, south, east, and west, could subscribe to the principles and ideals set forth in that Preamble to the Constitution of the United States of America.

CHAPTER XXVII

Kentuckiana, 1787-1788

*The most powerful weapon of ignorance—
the diffusion of printed matter.*

—TOLSTOI

An eager, expectant crowd gathered early on August 11, 1787, outside the courthouse at the corner of Main and Cross Streets in Lexington. The men discussed their favorite frontier subjects in a more casual manner than usual. They had something newer to talk about that morning—the coming of the printed word to the West.

In a back room of the two-story, double log building, John Bradford, pioneer publisher and editor, worked singlehandedly to meet his first deadline on *The Kentucke Gazette.* Many of his 180 subscribers were in the crowd waiting to receive their copies as fast as he could turn them out on his hand press.[1]

The statehood convention of May, 1785, had appointed a committee to arrange for a press in the district. They hoped it might ". . . insure unanimity in the opinion of the people . . . ." They knew it would ". . . give publicity to the proceedings of the convention." [2]

The trustees of Lexington saw a chance to steal a march on Danville, the convention town. They offered their fellow citizen, John Bradford, a choice public lot if he would undertake the task. At the same time they arranged for him to use half of the first floor of the courthouse for his "shop."

Bradford sent his brother and partner, Fielding Bradford, east to buy a secondhand press, type, ink, and paper, and to bring them down the Ohio on a flatboat. Fielding set up half of the first issue

213

The first printing house in Kentucky (office of the Kentucky Gazette, 1787).

in Limestone, while waiting for packhorses to carry the equipment "over the Great Buffalo Middle Trace" to Lexington.

John Bradford referred to the difficulties of that journey in his first editorial: "My customers will excuse this my first publication, as I am much hurried to get an impression by the time appointed. A great part of the types fell into pi in the carriage of them from Limestone to this office, and my partner, which is the only assistant I have, through an indisposition of the body, has been incapacitated of rendering the smallest assistance for ten days past." [3]

The first issue consisted of two pages, printed in three columns on a sheet of coarse paper about ten and a half by seventeen inches in size. It contained two original short articles, a few news items several weeks old, one advertisement. It announced that future issues would be "published weekly on arrival of mails from the East."

It would be difficult to exaggerate the timeliness and the importance of that weekly event to people so far from other centers of civilization. Like a free press anywhere, whatever touched the life or influenced the thinking of the people found expression in its tiny pages, censored only by the judgment and good taste of the publisher.

Its contents covered the entire range of human emotions and interests. The September 15, 1787, issue contained a notice to ". . . the Separate Baptists that their next general association will commence on the first Friday in October next, at Tates creek meeting house, and will continue Saturday and Sunday."

In the same issue, Charles Bland aired a private grudge in the advertising columns: "I will not pay a note given to Wm. Turner for three second-rate cows till he returns a rifle, blanket, and tomahawk I loaned him."

Nothing in the records of that period revealed the actual conditions of pioneer life more vividly than the advertisements in *The Gazette*. The Bradfords, needing a printer, found one by putting the following notice in their own paper: "Wanted Immediately. A Journeyman Printer, who understands the business, in its different branches."

Thomas Purvin of Strode's Station, a dozen miles away, applied for the job and got it. Of that first printer a neighbor had this to say: "Purvin had the palsy very bad; hands trembled so I didn't see how he could make out to set the type. . . had a good many children . . . taught school for some time; a teacher at Strode's." [4]

Pioneer industrialists found *The Gazette* invaluable in promoting their business ventures. Jacob Myers informed the public in the second issue that he was erecting a paper mill on a branch of Dick's River in Lincoln County near his grist mill.

"He flatters himself that in the execution of an undertaking which promises such advantages to the district, he will meet with the greatest encouragement from every good citizen who wishes to see arts and manufacture flourish." As his paper mill could not be operated without rags, he requested that ". . . all will be particular in saving all their old linen and cotton."

Joseph Robinson announced the erection of a tanyard near Mr. Isaac Ruddle's mills, ". . . where hides of all kinds except buffalo will be taken on the shares or otherwise." A "Diers" business had been set up in Bourbon County, and the dyer advertised for "Hemp, Flax, and Cotton thread to dye." [5]

The pioneer housekeepers must have welcomed this item in the September 22 issue: "JUST OPENED, And to be sold on the most reasonable terms for cash, at the house of Mr. John Clark, in Lexington, by George Tegarden, Consisting of a compleat assortment of linen and stufs. Also, coffee, bohe tea, chocolate, muscovado sugar, pepper, allspice, nutmeg, ginger, indigo, coperas, rosin, resins, rice, china and queen's ware, glass tumblers, West India rum, writing paper, cotton cards, eight penny nails, &c &c &c."

Trade in the West, according to the advertisements in *The Gazette,* was still carried on almost entirely by barter. Robert Barr announced that he ". . . will quit trade and take Bacon in exchange for drugs." A dry goods store would accept ". . . Bear, Otter, Beaver, Raccoon and Fox skins, Country made Linen and Sugar," in exchange for its wares.

On January. 7, 1788, appeared a notice for subscriptions ". . . to build a new addition to the Presbyterian meeting house at Lexington, to pay in pork or corn."

In the same issue, a letter from John Filson announced the proposed establishment of a school in Lexington, ". . . where the French language with all the arts and sciences" would be taught. The next week Elijah Craig advertised a boarding school for boys at Georgetown. "For diet, washing and house-room for a year, each scholar pays three pounds in cash, or five hundred weight of pork on entrance, and three pounds cash on the beginning of the third quarter."

Some subscribers of *The Gazette* evidently found it difficult to pay the modest price of "eighteen shillings per annum." For their benefit the publisher stated that he would accept ". . . Beef, Pork, Flour, Wheat, Rye, Barley, Oats, Indian Corn, Cotton, Wool, Hackled Flax or Hemp, Linen or Good Whiskey" in place of money.[6] Later, he offered, a 20 percent discount if the bill was paid in two days.

Among the numerous real estate advertisements were announcements of new "towns" to be laid out, as well as frequent warnings against buying certain tracts of land. The first woodcut in *The Gazette,* a picture of a tree, appeared above an advertisement of land for sale.

A notice of apportioning land grants was signed "Geo. R. Clark." The following "development" also bore Clark's name; "A settlement at or near the mouth of Severn creek, on the north side of the Kentucke river . . . the local situation of this settlement, if compleated, will render it an object worthy attention. G. R. Clark, John Crittenden." [7]

The most frequently mentioned items in the "lost and found" column were livestock and runaway servants. One honest person advertised finding a horse that ". . . had on a small bell." This interesting item appeared in the issue for January 12, 1788: *"Two Dollars* REWARD To any person that will deliver me a saddle and bridle which I lost off my horse at Lexington at December court, or leave the same at the printing office. Samuel Thompson."

The Indians naturally received a great deal of free publicity. In his second editorial John Bradford stated as one of the purposes in publishing the paper: "First, it will give a quick and general information concerning the intentions and behaviour of our neighboring enemies and put us upon our guard against their future violence." That same issue contained letters to and from Colonel Logan on the whereabouts of a band of savages.

People were evidently just as desirous then as now of seeing their writings in print. One contributor wrote John Bradford: "I sent you a piece and requested you to publish it as soon as convenient. It has not yet appeared in your paper, and . . . I am certain several pieces of less importance that you have received since mine have been published." [8]

The Gazette, it appears, was too slow in starting a woman's department to please some of its readers. A long article in the issue of October 20, 1787, signed "Abigail Trueheart," read: "To the Good Women of Kentucke. You certainly have observed, that in many pieces that crowd our press, not a single sentence is addressed to our sex."

Some articles brought forth vigorous protests against making the paper ". . . a scene of war, a vehicle of scandal, in consequence of every private quarrel."

The well-preserved old pages of *The Gazette* reveal that wilderness travel was still not undertaken lightly. The issue for April 12, 1788, carried one of many similar announcements: "NOTICE is hereby given that a company will meet at the Crab-Orchard on

Sunday the 4th day of May to go through the wilderness, and to set out on the 5th, at which time most of the Delegates to the state convention will go."

People planning to make the trip frequently advertised that they would carry letters for others. John Bradford, however, unofficially handled all inbound mail himself, without pay, until Kentucky became a state.

The transportation of goods in a country that still depended mainly upon trails and buffalo traces was a very difficult and expensive undertaking. John Clark informed the public through *The Gazette,* that he wanted ". . . A number of packhorses of 4 or 5 waggons to go to Bullitt's Licks for a quantity of Salt, of which I will give one third to any person or persons, that will engage to bring the salt or part of it to Lexington."

The Westerners, starved for news of the outside world, would read the issue of September 22, 1787, with great interest. It had only one large sheet, with reprints of events abroad on the following dates: The Hague, April 25; Vienna, May 16; Paris, April 18; St. Petersburg and Tunis, January 4; London, June 13.

Yet of far more concern to its readers was the information which *The Kentucke Gazette* supplied of events closer home. In two October issues in 1787 the Bradfords printed the full text of the new Constitution of the United States. A November issue carried the full text of the ordinance for governing the Northwest Territory, passed by the old Congress on July 13, 1787, and reprinted from *The Pittsburgh Gazette.*

Of even greater importance to pioneer readers was the opportunity the paper offered for people to express their own views on public affairs and to read those of others. The momentous question, "To sever or not to sever?" was vigorously argued for and against in the pages of *The Gazette,* sometimes with more heat than light. An antiseparation citizen wrote (in the second issue), "As most of us are farmers and unskilled in policy . . . we are able to give but a random guess at the propriety of a separation . . . we can see difficulties on both sides and would wish to avoid the worst."

In September and October, readers of *The Gazette* scanned

its pages to learn what their own latest convention, which met in Danville on September 17, 1787, had done.

It was a harmonious meeting, probably because Wilkinson, who usually contrived to stir up uneasiness and dissension, was absent. The delegates, with only two of the thirty-four members opposed, soon ". . . came to a Solemn Voate on the Business of a separation." [9]

John Brown represented the District of Kentucky in the last year of the Continental Congress. From a miniature painted by John Trumbell in 1792. Courtesy Gallery of Fine Arts, Yale University.

In addition to the customary addresses to Virginia and to the people of the district, they wrote one to the Continental Congress, asking for the admission of Kentucky into the Confederation of States. In their petition to Virginia, the delegates requested the assembly to send a Kentuckian to present their address to the Congress.

They were confident that this would be the last meeting for the purpose of asking for separate statehood. They, therefore, selected a date (December 31, 1788) on which Virginia's authority over the District of Kentucky should cease. After voting to call for an election of delegates to meet in the spring to form a constitution for the new state, the fifth convention was adjourned.

Kentucky had again done its part. Soon *The Gazette* informed its readers that the Virginia Assembly had appointed John Brown of Danville as a special representative of Kentucky to the Continental Congress.

That young Virginian had fought under LaFayette and studied law with Thomas Jefferson. Shortly after his arrival in Kentucky in 1782, the voters of Lincoln County had elected him as a state senator to the Virginia Assembly. From Richmond he went to New York, where the Congress was then meeting, to present Kentucky's petition for statehood.

Virginia had set July 4, 1788, as the final date for the Congress to act upon Kentucky's request. On the last day of February, John Brown offered a resolution that it be adopted.

The members of that Congress, however, had lost all interest in doing anything about the government. Their time was running out. The state legislatures were voting that year on the adoption of the new Federal Constitution. As soon as nine of them had ratified it, the old Continental Congress would cease to exist as a lawmaking body.

John Brown became desperate as weeks and months passed with no action on Kentucky's petition. At his urgent request, a committee was finally appointed to draw up an act to admit Kentucky. For two months no further action was taken on the subject. Then, on July 2, the committee was dismissed!

With only two days left, Brown offered a motion to ratify the compact to which both the District of Kentucky and the State of Virginia had already agreed. The Congress put off considering that motion until the next day.

On that day, July 3, 1788, it received word that New Hampshire, the ninth state to vote on the subject, had ratified the Federal Constitution. The old Continental Congress in its dying hours, resolved that Kentucky ought to be admitted into the Union—but that the new Congress should do it. The deadline, July 4, had come and gone, and Kentucky's petition had not been granted.[10]

When they read that news in *The Gazette,* the people of Kentucky realized that the end of the trail to statehood, on which they had set out so hopefully four years earlier, was still a long way off.

Might it not be, some thought and said, that they had missed the right turn somewhere along the way? Or, more probably, that they were on the wrong trail altogether?

CHAPTER XXVIII

At the Crossroads

*There is no more perfect endowment
in man than political virtue.*
—Plutarch

News that the Continental Congress of the United States had adjourned without acting on Kentucky's petition reached Danville on July 28, 1788, just as the delegates to the sixth convention had assembled. Instantly, the meeting was in an uproar.

Some wanted to go ahead and set up a separate state government at once. But, after much heated debate, the judgment of those who counseled further efforts at agreement finally prevailed.

The conservatives, however, won nothing except delay. The independence-at-once party had its way in writing the message to the people of the district.

In it, they asked voters to consider four objectives in choosing their delegates to the next convention, to be held in November. These were: (1) to obtain the admission of the District of Kentucky "as a separate and independent member of the United States of America"; (2) to secure the navigation of the Mississippi River; (3) to form a constitution of government for the District; (4) ". . . to do and accomplish whatsoever . . . may in their opinion promote its interests." [1]

To give the greatest possible publicity to these resolutions, the convention ordered that they should be printed in *The Gazette* every week until the time set for the election.

If *The Gazette* had taken a poll of public opinion in the West that summer, its first question would have been, without a doubt,

"What do you think will best promote the interests of the District of Kentucky?"

The replies would have been unanimous: "The free navigation of the Mississippi."

To its next probable query, "What, in your opinion, is the best way to secure the use of that river?" the answers would have varied widely.

Some thought that General Wilkinson, back in Lexington and living in grand style, had the right one. "Look at him," they said. "His agents are going all through the country, buying up our surplus products; anything we have to sell. Here's his notice in *The Gazette*: 'To purchase tobacco, tallow, butter, well cured bacon, ham, lard, and smoked briskets of beef. [2]

"They say he sends half a dozen loaded boats down the Mississippi at a time, all armed with swivels and three-pounders. Wilkinson knows what the West needs. Trade! Why couldn't the Congress do for us what he is doing? It just wants to hold us back. That's why."

"Your fine friend knows how to look out for himself," some of the General's critics replied. "He buys our tobacco for two cents a pound and sells it to the Spaniards for ten."

"Spain does not bestow her favors for nothing," said those who were better informed. "Don't you know that the people in New Orleans do not have free use of the only printing press in the city? They must get permission from their government before they are allowed to stick a paper against the wall to advertise their goods or try to recover anything they have lost. Would you sell your liberty for Spanish Gold?

"No! No! Kentucky wants no separate deal with Spain. What we should do is to organize a new government, at once. That is what Virginia and the other colonies did in '76; and with far less reason.

"Virginia has twice given its consent. Why waste time by asking it again? When we have once declared our independence, the new Congress will not dare refuse to take us into the Union."

Such were the views expressed by Harry Innes, John Brown, Caleb Wallace, Benjamin Sebastian, and many other leading citizens.[3]

A very different suggestion came, of all places, from Detroit. It was made by the notorious Dr. John Connolly, once the owner of a large part of the site of Louisville. He arrived in Kentucky in October, 1788, presumably on business connected with his former land interests in the district.

The West did not need to bargain with Spain or to plead with the Congress, he hinted broadly in private conversation with Wilkinson and few other men in Lexington. Great Britain had two regiments of soldiers at Detroit. It could supply Kentucky with arms, ammunition, clothing, money. With Britain's help by land and sea, the western settlers could open the Mississippi and take New Orleans from Spain.

Connolly's suggestion met with a cold reception. Its adoption would ruin Wilkinson. His other hearers vividly recalled the massacres at the Blue Licks and Ruddle's, and countless other outrages committed by the Indians under British leadership. They warned him to leave Kentucky at once, before the public identified him and dealt with him as an English spy.[4]

The more conservative leaders—Thomas Marshall, George Muter, John Edwards, and others—had a different plan. There was only one road for free men to follow to reach a political goal, if they wished to remain free, they warned the people. That was the road of law and order.

"This District is a part of Virginia. And Virginia is a part of the United States. The people in Kentucky have no legal right to form a separate state without the consent of both governments.

"But suppose they were so rash as to try it. How long could they remain independent, between Spain on the south and Britain on the north? Let us be patient a little longer. Give the new Congress a chance."[5]

Those, in the main, were the proposals for the voters to consider in choosing delegates to the November convention. No sane man would have dared to suggest any bargain with Great Britain. The conservatives called the "Country Party," argued for the constitutional procedure to attain statehood, but Wilkinson and his followers, known as the "Court Party," demanded immediate independence.

Their boldness alarmed many citizens, who feared what the next convention might do under the broad powers voted to it in July. An increasing number seriously questioned the wisdom of separating from Virginia on any terms.

In mid-October *The Gazette* published a long letter signed by Judge George Muter, addressed to the voters of Fayette County. He cited a recent Virginia law which stated that any persons who attempted to set up a new government out of any part of that state, without its consent, would be guilty of "high treason."

The Federal Consitution, he reminded them, declared that ". . . no new state shall be formed . . . within the jurisdiction of any other state . . . without the consent of the Legislature of the States concerned, as well as of the Congress"; furthermore, it forbade all states to form any treaty of alliance with any foreign country.

He earnestly advised his fellow citizens to instruct their delegates to send ". . . a decent and manly memorial" to the Virginia Assembly and to the Congress, asking them to ". . . procure for the people of the western country the navigation of the Mississippi." Finally, he warned them, for their own protection, to limit the time and the powers of any future convention.[6]

Judge Muter's timely letter cleared the murky political atmosphere. Many who had looked with favor on the new state scheme suddenly realized where such a course would lead them. The Spanish alliance plotters quickly sensed a change in sentiment and trimmed their public speeches accordingly.

During the five election days, a large majority of the Fayette voters—whether disgusted, uncertain, indifferent, or fearful—stayed away from the polls. Those who did vote evidently took Muter's warning to heart. Even Wilkinson, the most popular candidate, would have lost the election if he had not given his word that he would follow instructions.[7]

Yet he dominated the November convention from beginning to end. As usual, he was chairman of the Committee of the Whole and a member of nearly every other important one.

The first contest between the two parties was over the powers of the convention. "The same that was given it by the sixth convention: to do whatever would promote the interests of the District between this date and January, 1790." That was Wilkinson's argument.

His opponents had no intention of letting the convention set itself up as a dictatorship over the destinies of Kentucky for fourteen months. "We were elected for the sole purpose of again applying to Virginia for statehood," they firmly stated. When the question came to a vote, a majority agreed with them.

But the resourceful general had just begun his campaign. He asked for and obtained permission to read a long essay, addressed to the governor of Louisiana, on the natural advantages of the western country, ". . . its rich productions, and its imperious claims to the benefits of commerce through the Mississippi, its only outlet." [8]

Then he read a memorial "To the United States in Congress Assembled" on the subject of opening up the Mississippi to American trade. He had worded those addresses so cleverly, to conceal his real purpose, that the convention thanked him ". . . for the regard which he therein manifested for the Interest of the Western Country."

He followed up that advantage by moving for the adoption of a resolution to the people of the district, ". . . to furnish this convention, at its next session, with instructions in what manner to proceed on the important subject to them submitted."

The leaders of the "Country Party," dismayed at this clever ruse to thwart the purpose for which the convention had already voted, sent Joseph Crockett galloping to Lexington. He came back, posthaste, with hundreds of signatures on a petiton protesting against any illegal or hasty action by the convention.

Wilkinson lost that master maneuver, but he had won what he evidently most wanted: continued confusion and political uncertainty. His activities at Danville that month would provide good reading for the "Intendant of Louisiana" in New Orleans.[9]

The stormy session closed with the adoption of a brief request to Virginia in line with Judge Muter's advice. It asked

the assembly again to provide for statehood for the district, and
to use its influence with the Congress in order that a new state
be admitted ". . . according to the late recommendation of the
Congress of the old Confederation."

Nearly everyone felt that a serious crisis had been safely
passed when the seventh convention was adjourned, but the
partisan bitterness of the election campaign was increased by its
proceedings.

"We shall, I fear, never be safe," wrote Col. Thomas Marshall to General Washington, "until we have a separate state and
are admitted to the Union as a federal member."

To that the general replied, "The western settlers . . . stand
as it were on a pivot. The touch of a feather would turn them
any way." [10]

Virginia was as willing as Kentucky to end the long struggle,
but it tried to drive a hard bargain by adding two new conditions to its third Enabling Act. In one, Kentucky must agree
to pay a part of the state debt. In the other, Kentucky must
permit Virginia to keep all land that had been granted to its
soldiers, but not yet located by them, whenever the district
should become a state.[11]

Those conditions were a great deal more than "the touch of
a feather." The first appears reasonable enough, as some of
the debt was contracted in the defense of Kentucky. But the
second, if accepted, would deprive the new state of all unappropriated public lands from which to raise money for operat-
ing its own government.

Kentucky, however, was in no mood to accept either condition. Its eighth convention, meeting in Danville on July 20, 1789,
voted to ask Virginia for the identical terms to which both
parties had previously agreed. At the same time, it sent a vigorous protest against an order to discharge all scouts and rangers,
as that would leave the frontier unprotected for hundreds of
miles.

By this time, however, the new federal government had
been organized. General Washington was president of the United
States of America. Knowing the tense situation in the West, he

tactfully directed General Knox, his secretary of war, to give Judge Innes permission to restore the scout and ranger service. This order had the desired effect of restraining the hostile activities of the Indians. It also promoted a more favorable public sentiment in Kentucky, for between 1788 and 1790 more horses had been stolen and more people murdered than in any two preceding years.

President Washington also recognized the judicial needs of the District of Kentucky by appointing Harry Innes as a federal judge, at the same time naming others to similar positions in the thirteen states.

Kentucky's astonishing growth in population practically demanded that consideration. The first census of the United States, taken in 1790, showed that more than seventy-three thousand people were living in the District of Kentucky that year. That was far beyond the sixty thousand required for statehood by the Northwest Ordinance of 1787. The federal government could no longer safely treat the District of Kentucky as a colonial province or deny it a place in the national councils.[12]

The district had also come of age in other ways than mere numerical growth. It represented a cross-section of the nation; it included people from every social, political, economic, and religious group and class, who had come from every region in the Union.

From the first clearing in the wilderness, the first West had attracted men of culture and education and more than its proportionate share of capable and experienced leaders. Fortunately for the future of the nation, the patriots among them usually outnumbered or outwitted the schemers and traitors.[13]

The end of the long trail to independent statehood was almost in sight when five delegates from each of the nine counties met at Danville in July, 1790, to consider Virginia's latest act of separation. These included five from Fayette County's more than eighteen thousand people and five from Mason's less than three thousand. There was no equal representation yet, under Virginia law!

Virginia had omitted, in its latest Act, the former requirement that Kentucky should pay a part of the state debt. It had set a time limit, May 31, 1792, for locating lands already granted, but it was still inclined to bargain. A new condition would require ". . . the proposed state" to pay all the costs ". . . of the several expeditions carried on from the Kentucky District against the Indians, since the first day of January, one thousand seven hundred and eighty-five." [14]

Had this convention of Kentucky delegates been in the same frame of mind as the preceding one, it would have rejected outright this harsh requirement of the Virginia Assembly. Even so, the vote to accept Virginia's terms—twenty-four to sixteen—was far from unanimous, as it had been in some of the earlier Conventions. But it was clearly ". . . the will of the majority."

The Convention's address to the new Congress in Philadelphia asked admission into the Union before the first day of November 1791. Its final act, however, was to order an election of delegates ". . . to frame and establish a constitution," setting June 1, 1792, ". . . as the period when the said independence shall commence." [15]

Kentucky was taking no chances on a deadline again running out. It intended to give slow-moving Congresses and Conventions plenty of time. In this instance it gave them more than was needed.

On Washington's recommendation, the Federal Congress voted on February 4, 1791, to admit Kentucky into the Union on June 1, 1792. Its act, the first of its kind in history, reads in part as follows:

> An act declaring the consent of Congress, that a new State be formed within the jurisdiction of the Commonwealth of Virginia and admitted into this Union by the name of the State of Kentucky . . .
>
> AND BE IT FURTHER ENACTED AND DECLARED, That upon the aforesaid first day of June, one thousand seven hundred and ninety-two, the said new State by the name and style of the State of Kentucky, shall be received and admitted into this Union, as a new and entire member of the United States of America.[16]

John Brown had been right, however, in his prediction in a letter to Judge Muter on July 10, 1788: "The jealousy of the growing importance of the Western country, and an unwillingness to add a vote to the southern interest, are the real causes of opposition. . . . The eastern states would not, nor do I think they ever will, assent to the admission of the district into the Union, as an independent State, unless Vermont or the province of Maine is brought forward at the same time." [17]

Two weeks after it passed the act to admit Kentucky, the Congress voted to make Vermont a state. It entered the Union on March 4, 1791, more than a year before the date Kentucky had set for its own statehood to begin.

Yet neither that, nor anything else, could dampen the joy of Kentucky's people over reaching the end of their long trail to independence. They had stated their purpose at the start—equality within the Union and within the framework of the law provided for achieving new status.

To that purpose they had doggedly held through nine conventions in six long years. They had endured delays and disappointments, had resisted threats and temptations with a patience and determination that must at times have surprised themselves as much as they did outsiders.

Now, at last, solely by democratic and legal processes—freedom of speech and press, of debate, petition and suffrage—with little help from Virginia and with less than none from the other states, they had reached their goal at last.

From an uninhabited wilderness to independent statehood in seventeen years!

CHAPTER XXIX

Our Country Then

The land was ours before we were the land's. She was our
land more than a hundred years before we were her people.

—ROBERT FROST

What kind of place was this so-very-new United States of
America, the country of which the people of Kentucky sought to
become a part in 1790?

Its total area was 820,377 square miles. Its western boundary
was the Mississippi River.

On its southern border, Spain again held title to Florida, to
"West Florida," a strip along the Gulf Coast, to Louisiana, and
to everything west of the Mississippi River to the Pacific Ocean.

England owned Canada and still occupied Detroit and other
ports on the Great Lakes.

Within the boundary lines of the new nation, Massachusetts had
control of the Province of Maine; Vermont nominally belonged
to New York; Virginia included West Virginia and the District
of Kentucky. Tennessee, which North Carolina had ceded to the
United States, and that part of Alabama and Mississippi north
of the Spanish claim were known as the Southwest Territory.
Virginia had ceded the vast Northwest Territory to the United
States government.

The year 1790 was a very critical one in the history of the
United States of America. It was a time of testing, a time to
find out whether a group of "self-willed commonwealths" could
ever work together under a system that would require mutual
give-and-take on the part of every member.

Article 3rd

Section 1. In elections by the Citizens all free
males Citizens of the age of twenty one years having resided in the State two years or the county
in which they offer to vote one year next before
the election shall enjoy the rights of an elector
but no person shall be entitled to vote except
in the county in which he shall actually re-
side at the time of the election.

All elections shall be by ballot.

Electors shall in all cases except
treason felony and breach or surety of the peace
be privilged from arrest during their attendance at
elections and in going to and returning from them

Article 11th

Section 1. The house of representatives shall have
the sole power of impeaching.

All impeachments shall be tried
by the senate; when sitting for that purpose
the senators shall be upon oath or affirmation.
No person shall be convicted without the con-
currence of two thirds of the members present

The Governor and all other civil
officers

*Photostat of page 33 of the original draft of the first Constitution of
Kentucky, April 19, 1792. Courtesy Kentucky Historical Society.*

A site for the national capital must be selected. On June 9, 1790, the Congress, then meeting in New York in rented quarters, voted in favor of a site on the Potomac River, to be called the "District of Columbia." To get a majority vote for that bill, however, its sponsors had to agree that the federal government, for the next ten years, should be located in Philadelphia, with the State House on Chestnut Street as the national Capitol.

In May, 1790, after due deliberation, Rhode Island had made a few changes in its Charter from Charles II and joined the federal team, making it a "baker's dozen." Vermont was poised for admission in 1791. Kentucky's application had been approved, effective in 1792.

The time had come, as required by the Constitution, for an official counting of noses, a census of all the people then living in the United States of America.

Some states had never taken a census. Others had done it regularly. Now, a national census was necessary for two compelling reasons. For one, the federal government owed $3 million for money borrowed by the Continental Congress during the Revolutionary War. Some states had paid their quota. Some had not, partly because they did not know how much they owed, since the amount depended upon their comparative population.

Then, there was the troublesome problem of apportionment, one that is still very much with us. How many representatives could each state send to the Congress? What should be the boundaries of each Congressional district? That also depended upon the state's population and just where the people lived within its borders.

Federal marshals and the enumerators went forth, with their pens and record books, into every field and shop, every cabin and mansion, turning in some very interesting and surprising reports.

These reports showed a total of 3,929,625 people. Of that number, about four people in every five (80.8 percent) were of white European stock and the remaining one-fifth of African descent.[1] Of every one hundred white people, ninety were of English,

Scottish or Irish ancestry. On the basis of family names, the census reported only forty-four Hebrews in the country.

English-speaking people lived in every part of the country. New England was almost as British as England itself. People from Scotland lived mainly in Pennsylvania, although some were in the uplands of the Southern states. Irishmen could be found from Pennsylvania to South Carolina.[2]

The remaining 10 percent of white people were mainly of Dutch, German, Scotch-Irish and French ancestry. The Dutch lived in New York. Most of the Germans were in Pennsylvania. The Scotch-Irish (people who had moved from Scotland to northern Ireland), and some Swiss and Moravians from Central Europe also lived in Pennsylvania and in North Carolina. A few French people lived in every state except New Hampshire and New Jersey.

In Kentucky and Tennessee, the proportion was about eighty-three English, eleven Scottish and two of Irish stock in every one hundred white people.

The people of African descent in the United States then numbered 697,624, about one-fifth of the total population. They or their ancestors had been brought to the United States either directly from Africa or from islands of the West Indies. More than fifty-nine thousand of them were free. No Negroes lived in Maine; all of those in Vermont and Massachusetts were free.

Only 3,703 lived in New England; forty-five thousand were in the Middle States. In the Southern States, where their labor was profitable in the cultivation of the staple crops, they numbered more than one-third of the total population.[3]

In the other states, the demand for labor was supplied to some extent by "redemptioners," people whose passage from Europe had been paid by someone in America. They worked without pay, except for "board and keep," for a definite number of years. Many of them fled to the wilderness or to the new West beyond the mountains to escape from their bondage.

Of the nearly 4 million people reported in that first census, ninety-seven in every hundred lived on farms or in rural areas. Most of them lived in the Atlantic coastal region or in the rolling

Piedmont country east of the mountains. Some, as we have seen, had crossed the mountains and lived in the valleys of the westward-flowing rivers and in the central parts of Kentucky and Tennessee.[4]

The average for the entire country was about ten persons to a square mile. But the population was not evenly distributed. There was thousands of square miles of land with no settlements. Rhode Island had the densest population of any state, and the mythical center of population was twenty-three miles east of Baltimore.[5]

For obvious reasons, the census authorities made no attempt to count the Indians still living within the boundaries of the United States. A few hundreds lived peaceably along the Penobscot River in Maine and in the region of Cape Cod. Thousands probably still roamed the vast forests of New England.

Remnants of the once-powerful Iroquois tribes lived in the central lake region of New York and along the upper part of the Susquehanna River in Pennsylvania. Roving bands of Indians still kept the settlers uneasy in the western parts of those two states. In South Carolina, the Catawbas owned and occupied a tract of land fifteen miles square on both sides of the Catawba River.

The situation was very different on the western side of the Appalachian mountains. General St. Clair, the territorial governor of the Northwest Territory, estimated the white population in that region in 1790 at four thousand people, hedged about by sixty-five thousand Indians who lived in the valleys of the rivers flowing into the Ohio.

Life apparently went on as usual in the whitewashed log houses of the old French towns—Vincennes, Kaskaskia, Cahokia. The men continued to hunt and trap animals and to work on their strip farms in the ancient European pattern.

The fort at the site of Cincinnati, however, built in 1780, held only a garrison. General Israel Putnam, our first surveyor-general, with some of his Massachusetts soldiers, had built a stout fortification in 1788 on high ground at the site of Marietta, on the west bank of the Muskingum River. But the record states, significantly, "No white child was born north of the Ohio before 1790."[6]

The largest tribes within the United States at that time were the Creeks, Chickasaws, Cherokees, Choctaws, Chippewas, living in the Southwest Territory (Tennessee, Alabama, Mississippi). They had an estimated four thousand to eighteen thousand warriors. (Squaws and papooses did not count!) All the tribes had horses and cattle, and some had captured Negro slaves. Some had learned to use the plow. The leader of the Creeks, an intelligent, well-educated half-breed, made a treaty with the United States government (August 7, 1790) which gave them the right to deal with any citizen of the United States ". . . who shall attempt to settle on any of the Creeks' land" as they pleased.[7]

Agriculture was naturally the major occupation in the America of 1790. The earliest settlers brought barley, rye, oats and wheat and raised those grains wherever the climate was favorable. Maize, or Indian corn, "the greatest food gift on this planet," maturing in one hundred days, soon became their major crop. They raised it in every section, on farms and in city gardens.

Farming methods and tools used in the fourteen states were much the same as in pioneer Kentucky, but with one notable difference. In the states, no one then had to stand guard with a loaded rifle in his hand while others cut down the trees, cleared away the brush, cultivated the ground, and sowed or planted the seed.

The hand implements—hoe, fork, spade and shovel—were much the same as those now in use. The wooden plow had a strip of steel fastened to the bottom edge of the mould board. The harrow had wooden teeth. Wheat and other small grains were cut with a long curved cradle, or a sickle. A good worker, following the reaper, "could scoop up a swath, bind it into a sheaf, toss it into the air, and bind another before the first sheaf hit the ground."

The method of threshing grain was almost as primitive as in Biblical times. One worker held the sheaf by the stalks while another beat the grains of wheat loose with a long-handled wooden flail. Then they tossed the straw to one side, swept up the wheat from the threshing floor, and stored it in sacks. The shield of New York bears a picture of a flour barrel beside that of a beaver, but Pennsylvania led in the production of wheat and flour.[8]

Tobacco, one of the most demanding plants raised by mankind, was cultivated by slave labor in Maryland, Virginia, and North Carolina. From the carefully prepared seedbeds in early spring to the packed hogsheads in early winter, it was never off the planter's mind.

Nearly every plantation had its own wharf and one or more stout river boats (something like Indian pirogues). The casks or hogsheads of cured tobacco were rolled down to the wharf, then loaded onto the boats and taken downstream to the nearest seaport. There they were stored in a warehouse for export, and a "warehouse receipt" was issued to the owner.[9]

One naturally thinks of cotton in connection with agriculture in the Southern states. That plant, however, had not become the king of Southern crops in 1790. Eli Whitney's cotton gin was still some years in the future. Until that was developed, it took an adult worker two years to separate enough fiber from the black cotton seed to make one bale of cotton. Even with slave labor, the fiber was too costly for general use. Before the use of the cotton gin became general, cotton was rarely used in home weaving, and was never an article of extensive domestic manufacture. The domestic fiber crops, flax and hemp, were raised exclusively in New England.[10]

Rice, which was a new plant to the Europeans who settled in South Carolina, had become their major crop before the Revolutionary War. The climate was ideal for its cultivation. The planters diked up the almost level fields of the Coastal Plain to keep enough water on the ground for its growth.

At harvest time, they gathered their crop by using "rice boats." These were large flat-bottomed rafts, twenty to eighty feet long, ten to twelve feet wide. They were propelled by poles and steered by one huge oar at the stern. As the boat floated on the water, workers standing in it along the sides pulled the heads of the tall stalks of rice over the edge and shook or beat the ripened grains onto the floor. The boat moved slowly from one end of the field to the other until all the harvest had been gathered.[11]

Yet people must have other food besides grain. To the familiar European garden vegetables America added the native white potato, which would grow in all sections, and its cousin, the sweet potato, or yam, grown in the warmer South.

Emigrants to America from the British Isles and other countries in Europe brought with them the domestic fowls and animals with which they were familiar. Horses, cattle and swine were raised in all the states. The raising of sheep was a specialty in New England.

The mule, as a work animal, was not widely known or used at that time. General Washington is said to have maintained a horse-breeding establishment on his plantation at Mount Vernon. He was also the nation's first breeder of quality mules. In 1787, the Marquis de Lafayette is said to have presented him with a jack and some jennets, and eight years later the king of Spain is reported to have favored him with similar gifts.[12]

Of the forty-seven cities enumerated in 1790, only five, all with excellent harbors, had a population of more than eight thousand people. New York came first, with 32,335. Philadelphia was second with 28,522, Boston third with 18,038, followed by Charleston with 16,357, and Baltimore with 13,503. If Germantown and other suburbs of Philadelphia had been included, that city would have topped the list with a population of 42,444.

Salem, in Massachusetts, missed the "Over 8,000 Club" by less than one hundred people. Richmond, the capital of Virginia, the state with the largest population, numbered only 3,761 people. No place in North Carolina had as many as two thousand.[13]

How did those townsfolk make a living? Take Philadelphia as an example. In that city, forty-one workers in every hundred were employed in manufacturing and mechanical work. They worked in little shops, however, with hand tools and nearly every "master craftsman had a young apprentice, learning his trade and living with the family."

The next largest group (thirty-three in every hundred), was employed in trade and transportation. Domestic and personal services accounted for sixteen of every one hundred workers;

and the professions of law, medicine, ministry, and teaching, for eight. A few people, although they lived in town, were busy with some form of agricultural work outside its borders.[14]

From the large number of silversmiths reported in the census, one might think that silver ore was an important mineral within the United States in 1790, but such was not the case. Silver flowed into Europe from Spanish North and South America; and from Europe it came back to the American colonies in foreign trade as coin. Most domestic trade was carried on by barter, for Americans wanted to keep their coin, if possible.

Since there were no convenient banks in which to deposit it, no stocks or bonds to buy, they sometimes took their foreign coins to a silversmith and had them converted into goblets, platters, snuffboxes, candlesticks, candelabra, vases, and flat tableware. In this form people could use, enjoy and keep their silver. When a mint to coin money was established in 1792 in Philadelphia, they could, if they desired, have their silver converted into American silver coins.[15]

Nature, in forming this favored land, had not failed to provide it with sufficient mineral wealth for modern mankind's use. Iron ore, in the form of bog ores, was present in nearly every state. It was smelted with charcoal and limestone in small, local furnaces.

Rich deposits of iron ore were found in one-half of the counties of Pennsylvania. Furnaces on the south side of the James River in Virginia produced about five thousand tons of pig iron annually. Iron was New Jersey's greatest source of wealth. The nation's production in 1790 met the domestic demand and left thirty-five hundred tons of pig iron for export.[16]

Small quantities of lead ores in Montgomery County, New York, in New Jersey, and in the mountains of Virginia about met the nation's needs for that mineral. Saltpeter from the caves of Virginia supplied one of the ingredients for making gunpowder.

Large deposits of sodium chloride (rock salt) provided New York with an important mineral industry. Locally, it met domestic needs in the forms of baking soda and caustic sodas, chlorine and hydrochloric acid. It was also used in the manufacture of glass, pottery, soap, and textile dyes. In the form of rock salt, New York exported it to the countries of western Europe and, also, to Japan and China.[17]

Building stone, clays for brick and pottery, sands for mortar and glass were found in abundance in nearly every state. By 1790 there were several large-scale glassmaking establishments in New York, New Jersey and Pennsylvania.

Bituminous coal was little known or used in 1790. All heating, cooking and manufacturing then was done with wood, or charcoal derived from wood. Of the vast deposits of anthracite, or "stone coal," as the very few who had discovered its existence called it, no living person then had the remotest knowledge. And the pools of liquid oil, or petroleum, that lay deep under the surface below the coal beds held substances not even dreamed of in 1790.[18]

The period did not lack its Horatio Alger stories. In England, a young worker named Samuel Slater set himself the task of memorizing the size and shape of every bar, piston, nut, bolt, screw, wheel, and wire of the cotton spinning and weaving machinery in the factory where he worked. With that valuable information stored in his head, he left England in disguise, since no factory worker was permitted to leave the country. He landed in Pawtucket, Rhode Island, in 1790. There he had no difficulty in finding men eager to invest in his project of building a spinning and weaving mill.[19]

Samuel Slater started more than the first successful steam-power factory in America. With him, the Industrial Revolution, with all its potentialities for good and evil, had also crossed the Atlantic.

Before the Revolutionary War, practically all land traveling was done by foot or by horse, along bridle paths or "blazed" trails. A stagecoach system was set up in 1790. New England roads converged on Boston from many directions. A map of Rhode Island and Connecticut of that time shows a network of highways.

New York had a post road to Albany, and from there into the Mohawk Valley, and many into New Jersey. Philadelphia was a center of roads. The long route to Pittsburgh went through Lancaster, Harrisburg, Carlisle, Shippensburg and Bedford. In the South, the most important roads followed the coast. Bridges were almost unknown south of the Potomac River. If a stream could not be forded, the traveler had to wait until the water ran down. In Delaware and all southern states, "the roads were poor even in thickly settled districts; and at a distance from the coast they degenerated into trails or ceased entirely." When it required four days to drive from Boston to New York, taking into consideration the condition of the roads, and the night stops at taverns, no one undertook a long journey lightly or unadvisedly.[20]

By 1790 the stagecoach had become the common mode of land travel between New England and the Middle States. These coaches made regular runs of three trips weekly between Boston and New York and Philadelphia; five trips weekly, between Philadelphia and Baltimore and Alexandria. The most traveled road, from New York through New Jersey to Philadelphia, was generally in good condition. The road from New York to Newark was built of wood on soil so water-soaked ". . . that it trembled when stepped on." The highway from Philadephia to Baltimore, because of its heavy clay soil and deep ruts, through dense forests, was often impassable.

The kind of public coach then in use was something like an open wagon, ". . . hung with curtains of leather and woolen, which could be raised or lowered at pleasure. It had four benches & could seat twelve persons. Light baggage was put under the benches and the trunks were attached behind."

Many bridges crossed the rivers near large cities. Boston Bridge spanned the Charles River at a place where it is as wide as the Thames at London Bridge. It was then the longest bridge in the world. This period marked the beginning of the beautiful covered bridges that served the needs of travelers for more than a century and are now cherished as relics of our colorful past.

With the country's abundance of fine harbors, however, the easiest mode of travel was by boat. Every coastal town in Rhode

Island, Connecticut, and New Jersey had regular service by sailing sloops to New York with accommodations for passengers at night. But the charge for meals was so high that skippers were sometimes accused of delays, in order to profit through serving more meals en route.[21]

New England's soil never offered an overabundance to its people. But there were forests of tall, straight evergreens growing almost to the coastline. There were schools of cod and mackerel swimming almost within sight of the timberline, and sperm whales, coming up to breathe, sometimes within spyglass range. Those sea-bred Britishers really had no choice but to build ships and go fishing.

By 1790, Massachusetts alone had 539 vessels and 3,287 seamen engaged in the cod-fishing industry. It also had 1,000 men in vessels, chasing whales all the way from Newfoundland to Greenland, and other New England states were not very far behind.

Foreign commerce in 1790 offered one of the most promising fields for the exercise of business ability. All seaboard cities had merchants who owned clipper ships built in New England ports. These ships carried both the goods of their owners and of other merchants to Europe, South America, Africa, China, and India.

A Boston ship, the *Columbia,* sailed from that port in 1788, loaded with tools and trinkets. It rounded the southern tip of South America and sailed up the coast to the Pacific Northwest where its skipper traded his cargo with the Indians for sea otter furs. Then he sailed across the Pacific to trade his cargo of furs for tea in Canton, China. The *Columbia* returned to America by way of Africa, thus becoming the first United States vessel to circumnavigate the globe.[22]

The ports of Massachusetts handled more foreign tonnage than those of any other state. But all the larger cities thrived on foreign shipping. About one-fifth of all imports was landed at New York; but Philadelphia handled one-third of all goods shipped out of the United States.

Salem, Massachusetts, however, led in the Pacific and East

Indies trade, with forty ships carrying ginseng roots directly to China, and beef, pork, flour and wheat to ports along the route.

Boston's exports were more varied—rum, potash and pearlash went to Great Britain and the West Indies; lumber, fish, whale-oil and whalebone, soap, candles and pickled fish went to France and the Dutch West Indies.

New York, also, had a lively commerce with the West Indies, sending large amounts of wheat and flour, beef and pork, lumber and livestock. Philadelphia's exports had the greatest value of any, however, due to large quantities of wheat and flour, lumber, beef and pork, livestock, corn and corn meal.

Baltimore's exports, handled for the most part by foreign agents in foreign ships, went mainly to Great Britain and Holland; some wheat and Indian corn to Spain and Portugal. Charleston and Savannah had a large foreign commerce in the raw materials from the southern plantations and forests. Rice, tobacco and cotton, lumber, tar, pitch and turpentine, went mainly to Great Britain and Holland. The total volume of all overseas trade of the United States in 1790 was more than 725,000 tons.[23]

Our country had a flourishing press in 1790, with 103 newspapers (weekly or semiweekly) and seven periodicals. New England accounted for thirty-two; the Middle States, forty-two; the South, twenty-four. Six in New York and Pennsylvania were either in the Dutch or the German language. The list ranged from Philadelphia's venerable *The Pennsylvania Gazette* (1725 and long in existence as *The Saturday Evening Post*) to *The Kentucke Gazette* (1787). All were printed with hand-molded steel type on hand presses, such as John Bradford used in Lexington.

Their contents were much the same as his—local advertisements, notices, auctions, sales, clippings from other papers, letters. They printed very little about local events, but they had vigorous editorials and full reports of congressional doings, along with a few broad jokes and anecdotes.

The weeklies carried long political and religious articles, but none had anything remotely resembling our popular "Sports" and "Comics" and rarely any illustrations. None printed more than one thousand copies. They were distributed in the towns by newsboys; through the rural districts by postboys on horseback as they did their other errands. Stagecoach drivers took subscriptions and distributed the papers on their regular schedules.

Where did these publishers of 1790 get the paper to print their newspapers? Mainly from Pennsylvania, but not from its forests. There was no wood pulp paper then. Every sheet was made of rags, gathered by the men who went through the streets and alleys, pushing their little cars and calling, "Rags! Old iron! And bones!"

Fifty-three paper mills within range of the Philadelphia market produced seventy thousand reams of paper in 1790. It was good paper, as good as the best imported stock. Both paper and ink were lasting. The pages of the old *Kentucke Gazette* are almost as white and the print almost as clear as when they were pulled from the press in 1788.[24]

The post-office department was a going concern serveral years old in 1787 when the Federal Constitution was written. By 1790, the United States had seventy-five post offices, and 1,875 miles of post roads. The main post road began at Wiscassat, in Maine, and followed the coast through Boston, Springfield, Hartford, to New York, Philadelphia, Baltimore and Alexandria. From there it was a long stretch to Wilmington and Charleston, ending at Savannah, Georgia.

Crossroads branched off inland from the main route. But many important towns, even entire states, had no communication by post. Most mail was carried by stagecoach. Some, however, went by post riders. There was no regular schedule of departure farther south than Alexandria, Virginia.

Postage charges depended upon the distance. They were collected upon delivery and paid only in specie, which varied from state to state. In 1790, there was no postal department for Vermont, Kentucky and the "Southwest Territory." Three states (New York, Georgia, North Carolina) had one post office each. There were no corner post-boxes, no stamps, no envelopes. The writer folded the letter paper, wrote the address on it with a goosequill pen, tied a string around it, sealed it with softened red wax, and stamped his seal upon it. Then it was taken to the coach driver or post rider, who collected the charges when he delivered it.

The Postmaster General today, however, might well envy his predecessor in 1790. When *he* balanced his records at the end of the year, they showed a *surplus* of $5,775.00! [25]

The finances of our nation were in almost hopeless confusion during the Revolution and throughout President Washington's first administration. Our government had no mint for coining money. Trade in the states, like that beyond the mountains, was almost entirely by barter. The commonest coin in use was the Spanish silver "milled dollar," a "piece of eight," secured in trade with the Spanish islands in the West Indies.

A coin collector could have had a field day with the many kinds of gold money in circulation: British guineas, French Pistoles, Portuguese dores or Johannes (Joe's). The majority of the people, accustomed to the English system, still thought in terms of pounds, shillings and pence, even after our own decimal monetary system, based on the one-hundred-cents dollar, was established in 1785.

Paper money, issued both by the Confederation and the states was refunded, when due, by newer issues. In Virginia, "tobacco money" (public warehouse receipts for tobacco in storage), was worth the known value of tobacco.

In 1790, there were only three banks in the United States—the Bank of North America in Philadelphia, the Bank of New York, and the Bank of Massachusetts in Boston. Only one had any direct relation with the federal government. [26]

Education at that time was entirely a local affair. In New England every Massachusetts town with fifty householders was required to employ a schoolmaster to teach reading and writing; those with one hundred families must maintain a grammar school. In winter, the district school was taught for two months by a man; in summer, for two months by a woman.

The books in use included little more than Noah Webster's *Speller,* Webster's *Selections,* Morse's *Georgraphy* and *The Youth's Preceptor.* The groundwork of all reading was the Bible.

Although the Middle States had fewer laws about compulsory education than did New England, public schools were common. They had very few freeborn illiterates. In Pennsylvania and New

Jersey the German language was taught in the public schools. Literacy was as high among the Germans as among the English. The Dutch language was used in schools in New York.

The South, with its scattered population, had very few public schools, and the larger towns had few academies. Wealthy men sent their sons to northern colleges or to Europe to complete their education. They employed governesses to teach their daughters at home. Most of the people in thinly settled regions were illiterate, and, of course, very few slaves were ever taught to read and write.

In the United States in 1790 there were only three professions—law, theology and medicine. New England majored in the first two. In Philadelphia, probably through Franklin's influence, some colleges offered courses in medicine and science, but there were only two medical schools and one law school in the nation. It was customary to get legal or medical training in the office of some well-known lawyer or doctor.

That word "science" needs explanation. An intelligent high school senior today knows more in that field of knowledge than the most learned man could have known in 1790. The latter did not know an *id* from an *ohm,* a *virus* from a *vaccine.* He had never heard of *Carbon 14* or of *X-Rays.*

Benjamin Franklin had done something interesting with a kite and a key in a thunderstorm. In 1790 he invented the lightning rod. He also invented bifocal spectacles, but that was about as far as science had gone at that time.

The 1790 Census listed fourteen colleges or institutions of higher learning, ranging from Cambridge's venerable Harvard (1636) and William and Mary at Williamsburg, Virginia (1693) to Georgetown University in Maryland (1789). It did not list little Transylvania in Kentucky (1787). Its curriculum, however, may not have been up to present college standards.

None of those institutions had more than two hundred students. The average was nearer fifty. All leaned heavily on the classics— the Latin and Greek languages and their literature. The graduates could probably converse in both and could quote long passages from their favorite authors.[27]

Early settlers in the United States had been largely Protestants, though Maryland was founded as a Catholic colony by a group of persecuted English Catholics. Many of the Protestants had also been persecuted in England, so the people of various sections had that common background. Out of it grew a demand for freedom in religious matters. That demand had been the prime influence in the founding of Massachusetts, Pennsylvania, and Rhode Island.

This religious influence is recognized in a quotation on the west gateway at Harvard University. The words are taken from Colonial records:

AFTER GOD HAD CARRIED US SAFE
TO NEW ENGLAND
AND WEE HAD BUILDED OUR HOUSES
PROVIDED NECESSARIES FOR OUR LIVELIHOOD
REARD CONVENTIENT PLACES FOR GODS WORSHIP
AND SETTLED THE CIVILL GOVERNMENT
ONE OF THE NEXT THINGS WE LONGED FOR
AND LOOKED AFTER WAS TO ADVANCE LEARNING
AND PERPETUATE IT TO POSTERITY
DREADING TO LEAVE AN ILLITERATE MINISTERY
TO THE CHURCHES WHEN OUR PRESENT MINISTERS
SHALL LIE IN THE DUST

The great beginning schoolbook of the seventeenth century was *The New England Primer;* and there, says one educator, "the Puritan mood is caught with absolute faithfulness. Here was no easy road to knowledge and salvation, but with prose as bare of beauty as the whitewash of their church, with poetry as rough and stern as their storm-torn coast, with pictures as crude and unfinished as their own glacial-smoothed boulders, between stiff oak covers which symbolized the contents, the children were tutored."

By the beginning of the Revolutionary War, the Anglican, or

Episcopal, faith had been declared the "established" religion in seven of the colonies, and the Congregational was the "established" religion in three of the New England colonies. Only three colonies had declared for freedom of religion.

Yet, when the Constitution of the United States was written, delegates from all the states incorporated in it two items relating to religion. They guaranteed the free exercise of religious faith to all people and forbade the establishment by Congress of any state religion or the requirement of any religious test as a prerequisite to holding any office under the control of the federal government.[28]

Such were conditions in the United States of America, to which Kentucky sought admission as a member. Each state, sometime between 1776 and 1792, had written its own constitution, as it changed from the status of a colony of England to that of independent statehood.

The political leaders of Kentucky, during its long struggle for independence, had had ample time to read and study those new constitutions. We cannot consider here every feature or variance found in them from state to state. Two provisions, however, concerned every citizen. These were the qualifications for voting in elections and those for holding elective office. What guidance did they provide for a new state in deciding its own policies?

In every state except Vermont, an adult male citizen must own a "freehold" or pay his taxes if he owed any, before he could vote. The property requirement varied in amount; the minimum was a "freehold" (so many acres of land, or a house and lot). The tax might be large or small, but still its payment was required.

To qualify as a candidate for elective office in eleven states, a man must own a certain amount of real estate. The amount varied according to the importance of the office. In Virginia, for example, a candidate for governor must own five thousand acres of land.

A man's religious beliefs, which had been the main influence in the founding of several colonies, were still, in some states, a factor in his political rights as a citizen. In Rhode Island and Maryland, a property owner had to be a Christian in order to vote or to become a candidate for elective office. In New Hampshire, besides being a "freeholder," he must be a Protestant. Vermont, the newest state, had no property restriction on voting, but a candidate for an elective office must be a Protestant.[29]

Such were the precedents when the Kentucky delegates met in Danville in their tenth and final convention to adopt a constitution for the fifteenth state.

CHAPTER XXX

"The First Republic in the Western Waters"

We here highly resolve . . . that this nation, under God, shall have a new birth of freedom, and that government of the people, by the people and for the people, shall not perish from the earth. —ABRAHAM LINCOLN

Sixteen of the forty-five delegates who met in Danville on April 3, 1792, to frame a constitution for Kentucky had had experience in previous conventions, either in Kentucky or in Virginia. In earlier meetings, they had reached agreement on many subjects. A recent resident, Colonel George Nicholas, was a lawyer skilled in political argument. He came with twenty-one resolutions prepared for discussion.

On April 19, the goal toward which Kentuckians had been moving for eight years was reached. Kentucky's first constitution, largely the work of Nicholas, had been written, adopted, signed and sealed.[1]

Two days later *The Kentucky Gazette* carried a notice for elections to be held on May 1. In the next issue, April 28, 1792, the qualifications for voting were printed. John Bradford's post rider, Edward Bullock, set out on his twice-a-month mail route with copies of those two issues and letters that had arrived at Bradford's pioneer post office in his bulging saddle bags. Before his next round, Bradford had printed copies of "The Constitution of the State of Kentucky" for sale.[2]

Readers of that document would find in it many novel features, by comparison with the constitutions of the fourteen other states. It made population, not counties, the basis of representation. Its

"Bill of Rights" guaranteed freedom of religion, speech, press and assembly, and set forth other ". . . general, great and essential principles of liberty and free government."

For the first time in history, a written constitution gave the rights to vote and to hold an elective office ". . . to all free male Citizens of age of twenty-one" without any property or religious qualifications or restrictions whatsoever. It would be years before Negroes and women were so privileged, but one step had been taken. Electors should vote by ballot, and they were privileged from arrest ". . . during their attendance at elections and in going to and returning from them."

The Constitutional Convention had not argued over those bold innovations. Then, as if afraid of such a heady breath of freedom, the delegates cautiously limited the scope of the franchise. Kentucky electors could vote directly only for members of the lower house of their General Assembly. For choosing their governor and their state senators, the delegates at that convention adopted the federal Constitution's method of selecting the president of the United States. Voters would cast their ballots for electors, and those so chosen would then vote for the governor and the state senators.

The Constitutional Convention delegates turned their backs on democracy entirely when they devised the laws to safeguard their property rights. Only three of them at that time owned no Kentucky lands. The holdings of ten members ranged from ten thousand to eighty-eight thousand acres. A majority voted to give the sole right to try law suits involving land titles to the Court of Appeals, whose judges would be appointed by the governor.

That constitution of 1792 contained not one word about education, the essential partner of democracy, but it had many on the subject of slavery. Seven preachers in the convention, ably led by the Reverend David Rice, tried hard to get an antislavery resolution adopted.

Although twelve delegates owned no slaves, another twelve had ten to fifty each. Only sixteen of the forty-two members present (three from Jefferson County not voting) were ready to take that liberal stand for human rights as opposed to property rights.[3]

A majority did agree to forbid the importation of slaves into the state for sale and to permit owners to free their slaves if they so desired. The proslavery group, however, under the leadership of Nicholas, won the point that if slaves were ever freed by law, the state should pay the owners for them. This was similar to the plan which Abraham Lincoln, a son of Kentucky, proposed nearly seventy years later as a solution to the slavery problem of the nation.

Being a human document, that first Constitution of Kentucky was full of compromise and far from perfect. It was ". . . made for present use rather than futurity, for the then condition of the country, more than for one materially different." [4] Its framers frankly admitted that fact when they provided for changes to be made or a new constitution to be written in five years if the people so desired.

There were no differences of opinion, however, as to the kind of man that a frontier state needed to head its government. He must, of necessity, be a border chieftain, an early resident, a leader whom the Indians feared and the citizens trusted. No man in Kentucky could better meet these requirements than the electors' almost unanimous choice—sturdy, honest, capable, forty-two-year-old Isaac Shelby, affectionately known as "Old King's Mountain."

On June 4, 1792, the day of his inauguration, every road leading into Lexington was thronged with people—on foot, on horseback, in wagons. Some had been traveling for days along the stump-filled dirt roads, through forests heavy with the scent of yellowwood blossoms. They had splashed across the shallow fords, crossed the deep streams in canoes or flatboats; stopped overnight with friends or relatives in stations or villages along the way.[5]

As they journeyed, the words "Do you remember?" and "I recollect," were constantly on their lips. Ten years earlier, in 1782, the year of the tragedy at the Blue Licks and elsewhere, they could have traveled a whole day without seeing a clearing.

Isaac Shelby (1750-1826), first governor of Kentucky.
From a steel engraving in the National Portrait Gallery.
Courtesy the Filson Club.

For safety then, everyone in Kentucky had to live in one of the crowded stations or forts. Now the travelers saw sturdy houses, young orchards, and neat gardens.[6]

Naturally they discussed politics—the new constitution and its various provisions as it affected them personally, the new governor and the legislature's probable choice for United States senators, some of the changes they would like to make in five years.[7]

Lexington folks had risen earlier than usual that morning. By sunrise, crowds in holiday mood pushed and jostled each other on the unpaved streets. At one corner a squad of militia drilled and marched. At another, a band of cavalry wheeled and cavorted. The sounds of bugles, fifes, and drums filled the air.

In all that throng, who might yet be found who had had a share in the beginning of this marvelous development of the first West? James Harrod, still straight of back and black of hair, could be there; Simon Kenton, with a lifetime of sharing adventures crowded into his thirty-seven years; Benjamin Logan, tall and dignified, the founder of one of the earliest stations; Squire and Daniel Boone, vigorous and keen of eye, at forty-eight and fifty-eight; Robert Patterson, founder of the town where the state legislature was now meeting.[8]

As these pioneers of the wilderness looked into each others' eyes, they had no need to ask, "Do you remember?" They saw things not visible to those about them—the uncharted forest, the herds of wild game, the painted savages, the gallant comrades whose deeds and deaths had helped to make this day possible.

A volley of gunfire and the roar of an old six-pounder brought everyone sharply back to the present. The crowds surged toward the Danville road. They shouted as they saw Shelby, riding at the head of a long processsion of horsemen, dressed in his usual frontier outfit, with holsters and saddlebags.

The procession halted at the edge of town where a delegation of Lexington men met them. John Bradford read a speech welcoming the governor to the city, after which a judge swore him in as the state's chief executive. Shelby's voice rang out clearly as he repeated the oath of office. "I do solemnly swear that I will be faithful and true to the Commonwealth of Kentucky as long as I continue a citizen thereof and that I will faithfully execute to the best of my abilities the office of governor according to law."

The valley of the Elkhorn River rang with the volley and cheers that followed his words. Then the procession fell into line behind the governor and his escort. To the accompaniment of fifes and drums and the clanging of the town's bells, they marched to the *Sign of the Eagle* tavern at the corner of Main and Upper Streets.

There the governor reviewed a parade of the Light Infantry and the Troop of Horses. The inaugural ceremonies ended with another round of volleys from rifles and the six-pounder. The crowd counted aloud: "One!. . . Two! . . . Twelve! . . . Thirteen!" That was for the old states in the Union.

"Fourteen! That was for Vermont.

"Fifteen! That was for Kentucky.

"Another? That's for Shelby!" the crowd shouted. "Hurray for Kentucky and Governor Shelby!" [9]

Isaac Shelby was one of the few men in pioneer Kentucky who lived and died on his original preemption claim. This drawing shows his home, built of stone in 1783. Courtesy the Filson Club.

Two days later the eleven senators and the forty representatives met to receive the governor. "He entered the handsome State House—a new two-story brick building designed for a Market House but hurriedly changed early in 1792 when Lexington saw a chance of becoming the capital of the new state. Proudly floating in the breeze on a pole next to the State House was a fifteen-star flag made by some unknown 'Betsy Ross' for the occasion."[10]

Shelby as usual wore his frontier outfit. But his bow, his manner, his speech to the first General Assembly of Kentucky were as courtly as Washington's had been three years before when he opened the first Federal Congress in New York, and the formality did not seem out of place to those one-time subjects of King George III.

"The General Assembly, responding to the Governor's address, wished him the enjoyment of uninterrupted health and that his administration may be truly advantageous to the first republic in the western waters." [11]

At its first meeting, the assembly named the Rev. John Gano as chaplain. It directed the treasurer to borrow money if he could. It selected an auditor and confirmed the Governor's appointments for his cabinet and for the judges of the Court of Appeals.

"The joint ballot of both houses were taken for two senators to represent this state in the Senate of the United States, and John Brown, Esqu., of Woodford Co. . . . and John Edwards, Esqr., of Bourbon County, were elected." [12]

The legislators also had to tackle the thorny problem of raising money to run the government. The state had begun its career without one penny of public funds. Virginia already had disposed of most of its choicest lands. All monies paid to complete land titles had gone into her treasury.

Kentucky must depend upon taxation as its chief source of revenue. Yet what could the lawmakers tax? Many people were desperately poor. Some leaders had even opposed statehood because they feared that Kentucky could not afford the luxury of independence.

Hopefully, the lawmakers levied two shillings on every one hundred acres of land and on every slave fit for work; on horses, mares, colts, and mules, eight pence each; on every head of cattle, threepence; on chariots, coaches, and other riding carriages, from four to six shillings a wheel; on every ordinary [tavern] license, three pounds; and on every billiard table and retail store, ten pounds.[13]

That first legislature must also decide upon a permanent place for the capital. For this it appointed a committee of five members to take bids and to visit the sites offered for a capitol building.

Lexingtonians confidently awaited the committee's decision. Their town was the largest, the most centrally located in the heart of the richest land. It had taverns and stores, schools and churches, a weekly newspaper. It boasted two stone houses, half a dozen of brick, and scores of comfortable log and frame buildings. It had built that fine State House where the legislature was meeting. Besides, was not its own citizen, Robert Todd, a member of the committee?

One Lexingtonian, Andrew Holmes, had other plans for the capital. He owned much land in Frankfort on both sides of the Kentucky River, thirty miles west of Lexington. As an inducement to get the capital located there he made the committee a truly remarkable offer.

The government could have the use of a house and a warehouse he owned in Frankfort for seven years; he would give it eight public lots and the choice of thirty unsold lots; he would provide ". . . 10 boxes of 10 x 12 window glass; 1500 lbs. nails, 50 pounds sterling worth of locks and hinges."

He would furnish stone and timber and ". . . the use of his sawmill, carriage, wagon and two good horses." In addition to Holmes' personal offer, eight citizens of Frankfort agreed to put up their bond to give the state $3,000 in gold or silver.[14]

Robert Todd owned more than one thousand acres of rich land near Lexington. Yet his hometown's bid fell far short of that made by Frankfort, and Todd voted with two other members of the committee of five for the little town on the Kentucky River as ". . . the most proper place for the seat of government."

In choosing a design for the Great Seal of the new state, Governor Shelby may have recalled John Dickinson's old Revolutionary "Liberty Song:"

"Come, join hand in hand, Brave Americans all;
By uniting we stand, By dividing we fall."

He directed that the seal should be ". . . engraved with the following device: Two friends embracing, with the name of the state over their heads, and round about them the following motto, "United we stand, Divided we fall!" The engraver might appropriately have clothed those two friends in deerskin and moccasins; instead, he chose the full dress of the period, from powdered wigs to buckled shoes.[15]

When the fifteenth state began its independent career, English troops still held Detroit and other lake posts; Spain controlled the Mississippi, the West's only outlet to the world's markets. It could close that outlet at will.

Closer home, the Indians hung upon Kentucky's borders and prowled its forests. On November 6, 1792, ". . . . the Kentucky Militia, commanded by Maj. Adair, were attacked near fort St. Clair . . . by double their number . . . Maj. Adair had six men killed and five wounded, and lost the greater part of their horses, but kept the field." [16]

Kentucky no longer stood alone. On that same day the governor addressed the second session of the Legislature. He told the assembly that he had written to the commanding officer of the army of the United States regarding measures for the protection of Kentucky.

In reply he had received a letter from ". . . the honorable the Secretary of War. It is with pleasure I inform you that the Secretary's letter contains an assurance by order of the President . . . that he will hold the protection of this country as a primary object of his attention." [17]

Yes, it was a good thing to be a member of the Union, people decided. It was reassuring to have friends in high positions. In the past, they had been sorely needed, but often wanting.

Yet Kentucky had won through without their help!

Statehood, however, had not solved all of the state's problems. For a long time plots and conspiracies to separate it from the Union would continue to breed distrust and suspicion within and beyond its borders. Tangled, overlapping land claims would burden its courts and distress many of its citizens for generations, but the Kentuckians had successfully solved their greatest problem, the legal establishment of political independence. In achieving that, they had held to democratic processes and principles. In framing their basic law, they had given a broader interpretation to the American ideal of government by the consent of the governed.

The new state could deal with other difficulties as they arose. Poor though they were in worldly goods, those citizens were rich in a unique heritage of political experience and exciting memories. They could face the future confidently, unafraid.

Already a yet newer West was beckoning. Kentucky's sons and daughters would go forth to people other wildernesses and erect other free states. They would have their native state to guide them, the record of its successes and failures, of its stubborn will to control its own destiny, but to stay within the law while doing it. They would have the fostering interest and care of the new federal government, steadily increasing in prestige and power.

The new tasks of democracy would not be easy, but succeeding generations would find them less difficult because of the trail towards freedom which their forefathers had blazed in Kentucky, the land where the West began.

NOTES TO CHAPTER I

[1]Lucien Beckner, "Eskippakithiki, The Last Indian Town in Kentucky." Reprint, *The Filson Club History Quarterly,* (hereafter cited as *Hist. Quart.*), Oct., 1932, pp. 355-382; Charles A. Hanna, *The Wilderness Trail* (Vol. 2, New York: G. P. Putnam & Son, 1911), II,130,215 (note). (The site of Eskippakithiki is eleven miles east of Winchester, Kentucky.)

[2]Hanna, *op. cit.,* "Lyman C. Draper's Account of John Finley," II,213-231,252-256; Lucien Beckner, "John Findley, The First Pathfinder of Kentucky," *Hist. Quart.,* Apr., 1927, pp. 213-219. (The name is also spelled "Finlay," "Findlay").

[3]*World Almanac* (New York: N. Y. *World-Telegram,* 1958), p. 531; Hanna, *op. cit.,* pp. 215-6 (f. n. #2), "The Iroquois name for the level region or prairie surrounding the Indian village was *kenta-ke*"); Lucien Beckner, Letter of 21 March, 1951, Thomas P. Field, "Place Names of Kentucky", *Hist. Quart.,* July, 1960, p. 243.

[4]John Bakeless, *Daniel Boone, Master of the Wilderness,* (New York: Wm. Morrow & Co., 1939), pp. 21-26.

[5]William Waller Hening, (ed.), *Laws of Virginia, Statutes at Large* (Vol. 13, Richmond: Franklin Press, 1820), VII, pp. 663-669.

[6]Temple Bodley, *History of Kentucky,* (Vol. 4, Chicago-Louisville: S. J. Clarke Pub. Co., 1928), I, pp. 66-71.

[7]John P. Kennedy (ed.), *Journals of the House of Burgesses of Virginia,* 1770-1772, (Richmond: Virginia State Library, 1906), XV, xvi; Clarence W. Alvord, *The Mississippi Valley and British Politics* (Vol. 2, Cleveland: The A. H. Clark Co., 1917), II, 83-85. (The "Louisa" is the present "Levisa," a branch of the West Fork of the Big Sandy. Either by error or intention. the treaty boundary was located at the Kentucky River, and the name "Louisa" then applied to that stream).

[8]John Filson, *The Discovery, Settlement and Present State of Kentucke,* (Wilmington: James Adams, 1784), pp. 50-51.

[9]*Ibid.,* p. 56.

[10]*Ibid.* pp. 51, 55-56.

[11]*Ibid.,* pp. 56-57; Willard Rouse Jillson, *Filson's Kentucke,* The Filson Club Publications No. 35 (Ed. I, Louisville; John P. Morton & Co., 1929), pp. 131, 132.

[12]Seymour Dunbar, *History of Travel in America,* Vol. 4, Indianapolis: Bobbs-Merrill Co., 1915), I, 124; Bakeless, *op. cit.,* pp. 67-69.

[13]Hanna, *op. cit.,* II, 230-231, 252-256; Bakeless, *op. cit.,* pp. 70-74; Wisconsin State Historical Society, *Draper Manuscript Collections* (hereafter referred to as *Draper MSS*), Nos. 22C5, 6C7-29, 6S79-83 (microfilm copies, The Filson Club, Louisville, Kentucky); *The Virginia Gazette,* Dec. 23 1773.

NOTES TO CHAPTER II

[1]Lucien Beckner, "Captain James Harrod's Company," *Kentucky Historical Society Register,* Frankfort, (hereafter cited as *The Register*), Sept. 1922, pp. 280-282; Kathryn Harrod Mason, "Harrod's Men—1774," *Hist. Quart.,* Jy., 1950, pp. 230-233.

[2]Richard H. Collins, *History of Kentucky* (Rev. Ed., Vol. 2, Louisville: J. P. Morton & Co., 1876), II, 517-519, 617-620; Kathryn H. Mason, *James Harrod of Kentucky*, (Baton Rouge, La., St. University Press, 1051), pp. 42-52.

[3]R. C. Ballard Thurston, Personal Interview, The Filson Club, 1938; Denske Dandridge, *George Michael Bedinger, A Kentucky Pioneer*, (Charlottesville, Va., The Michie Co., 1909), pp. 105-111.

[4]J. Bakeless, Daniel Boone, pp. 77-80: Reuben Gold Thwaites and Louise Phelps Kellogg (eds.), *Documentary History of Dunmore's War*, (Collections Wisconsin State Historical Society, Madison: 1905), pp. xv, xvi; Clarence W. Alvord, *The Mississippi Valley and British Politics*, II, 188-193; John Filson, *The Discovery, Settlement and Present State of Kentucke*, p. 58.

[5]Temple Bodley, *History of Kentucky*, Vol. 1, 92-95; Thwaites & Kellogg, *op. cit.*, pp. 253-257, 267-268, 301-304.

[6]George Elliott Howard, *Preliminaries of the Revolution, 1763-1775*, in *The American Nation: A History*, edited by A. B. Hart (Vol. 8; New York: Harper & Bros., 1905), VIII, 241; Constance Lindsey Skinner, *Pioneers of the Old Southwest* (New Haven: Yale University Press, 1919), pp. 122-125.

NOTES TO CHAPTER III

[1]John Filson, *The Discovery, Settlement and Present State of Kentucke*, pp. 58-59.

[2]John Bakeless, *op. cit.*, *Daniel Boone*, pp. 84-85; Archibald Henderson, "Creative Forces in American History: Henderson and Boone," *American Historical Society Review*, XX, 105; Archibald Henderson, "The Transylvania Company Personnel," *Hist. Quart.*, Oct., 1947, pp. 327-328, 331; William Henry Perrin, *History of Fayette County, Kentucky* (Chicago: O. L. Baskin & Co., 1882), P292; *Draper MSS.* No. 2C106 (Capt. Nathaniel Hart.)

[3]Filson, *op. cit.*, p. 59; William Ayres, *Historical Sketches*, (Pikeville: Sun Publishing Co., 1925), pp. 168-170.

[4]William Allen Pusey, *The Wilderness Road to Kentucky* (New York: George H. Doran Co., 1921), pp. 19-23, 39,55; Thomas Speed, *The Wilderness Road*, Filson Club Publications No. 2 (Louisville: John P. Morton & Co., 1886), p. 19; Archer Butler Hulbert, *Boone's Wilderness Road* (Cleveland: A. H. Clark Co., 1903), p. 177.

[5]Ellen Churchill Semple, *American History and Its Geographic Conditions* (Boston: Houghton Mifflin Co., 1903), pp. 67-68; Arthur McQuiston Miller, *The Geology of Kentucky* (Frankfort: State Journal Co., 1919), pp. 187-189: Willard Jillson, *The Topography of Kentucky* (Frankfort: State Journal Co., 1927), pp. 155-156.

[6]William Ayres, *op. cit.*, p. 169; George W. Ranck, *Boonesborough*, The Filson Club Publications No. 16 (Louisville: John P. Morton & Co., 1901), Appendix G, p. 163.

[7]George W. Ranck, *op. cit.*, p. 164.

[8]Archer Butler Hulbert, *op. cit.*, pp. 175, 183-186; Robert F. Kincaid,

The Wilderness Road (Indianapolis: Bobbs-Merrill Co., 1947), pp. 99-105; William Allen Pusey, *op. cit.,* pp. 26-27; Seymour Dunbar, *History of Travel in America,* Vol. 4 (Indianapolis: Bobbs-Merrill Co., 1915), I, 136-140.

NOTES TO CHAPTER IV

[1]Seymour Dunbar, *History of Travel in America,* I, 114-116; Archibald Henderson, *The Conquest of the Old Southwest,* (New York: Century Co., 1920), pp. 187-190.

[2]Constance Lindsey Skinner, *Pioneers of the Old Southwest,* pp. 131-134; Bakeless, *Daniel Boone,* pp. 85-87; Wm. P. Palmer (ed.), *Calendar of Virginia State Papers* (Vol. 11, Richmond: R. F. Walker, 1875), I, 272-273.

[3]Julia Alves Clore, "Personnel of the Transylvania Company," *Kentucky Progress Magazine,* Summer, 1934, pp. 336-337, 400; Henderson, *op. cit.,* pp. 222-228; *Draper MSS* No. 2CC23.

[4]Ayres, *Historical Sketches,* p. 170; Palmer (ed.), *op. cit.,* I, 283; Bakeless, *op. cit.,* pp. 85-88.

[5]Bakeless, *op. cit.,* pp. 85-88; John Haywood, *History of Tennessee,* (Knoxville: Heiskell & Brown, 1823), pp. 31-42; Ranck, *Boonesborough,* pp. 152-156.

[6]Skinner, *op. cit.,* pp. 129-134; Bakeless, *op. cit.,* pp. 86-87; *Draper MSS* No. 7C1-31 (Draper's notes on statements by persons present at the Treaty).

[7]Henderson, *op. cit.,* pp. 221-226; Filson, *Kentucke,* p. 80; C. Frank Dunn, Lexington, Ky., *(Personal Letter,* Aug. 3, 1951).

[8]John Richard Alden, *Southern Colonial Frontier, 1754-1775,* (Ann Arbor: University of Michigan Press, 1944), pp. 290-293; John P. Kennedy (ed.), *Journals of the House of Burgesses of Virginia, 1770-1772* (Richmond: Virginia State Library, 1906), pp. xv, xvi; (At Lochaber, 1770, the Cherokees had agreed that ". . . no alteration shall be made in the Boundary line . . . without the consent of the Superintendent or such other as shall be authorized by his Majesty . . . at a congress of said Indians held to said purpose, and not in any other manner.")

NOTES TO CHAPTER V

[1]Richard Collins, *History of Kentucky,* II, 498-501; (Richard Henderson's "Journal of an Expedition to Cantucky in 1775").

[2]Ranck, *Boonesborough,* (Richard Henderson's letter to his partners, June 12, 1775), pp. 184-193.

[3]Lewis H. Kilpatrick, "William Calk, Kentucky Pioneer," *Kentucky Magazine,* Vol. 2, No. 1 (Jan., 1918), pp. 33-42.

[4]William Calk, "His Jornal," (Photostat copy, library of the Filson Club, Louisville; from the original manuscript in Mt. Sterling, Kentucky); Hulbert, *Boone's Wilderness Road,* pp. 107-119; Speed, *The Wilderness Road,* pp. 41-49; Pusey, *The Wilderness Road to Kentucky,* pp. 19-23, 39, 55; Lewis H. Kilpatrick, "The Journal of William Calk, Kentucky Pioneer," *Mississippi Valley Historical Society Review,* Vol. 7, No. 4 (Mar., 1921), pp. 363-377.

[5]William Calk, *op. cit.*

[6]Ranck, *op. cit.,* pp. 184-193.

NOTES TO CHAPTER VI

[1]Ranck, *Boonesborough*, pp. 184-193; Bakeless, *Daniel Boone*, p. 99; *Kentucky Progress Magazine* (Frankfort), Summer, 1935, p. 391.

[2]Zachary F. Smith, *History of Kentucky* (Louisville: Courier-Journal Job Printing Co., 1886), 88-89; Collins, *History of Kentucky*, II, 497-499.

[3]Ranck, *op. cit.*, pp. 25, 26, 175; Lucien Beckner (ed.), "The Henderson Company Ledger by John D. Shane," *Hist. Quart.*, Jan., 1947, pp. 22-46.

[4]Ranck, *op. cit.*, pp. 177-179.

[5]William L. Saunders (ed.), *The Colonial and State Records of North Carolina* (Vol. 20, Raleigh, 1890, IX, (1771-1775), pp. 1129-1131; Collins, *op. cit.*, II, 512.

[6]William Calk, "His Jornal," (Photostat Copy, The Filson Club Library).

[7]Ranck, *op. cit.*, p. 174; Bakeless, *op. cit.*, pp. 99, 100; Emmet Field Horine, (ed.), *Pioneer Life in Kentucky, 1785-1800, by Daniel Drake, M.D.* (New York: Henry Schuman, 1948), pp. 36-38, 44-45.

[8]William Calk, *op. cit.*

NOTES TO CHAPTER VII

[1]Collins, *History of Kentucky*, II, 238, 307, 499, 501; Henderson, *Conquest of the Old Southwest*, p. 246.

[2]Robert M. McElroy, *Kentucky in the Nation's History*, (New York: Moffat, Yard & Co., 1909), p. 35; Bakeless, *Daniel Boone*, pp. 100, 101; Judge Charles Kerr (ed.), *History of Kentucky*, by Wm. E. Connolley and E. Merton Coulter (Vol. 5, Chicago: American Historical Society, 1922), I, 212.

[3]Collins, *op. cit.*, II, pp. 498-501; Bakeless, *op. cit.*, pp. 102-105.

[4]Bodley, *History of Kentucky*, I, 110, 111.

[5]Collins, *op. cit.*, II, 505-510; A. B. Hart (ed.), *The American Nation—A History*, VIII, 223-229, 237; Frederick J. Turner, "Western State-making in the Revolutionary Era," *Am. Hist. Society Review*, I, 76-81; John Mason Brown, *The Political Beginnings of Kentucky*, Filson Club Publications No. 6 (Louisville: J. P. Morton & Co., 1889), p. 24; Peter Force (compiler), *American Archives*, Fourth Series (Vol. 6, Washington: M. St. Clair Clarke & Peter Force, 1837-1843), IV, cols. 546-554.

[6]Hambleton Tapp, *The Sesqui-Centennial History of Kentucky* (Vol. 5, Chicago: American Historical Society, 1946), I, 85, 86; Force (comp.), *op. cit.*, IV, cols. 551, 552; Bakeless, *op. cit.*, p. 102.

[7]Skinner, *Pioneers of the Old Southwest*, pp. 136-138.

NOTES TO CHAPTER VIII

[1]Saunders (ed.), *The Colonial and State Records of North Carolina*, II, 1122-1125; Charles Kerr (ed.), *History of Kentucky*, I, 164.

[2]Saunders, *op. cit.*, IX, 1169-1170.

[3]Peter Force (comp.), *American Archives*, IV, cols. 553-554.

[4]Archibald Henderson, "Transylvania Company Personnel—James Hogg." *Hist. Quart.*, Jan., 1947, pp. 3-21.

[5]Ranck, *Boonesborough*, pp. 224-229; Saunders (ed.), *op. cit.*, IX, 545-546.

[6]Palmer (ed.), *Calendar of Virginia State Papers*, I, 275; Force (comp.), *op. cit.*, VI, cols. 1528-1529; Ranck, *op. cit.*, pp. 241-244.

[7]James Rood Robertson, *Petitions of the Early Inhabitants of Kentucky*, The Filson Club Publications No. 27 (Louisville: J. P. Morton & Co., 1914), pp. 36-41; Temple Bodley, *George Rogers Clark, His Life and Public Services*, (Boston: Houghton Mifflin Company, 1926), pp. 28-30.

[8]James Alton James (ed.), *Collections of Illinois State Historical Society, George Rogers Clark Papers, 1771-1778* (Springfield: Ill. State Hist. Library, 1912), VIII, 213, 214.

[9]Hening, William Waller (ed.), *The Statutes at Large, Being a Collection of all the Laws of Virginia* (Vol 13; 1775-1778, Richmond: J & G Cochran, 1821), IX, 257-258; Bodley, *History of Kentucky*, I, 130-137; McElroy, *History of Kentucky*, pp. 51-60.

[10]Hening, *op. cit.*, IX, 571-572; Force, *op. cit.*, IV, col. 1044; John Richard Alden, *Southern Colonial Frontier, 1754-1775*, pp. 290-293.

NOTES TO CHAPTER IX

[1]Ranck, *Boonesborough*, p. 141.

[2]Collins, *History of Kentucky*, II, 616; Denske Dandridge, *George Michael Bedinger, Kentucky Pioneer*, p. 195.

[3]Collins, *op. cit.*, II, 29; Dandridge, *op. cit.*, p. 165; Joseph Doddridge, *Notes on the Settlements and Indian Wars Of the Western Parts of Virginia and Pennsylvania from 1763 to 1783* (Pittsburgh: Ritenour & Lindsey, 1912), pp. 83-93.

[4]M. J. Spaulding, *Sketches of the Early Catholic Missions of Kentucky* (Louisville: B. J. Webb & Brother, 1844), p. 24.

[5]Ranck, *op. cit.*, pp. 45, 49, 237; Skinner, *Pioneers of the Old Southwest*, pp. 37-42, 46-48; Doddridge, *op. cit.*, pp. 121-125.

[6]Horine (ed.), *Pioneer Life in Kentucky, by Daniel Drake, M.D.*, pp. 43-46, 54-56, 86-87.

[7]Ranck, *op cit.*, pp. 49-52, 249-250; Bakeless, *Daniel Boone*, pp. 124-137; Collins, *op. cit.*, II, 526-527.

[8]Ranck, *op. cit.*, pp. 249-251; *Draper MSS* No. 11CC11; Charles W. Bryan, "Richard Callaway, Kentucky Pioneer," *Hist. Quart.*, Jan., 1935, pp. 35-50.

[9]Doddridge, *op. cit.*, pp. 102-106.

[10]Smith, *Hist. of Kentucky*, pp. 393-394; Dandridge, *op. cit.*, p. 161; Skinner, *op. cit.*, pp. 34-36; Dunbar, *History of Travel in America*, I, 106-113.

NOTES TO CHAPTER X

[1]William H. English, *The Conquest of the Territory Northwest of the River Ohio, 1778-1785, and Life of General George Rogers Clark* (Vol. 2, Indianapolis: Bobbs-Merrill Co., 1897), I, 465-466; James (ed.), *George Rogers Clark Papers, Ill. Hist. Colls.*, VIII, 214-215; *Draper MSS* No. 48J10.

[2]Collins, *Hist. of Kentucky*, II, 469-473; Humphrey Marshall, *History of Kentucky* (2nd. Ed., Vol. 2, Frankfort; Geo. S. Robinson, 1824), I, 27, 30, 49; *Draper MSS* No. 9CC23-24.

³English, *op. cit.*, I, 465-466; James (ed.), *op. cit.*, VIII, 218; Bodley, *George Rogers Clark*, pp. 38-40; Bakeless, *Daniel Boone*, pp. 141-155.

⁴Otto A. Rothert, "John Floyd—Pioneer and Hero," *Hist. Quart.*, Jy., 1928, p. 173.

⁵James (ed.), *op. cit.*, VIII, 20-23; English, *op. cit.*, I, 581; Bodley, *op. cit.*, p. 40; *Draper MSS* No. 48J12 (George Rogers Clark's "Diary").

⁶James (ed.), *op. cit.*, VIII, 20-23; English, *op. cit.*, I, 581; Bodley, *op. cit.*, pp. 43-48.

⁷James (ed.), *op. cit.*, VIII, 115; Bodley, *op. cit.*, pp. 43-45, f. n. #3.

NOTES TO CHAPTER XI

¹Miller, *Geology of Kentucky*, pp. 220-221, 341; *Register*, Vol. 26 (1928), p. 397; *Draper MSS* No. 57J25 (Daniel Trabue).

²Bakeless, *Daniel Boone*, pp. 156-167; Skinner, *Pioneers of the Old Southwest*, pp. 143-147, *Draper MSS* No. 11C28-282.

³Samuel M. Wilson, "Daniel Boone, 1734-1934," *Hist Quart.*, Oct., 1934, p. 151; Reuben Gold Thwaites, *Daniel Boone*, (New York: D. Appleton & Co., 1902), pp. 150-158.

⁴Bakeless, *op. cit.*, pp. 182-185; Thwaites, *op. cit.*, pp. 206-208; *Draper MSS* Nos. 4C44-47 (Abner Bryan), 11C27-32 (Ansel Goodman), 11C-62¹⁰⁻¹² (Jos. Jackson).

⁵Filson, *Kentucke*, pp. 65, 66, 67; Ranck, *Boonesborough*, pp. 71-76; *Draper MSS* No. 11C62,¹³⁻¹⁶ (Jos. Jackson).

⁶Filson, *op. cit.*, p. 68.

⁷*Ibid.*, p. 69; Louise Phelps Kellogg, *Frontier Advance on the Upper Ohio, 1778-1779* (Vol. XXIII, Coll. of the Wisconsin State Historical Society; Draper Series, Vol. IV; Madison: 1916), pp. 114-115, 126, 132.

⁸Ranck, *op. cit.*, pp. 80-104; Smith, *History of Kentucky*, ("Robt. B. McAfee MS"), pp. 101-104; *Draper MSS No.* 11CC12, 13, 14 (John Gass).

⁹Wilson, *op. cit.*, pp. 192-193; *Draper MSS* Nos. 11C60-61 (Ambrose Coffey), 57J32-33 (Daniel Trabue); Bakeless, *op. cit.*, pp. 230-237.

NOTES TO CHAPTER XII

¹James (ed.) *George Rogers Clark Papers*, *Ill. Hist. Colls.*, VIII, 116; Bodley, *George Rogers Clark*, p. 45, f. n. #2; *Draper MSS* No. 9CC28-29 (William Whitley's Narrative).

²James (ed.), *op. cit.*, VIII, 222; Bodley, *op. cit.*, p. 60.

³James (ed.), *op. cit.*, VIII, 119-122 (Clark's "Letter to George Mason"), 229 (Clark's "Memoir"); English, *Conquest of the Old Northwest*, I, 417-418.

⁴George W. and Helen P. Beattie, "Pioneer Linns of Kentucky," *Hist. Quart.*, Jy., 1946, p. 231; Reuben Gold Thwaites and Louise Phelps Kellogg (eds.), Colls. Wis. State Hist. Soc., Draper Series Vol. III, *Frontier Defense on the Upper Ohio* (Madison: 1912), pp. 298-300. (News of the French Alliance, conveyed in a letter to Clark from Pittsburgh, arrived at the Falls after Clark's expedition had left. William Linn, alone in a canoe, took the letter down the river and caught up with Clark's army near the mouth of the Tennessee River.)

⁵James (ed.), *op. cit.*, VIII, 119-122 (adapted from Clark's "Letter to

George Mason," and Clark's "Memoir".)

[6]Bodley, *op. cit.*, p. 75; James (ed.), *op. cit.*, pp. 123, 236.

[7]Bodley, *op. cit.*, p. 83; James (ed.), *op. cit.*, p. 126. (Exact date not given; ". . . about the last of August and first of September," according to Clark's "Letter to John Mason", p. 124).

[8]James (ed.), *op. cit.*, pp. 244-246; English, *op. cit.*, I, 493-496 (adapted from Clark's Memoir").

[9]James (ed.), *op. cit.*, pp. 249-252 (adapted from Clark's "Memoir").

NOTES TO CHAPTER XIII

[1]Morton V. Joyes, Sr., "Letter by Colonel John Todd, Jr., 1778," *Hist. Quart.*, Jy., 1928, p. 157.

[2]Fannie Casseday Duncan, *When Kentucky Was Young*, (Louisville: J. P. Morton & Co., 1928), pp. 152-160; Reuben T. Durrett, *The Centenary of Louisville*, Filson Club Publications No. 8 (Louisville: J. P. Morton & Co., 1893), pp. 29-32; History of the Ohio Falls Cities and Their Counties (Vol. 2, Cleveland; I. A. Williams & Co., 1882), I, 154-155.

[3]Reuben Gold Thwaites and Louise Phelps Kellogg (ed.), *The Revolution on the Upper Ohio* (Colls., Wisconsin State Historcial Society, Draper Series Vol. II, Madison: 1908), pp. 226-229, 252 (f.n. #99), 253; G. W. and H. P. Beattie, "Pioneer Linns of Kentucky." *Hist. Quart.*, Jy., 1946 pp. 223-226; J. Stoddard Johnston, *Memorial History of Louisville* (Vol. 2, Chicago: American Biographical Publishing Co., 1896), I. 39.

[4]Ranck, *Boonesborough*, pp. 235-236; Johnston *op. cit.*, Vol. I, 1-8; United States Geological Survey, Topographic Map, *Camp Taylor; A* McQ. Miller, *Geology of Kentucky*, pp. 78, 79, 216.

[5]Durrett, *op. cit.*, pp. 23, 26-28, 131-133, 163-164, 166; Johnston, *op. cit.*, I, 36-38; 40-46; Louisville Abstract Association, *Abstract of Old Deeds* (Photostat copies, The Filson Club Library), Nos. 1-4, 9, 10; Carl Bernstadt. "Certain Phases of the Origin of Louisville," *Hist. Quart.*, Jy., 1930, p. 107; Hening, *Virginia Statutes*, VII, 661, 663; W. H. Perrin, J. H. Settle, G. C. Kniffen, *Kentucky, A History of the State, 4th Ed.* (Louisville & Chicago: P. A. Battey & Co., 1887), p. 119.

[6]Alfred Pirtle, "Where Louisville Started," (Louisville: The Standard Printing Co., 1921), pp. 1-5; Durrett, *op. cit.*, p. 32.

[7]Durrett, *op. cit.*, pp. 32, 37-40; Johnston, *op. cit.*, Vol. I, 39-41.

[8]R. T. Durrett, "First Christmas Day in Louisville," *The Courier-Journal*, Louisville, August 2, 1893.

NOTES TO CHAPTER XIV

[1]James (ed.) *George Rogers Clark Papers* (Ill. Hist. Soc. Colls. Vol. VIII), p. 267; Bodley, *Clark*, pp. 106, 107.

[2]James (ed.), *op. cit.*, pp. 98, 99; English, *op. cit.*, Conquest of the Old Northwest, I, 287,437

[3]James (ed.), *op. cit.*, pp. 270-271 (Letter to Mason).

[4]James (ed.), *op. cit.*, p. 274; English, *op. cit.*, I, 330.

[5]James (ed.), *op. cit.*, pp. 159-160; Bodley, *op. cit.*, p. 118. (Bowman's "Journal").

[6]James (ed.), *op. cit.*, pp. 275-276; English, *op. cit.*, I, 301-303 (Clark's "Memoir").

[7]James (ed.), *op. cit.*, pp. 277-278; Henry S. Bartholomew (ed.), *2nd ed., Michigan Pioneer Collections*, Vol. IX, X (Lansing: Wynkoop, Hallenbeck, Crawford, 1908), IX, 489.

[8]James (ed.), *op. cit.*, pp. 160-161; Bodley, *op. cit.*, p. 128 (Bowman's "Journal"); English, *op. cit.*, I, 338.

[9]Sir Henry Hamilton, *Journal of the Vincennes Expedition*, 1778-1779 (photostat copy, The Filson Club; from *MS* in Harvard University) pp. 151-152; John D. Barnhard (ed.) *Henry Hamilton and George Rogers Clark in the American Revolution*, (Crawfordsville: R. E. Banta, 1951), pp. 102, 185-6, 188, 191-194, 195, 196, 249.

NOTES TO CHAPTER XV

[1]Alton James (ed.), Ill. Hist. Colls., Vol. VIII, *George Rogers Clark Papers*, pp. 148-149.

[2]Charles G. Talbert, "Kentucky Invades Ohio—1779," *Register*, Jy., 1953, p. 228; *Draper MSS* Nos. 58J7-8, 58J173-176, 59J223.

[3]Charles G. Talbert, *op. cit.*, p. 230; Charles G. Talbert, "William Whitley, 1749-1813", *Hist. Quart.*, Apr., 1951, pp. 103-106; *Draper MSS* No. 9CC23-24, 29, (Whitley's Narrative").

[4]Charles G. Talbert, *Register*, Jy., 1953, pp. 230-233; *Draper MSS* No. 12CC64-66 ("Josiah Collins"); Lucien V. Rule (ed.), "John D. Shane's Interview with Ephraim Sandusky" (*Draper MSS* No. 11CC131-145), *Hist. Quart.*, Oct., 1934, p. 223; Dandridge, *George M. Bedinger*, pp. 54-72; *Ohio Archeological and Historical Quarterly*, XXII, (Oct., 1913 "Bowman's Campaign of 1779"), *Draper MSS*, Bedinger "A", I, 19-31; pp. 502 ff.

[5]James (ed.), *op. cit.*, p. 146; Bodley, *George Rogers Clark*, p. 136; Talbert, *Register*, Jy., 1953, pp. 233-234.

[6]Henry S. Bartholomew (ed.), *Mich. Pioneer & Historical Collections*, X, 336 (Capt. Bird To Capt. Lernault).

[7]Lucien Beckner (ed.), "Shane's Interview with William Clinkenbeard," (*Draper MSS* No. 11CC54-66), *Hist. Quart.*, Apr., 1928, pp. 106-112.

[8]Edward Bryan, "Notes on Bryan's Station," *Register*, Jy., 1944, p. 269.

[9]J. Winston Coleman, Jr., *The British Invasion of Kentucky*, (Lexington: Winburn Press, 1951), pp. 4-15; Milo M. Quaife, "When Detroit Invaded Kentucky," *Hist. Quart.*, Jan., 1927, pp. 60-63; M. Agnes Burton (ed.), *Reprint, Mich Pion. & Hist. Colls.*, XIX, 538-539 (Capt. Bird to Maj. de Peyster).

[10]Maude Ward Lafferty (Mrs. W. T.), "A Revolutionary Tragedy: The Destruction of Ruddle's and Martin's Forts," Typescript, The Filson Club, 1931; Coleman, *op. cit.*, pp. 15-18. (Ruddle is also spelled "Ruddell", "Riddle.")

[11]Burton (ed.), *op. cit.*, XIX, 539.

[12]*Ibid.*, XIX, 553 (Maj. de Peyster to Lt. Col. Bolton); Bakeless, *Daniel Boone*, pp. 246-250; Coleman, *op. cit.*, pp. 19-33.

NOTES TO CHAPTER XVI

[1]Collins, *Hist. of Kentucky*, II, 328; M. W. Lafferty, "Ruddle's and Martin's Forts," Typescript, The Filson Club.

[2]Hening, *Virginia Statutes*, VII, 663-669; James Rood Robertson, "New Light on Kentucky History," *Proceedings, Mississippi Valley Historical Association*, IX, Part I (1915-1916), pp. 90-92; Filson, *Kentucke*, pp. 36-38; Samuel M. Wilson, *First Land Court of Kentucky, 1779-1780—Reprint* (Lexington: 1923), pp. 30-32; Marshall, *History of Kentucky*, I, 78-83.

[3]*The Register*, "Certificate Book," Vol. 21 (1923), p. 8.

[4]Bodley, *Clark*, pp. 165-166: James (ed.), *Ill. Hist. Colls.*, George Rogers Clark Papers VIII, 451 (adapted).

[5]Lucien Beckner, (ed.), "Shane's Interview with William Clinkenbeard," *Hist. Quart.*, Apr., 1928, pp. 126-127; John Bradford, "Historical Notes," Secs. 9 & 10, *"The Kentucke Gazette"* (hereafter cited as *The Gazette*), Oct. 20 & 27, 1826.

[6]Beckner (ed.), *op. cit.*, p. 127; Charles G. Talbert, "Wm. Whitley, 1749-1815," *Hist. Quart.*, April, 1951, p. 107; *Draper MSS* No. 9CC25-26 (William Whitley).

[7]R. C. Ballard Thurston, Personal Interview, The Filson Club, March, 1939.

[8]Beckner (ed.), *op. cit.*, pp. 127-128.

[9]James (ed.), *op cit.*, VIII, 451-453; Bakeless, *Daniel Boone*, pp. 253-255; M. Agnes Burton (ed.), *Mich. Pioneer & Hist. Colls.*, XIX, 614, 615.

[10]Charles G. Talbert, "Kentucky Invades Ohio—1780," *The Register*, Oct., 1954, pp. 294-298.

NOTES TO CHAPTER XVII

[1]Bodley, *Hist. of Kentucky*, I, 204 (*Draper MSS* No. 15S175).

[2]Beckner (ed.), "Shane's Interview with William Clinkenbeard," *Hist. Quart.*, Apr., 1928, p. 98.

[3]Dandridge, *George Michael Bedinger*, pp. 36, 38, 43-5.

[4]George Robertson, *Scrap Book on Law and Politics, Men and Times*, (Lexington: A. W. Elder, 1885), p. 272.

[5]George W. Ranck, "The Travelling Church" (Louisville: Baptist Book Concern, 1891), pp. 1-35; Collins, *Hist. of Kentucky*, I, 416; Mrs. Jennie M. Chinn, "Early Churches of Kentucky," *Typescript*, Ky. Hist. Soc. Library, Frankfort (1930); Charles R. Staples, "Pioneer Kentucky Preachers and Pulpits," *Hist. Quart.*, Jy., 1935, pp. 138-140.

[6]S. J. Conkwright, *History of the Churches of Boone's Creek Baptist Association of Kentucky* (Winchester: 1923), pp. 18-23; Ranck, *op. cit.*, pp. 21-23.

[7]Ranck, *op. cit.*, pp. 23-29; Kincaid, *Wilderness Road*, pp. 165-167; Speed, *Wilderness Road*, p. 40.

[8]Ranck, *op. cit.*, pp. 31-33; John Taylor, *A History of Ten Baptist Churches*, 2nd Ed., (Bloomfield: Will H. Holmes, 1827), pp. 42-45; J. H. Spencer, *A History of Kentucky Baptists from 1769 to 1885* (Vol. 2, Cincinnati: J. R. Baumes, 1885), I, 28; Miss Susan Darnaby (granddaughter of

Pioneer Edward Darnaby), Fayette County, Personal Interview, June 6, 1952; Staples, *op. cit.,* pp. 141-142.

NOTES TO CHAPTER XVIII

[1]R. T. Durrett, *The Centenary of Louiville,* pp. 34, 149.

[2]Collins, *Hist. of Kentucky,* II, 183; Carl Bernstadt, ". . . Origin of Louisville," *Hist. Quart.,* Jy., 1930, pp. 107-151; *Fayette County Deed Book F,* p. 378 (July 1, 1780).

[3]William Henry Perrin, *History of Fayette County* (Lexington: O. L. Baskin & Co., 1882), Part II, pp. 222, 223, 225; Charles R. Staples, *The History of Pioneer Lexington* (Lexington: Transylvania Press, 1935), p. 22.

[4]Brown, *Political Beginnings,* p. 41; Wm. W. Hening (ed.), *Virginia Statutes at Large, 1779-1881* (Richmond: Geo. Cochran, 1822), X, 315; Collins, *op. cit.,* II, 258; Marshall, *History of Kentucky,* I, 152.

[5]Lucien Beckner (ed.), "Shane's Interview with Jeptha Kemper," (*Draper MSS* No. 12CC127-133), *Hist. Quart.,* Jy., 1938, p. 155.

[6]Bodley, *George Rogers Clark,* pp. 173-180; James (ed.), *Ill. Hist. Colls.* VIII, 556; Charles G. Talbert, "A Roof for Kentucky," *Hist. Quart.,* Apr., 1955, pp. 145-151.

[7]W. P. Palmer & S. McRae (eds.), *Calendar of Virginia State Papers* (Richmond: James E. Goode, 1881), II, 47-49. (John Floyd's letter to Thomas Jefferson).

[8]*Ibid.,* II, 313; Bodley, *Hist. of Kentucky,* I, 298.

[9]William Macdonald (ed.), *Documentary Source Book of American History, 1616-1926* (3rd Ed., New York: The Macmillan Co., 1933), pp. 195-203; Merrill Jensen, *The New Nation: A History of the United States During the Confederation, 1781-1789* (New York: Alfred A Knopf, 1950), pp. vii, viii, 18-26.

[10]Gaillard Hunt (ed.), *Journals of the Continental Congress,* Vol. XXII (Washington: Government Printing Office, 1909), pp. 227-229; William Wirt Henry, *Patrick Henry—Life, Correspondence and Speeches* (Vol. 3; New York: Charles Scribner's Sons, 1891), II, 75-109; Temple Bodley, *Our First Great West—in Revolutionary War, Diplomacy and Politics,* The Filson Club Publications No. 36 (J. P. Morton & Co., Louisville: 1936), pp. 178, 194; Merrill Jensen, "The Cession of the Old Northwest," Miss. Valley Historical Society *Review,* Vol. XXIII, No. 1 (June, 1936), pp. 27-48.

[11]Robertson, *Petitions . . . Kentucky to Virginia,* No. 24, pp. 78-79.

[12]Henry, *op. cit.,* II, 92, 93; W. C. Ford (ed.), *Journals of the Continental Congress* (Washington: Government Printing Office) 1907, v. VII. 263; v. VIII, 204-205; G. Hunt (ed.), vol. XVII (1909), 808; vol. XX (1912), 704; vol. XXI (1912), 1057; vol. XXII (1914), 191.

NOTES TO CHAPTER XIX

[1]James T. Morehead, *Address in Commemoration of the First Settlement of Kentucky,* (Frankfort: A. G. Hodges, State Printer, 1840). pp. 147-148; Bakeless, *Daniel Boone,* pp. 265, 271; Samuel M. Wilson, *Battle of the Blue Licks* (Lexington: 1927), pp. 8, 9, 12, 16.

[2]Smith, *Hist. of Kentucky,* pp. 189-194; Collins, *Hist. of Kentucky,* II, 634; Bakeless, *op. cit.,* p. 265.

[3]Reuben T. Durrett (author & ed.) *Bryant's Station,* The Filson Club Publications No. 12 (Louisville: J. P. Morton & Co., 1897), pp. iv, v, vii, 18-24; Mann Butler, *A History of the Commonwealth of Kentucky* (Louisville: Wilcox, Dickerman & Co., 1834), p. 124; Maude Ward Lafferty, MS Excerpts from "Bryant's Station—Plan and Siege" by Dr. L. C. Draper (Draper MSS 13C77) George W. Ranck, "The Story of Bryan's Station" in Durrett, *op. cit.,* pp. 87, 88, 92-97.

[4]Bakeless, *op. cit.,* pp. 277-282; Durrett (ed.), *op cit.,* pp. 37-39, 53, 62, 75, 130; Ranck, *op. cit.,* pp. 95-97; John Bradford, "Notes on Kentucky," Sec. 13, *The Gazette,* Nov. 17, 1826.

[5]Bakeless, *op. cit.,* pp. 281-286; Morehead, *op. cit.,* p. 91.

[6]Bennett H. Young, "The Battle of the Blue Licks," in Durrett *op. cit.,* pp. 143-146; Wilson, *op. cit.,* p. 42.

[7]Filson, *op. cit.,* pp. 42-46, 57, 143; Young, *op. cit.,* pp. 151-162; Morehead, *op. cit.,* pp. 95-99.

[8]Filson, *op. cit.,* pp. 57, 58, 80; Bradford's "Notes", Sec. 14, *The Gazette,* Nov. 24, 1826; *Draper MSS* No. 12CC70.

[9]Bakeless, *op. cit.,* pp. 296-297; Kerr (ed.), *History of Kentucky,* I, 77-84; Bradford's "Notes," Sec. 14, *The Gazette,* Nov. 24, 1826; C. Frank Dunn (Lexington) Letters of Feb. 16 and 29, 1952, and unpublished notes.

[10]Palmer & McRae (eds.), *Calendar of Virginia State Papers,* III, 333, 334, Levi Todd; Filson, *Kentucke,* pp. 75-76; *Draper MSS* No. 52J34-37 (John Floyd to George Rogers Clark.)

[11]Young, *op. cit.,* pp. 181-186; Filson, *op. cit.,* pp. 78-80.

[12]*Draper MSS,* No. 12CC70 J. Collins; Young, *op. cit.,* p. 190.

[13]Lucien V. Rule (ed.), "Shane's Interview with Ephraim Sandusky," (*Draper MSS* No. 11CC141-145), *Hist. Quart.,* Oct. 1934, p. 224; Young, *op. cit.,* pp. 190-192; Filson, *op. cit.,* 90.

[14]Filson, *op. cit.,* pp. 77, 78; Palmer & McRae (eds.), *op. cit.,* III, 334; Young, *op. cit.,* pp. 194-196; *Draper MSS* No. 12CC50 (Mrs. Sarah Graham.)

NOTES TO CHAPTER XX

[1]Wilson, *Battle of the Blue Licks,* pp. 16, 66; Palmer & McRae (eds.), *Va. Calendar State Papers,* III, 301; C. Frank Dunn (Lexington), Unpublished Notes and Letters of Feb. 16 and 29, 1951.

[2]Young, *Battle of the Blue Licks,* pp. 119, 201, 202; Palmer & McRae, *op. cit.,* III, 301, 302.

[3]Lucien Beckner (ed.), "Shane's Interview with Mrs. Sarah Graham," (*Draper MSS* No. 12CC45-53), *Hist. Quart.* Oct., 1935, p. 236.

[4]Durrett (ed.), *Bryant's Station,* pp. 204-206; (Boone's Letter); Collins, *History of Kentucky,* II, 660-661; Wilson, *op. cit.,* pp. 49-50, Palmer & McRae (eds.), *op. cit.,* III, 275-276.

[5]Durrett (ed.), *op. cit.,* p. 214; Palmer & McRae (eds.), *op. cit.,* III, 303, 304 (Andrew Steele's Letter).

[6]Palmer & McRae (eds.), *op. cit.,* III, 337 (Arthur Campbell's Letter to Gov. Benjamin Harrison).

[7]*Ibid.*, III, 331-333 (William Christian's Letter).

[8]Bodley, *George Rogers Clark*, pp. 214-216; Wilson, *op. cit.*, p. 110.

[9]Kerr (ed.), *History of Kentucky*, I, 187; Smith, *History of Kentucky*, p. 222.

[10]James (ed.), *III, Hist. Colls.* (*George Rogers Clark Papers*), XIX, 150-153; Palmer & McRae (eds.), *op. cit.*, III, 216, 351; *Draper MSS* No. 63J121-124; (Clark's "Orderly Book"); Charles G. Talbert, "Kentucky Invades Ohio—1792," *Register*, Oct., 1955, pp. 293-298.

[11]Beckner (ed.), "Shane's Interview with William Clinkenbeard," (*Draper MSS* No. 11CC54-66), *Hist. Quart.*, Apr., 1928, p. 124.

[12]Palmer & McRae (eds.), *op. cit.*, III, 381; Butler, *A History of Kentucky*, pp. 536-537; (Clark's Letter to Governor Harrison at Richmond, Virginia).

[13]Bodley, *op. cit.*, pp. 361, 362; *Draper MSS* No. 54J49-50 (Clark's Letter to Sen. John Breckenridge, Nov. 5, 1805).

NOTES TO CHAPTER XXI

[1]Henry Steele Commager (ed.), *Documents of American History* (Third Edition; New York: Columbia University Press, F. S. Crofts & Co., 1944), pp. 105-107; Samuel F. Bemis, *A Diplomatic History of the United States*, (New York: Henry Holt & Co., 1936), pp. 16-21, 27-29.

[2]Francis Wharton (ed.), *The Revolutionary Diplomatic Correspondence of the United States* (Vol. 8; Washington: Government Printing Office, 1889), IV, 224-5, 270, 284, 313; V, 37, 163; Bodley, *Our First Great West*, pp. 231, 258, 335, 338; Samuel Cody Burnett, *The Continental Congress* (New York: The Macmillan Co., 1941), p. 546.

[3]Wharton (ed.), *op. cit.*, IV, 134-138; William Jay, *Life of John Jay* (Vol. 2; New York: J. & J. Harper, 1833), I, 107-109.

[4]Jared Sparks, *The Life of Gouverneur Morris*, (Vol. 3; Boston: Gray & Bowen, 1832), I, 225; Wharton (ed.), *op. cit.*, IV, 75.

[5]Wharton (ed.), *op. cit.*, IV, 135; Bemis, *op. cit.*, pp. 32-35.

[6]Wharton (ed.), *op. cit.*, IV, 75.

[7]Commager (ed.), *op. cit.*, p. 106 (Article 110.)

[8]Bodley, *op. cit.*, pp. 238, 240-243, 280-283; Wharton (ed.), *op. cit.*, V. 571, 848-850; VI, 48.

[9]Wharton (ed.), *op. cit.*, V., 541-542.

[10]*Ibid.*, V, 657, 838; VI, 23

[11]Justin Winsor (ed.), *Narrative and Critical History of the United States* (Vol. 8; Boston & New York: Houghton Mifflin & Co., 1881-1897), VII, 122-127; Wharton (ed.), *op. cit.*, I, 256; VI, 30-32; VIII, 165, 617; Burnett, *op. cit.*, p. 549; Jay, *op. cit.*, I, 123-125, 147-150; Merrill Jensen, *The New Nation*, pp. 6-18; Bemis, *op. cit.*, pp. 53-58.

[12]Wharton (ed.), *op. cit.*, VI, 112-113 (Franklin to Livingston, Dec. 5, 1782).

[13]Wharton (ed.), *op. cit.*, V, 185, 392, 845; Bemis, *op. cit.*, pp. 59-61.

[14]Macdonald (ed.), *Documentary Source Book*, pp. 205-209; Burnett, *op. cit.*, pp. 563, 589-594.

NOTES TO CHAPTER XXII

[1]*Papers of Thomas J. Clay, Clay MSS*, Library of Congress (quoted by Theodore Roosevelt, *The Winning of the West*, 1889 Ed., Vol. 3; New York: G. P. Putnam's Sons, 1889), II, Appendix J, pp. 409-410.

[2]Reuben T. Durrett, *John Filson, The First Historian of Kentucky*, Filson Club Publications No. 1 (Cincinnati: Robert Clarke & Company, 1884), pp. 5-16; Willard Rouse Jillson, *Filson's Kentucke*, Filson Club Publications No. 35 (Louisville: John P. Morton & Co., 1929), pp. 139-149; Samuel M. Wilson, "John Filson in Pennsylvania," *Hist. Quart.*, Oct., 1939, pp. 179-201; C. Frank Dunn, "John Filson and Transylvania Seminary," *The Register*, Oct., 1947, pp. 313-324.

[3]Durrett, *op. cit.*, p. 20.

[4]Jillson, *op. cit.*, p. 137.

[5]P. Lee Phillips, *The First Map of Kentucky by John Filson* (Washington: W. H. Lowdermilk & Co., 1908), pp. 1-22; Jillson, *op. cit.*, pp. 136-137, 151-152, R. C. Ballard Thruston, "Filson's History and Map of Kentucky," *Hist. Quart.*, Jan., 1934, pp. 17-38.

[6]P. Lee Phillips, *op. cit.*, pp. 10-12.

[7]Durrett, *op. cit.*, pp. 28-40; R. C. Ballard Thruston, *op. cit.*, pp. 1-16; Jillson, *op. cit.*, pp. 124-127.

[8]John Filson, *The Discovery Settlement and Present State of Kentucke*, p. 16.

[9]*Ibid.*, pp. 23, 24, 25.

[10]*Ibid.*, pp. 26, 27, 28.

[11]*Ibid.*, p. 21.

[12]*Ibid.*, p. 107; Jensen, *The New Nation*, pp. 113-115, 173; Bodley, *History of Kentucky*, I, 347; Kerr (ed.), *History of Kentucky*, I, 204.

NOTES TO CHAPTER XXIII

[1]Filson, *Kentucke*, pp. 12, 21, 40; Jillson, *Filson's Kentucke*, pp. 123, 124-5, 130; Archer Butler Hulbert, *The Ohio River, A Course of Empire* (New York: G. P. Putnam's Sons, 1906), p. 126.

[2]Filson, *op. cit.*, pp. 113-118; Jillson, *op. cit.*, pp. 135-136.

[3]English, *The Conquest of the Territory Northwest of the Ohio River, 1778-1785*, I, 723; Bodley, *George Rogers Clark*, pp. 175-6.

[4]Mrs. Jennie M. Chinn, "The Early Churches in Kentucky," MS in Kentucky Historical Society Library (1930); Collins, *Hist. of Kentucky*, II, 523.

[5]Willard Rouse Jillson, *Tales of the Dark and Bloody Ground* (Louisville: C. T. Dearing Printing Co., 1930), pp. 90-101 (Autobiography of John Rowan).

[6]Leland D. Baldwin, *The Keelboat Age on Western Waters*, (Pittsburgh: University of Pittsburgh Press, 1941), pp. 48, 49, 54; Williams, *Ohio Falls Cities*, I, 194; W. F. Marshall, "Robert Trent, River Pilot," *The Challenge* (Nashville, Tenn., Nov. 1, 1936, pp. 1, 6, 7; Robert Ross Trent, Nashville, Tenn., Personal Interview, 1935; Josephine E. Phillips, "Flatboating on the Great Thoroughfare," *Bulletin*, Ohio Hist'l and Philosophical Society, June, 1947, pp. 11-24.

[7]Mrs. Norvin Green (Mary Ann English), Typescript, "History of Elijah Nuttall and Family," and Personal Interviews, Louisville, *circa* 1910.

[8]Dunbar, *History of Travel in America*, I, 163, 164; *Draper MSS* No. 10J230 (Dr. John Croghan's "Diary").

[9]Williams, *op. cit.*, I, 194-198; Collins, *op. cit.*, II, 198.

NOTES TO CHAPTER XXIV

[1]R. C. Ballard Thruston, Family Papers and Personal Interviews, The Filson Club, Louisville, 1938.

[2]Marshall, *History of Kentucky*, I, 198.

[3]Lucien Beckner (ed.), "Shane's Interview with William Clinkenbeard," *Hist. Quart.*, Apr., 1928, pp. 98, 104.

[4]Lucien Beckner (ed.), "Shane's Interview with Jeptha Kemper," *Hist. Quart.*, Jy., 1938, p. 156.

[5]Calvin Morgan Fackler, *Early Days in Danville* (Louisville: Standard Printing Co., 1941), p. 52.

[6]Collins, *History of Kentucky*, II, 372; Reuben T. Durrett, *The Centenary of Louisville*, p. 84.

[7]Beckner (ed.), *op. cit.*, "Shane's Interview with Jeptha Kemper," p. 157.
[8]Collins, *op. cit.*, II, 370.

[9]*Ibid.*, II, 370.

[10]Lucien Beckner (ed.), "The Henderson Company Ledger by John D. Shane," *Hist. Quart.*, Jan., 1947, p. 46 (*Draper MSS* 17CC189-191).

[11]C. Frank Dunn, "Transylvania Seminary—Where?", *The Register*, Oct., 1947, p. 323; C. Frank Dunn, Lexington, Letter of May 30, 1951, "The 20 x 20 ft. log-frame building, on the grounds of the State Experiment Station farm, was razed in 1927."

[12]Charles R. Staples, "Pioneer Kentucky Preachers and Pulpits," *Hist. Quart.*, Jy., 1935, pp. 130, 139, 148, 153; Benjamin J. Webb, *Centenary of Catholicity in Kentucky* (Louisville: Charles A. Rogers, 1884), p. 12; Mrs. Jennie M. Chinn, *MS*, "Early Churches in Kentucky", Library, Kentucky Historical Society, Frankfort.

[13]G. W. and H. P. Beattie, "Benjamin Linn—Hunter, Explorer, Preacher," *Hist. Quart.*, Apr., 1946, pp. 139-144.

[14]Beckner (ed.), "Shane's Clinkenbeard," *op. cit.*, p. 119.
[15]*Ibid.*, p. 118.

[16]Beckner (ed.), "The Henderson Company Ledger," *op. cit.*, p. 33.

NOTES TO CHAPTER XXV

[1]William Littell, *Political Transactions in and Concerning Kentucky*, Reprint, with Introduction by Temple Bodley, Filson Club Publications No. 31 (Louisville: J. P. Morton & Co., 1926), pp. 8-13, 34.

[2]Littell, *op. cit.*, pp. 63-67; Brown, *Political Beginnings of Kentucky*, p. 62, f. n. #31.

[3]Johnston, *History of Louisville*, I, 53-55; Williams (Pub.), *Ohio Falls Cities*, I, 166, 190-191; Louisville Abstract Association, "Abstracts of Old Deeds" (Photostats, The Filson Club), Nos. 1-4, 9, 10; Carl Bernhardt, "Certain Phases of the Origin of Louisville," *Hist. Quart.*, Jy. 1930, 107. (The area involved extended along the Ohio from First to Twelfth

Street, thence to Broadway and Eighteenth Streets, from there, up Broadway to Shelby Street.)
[4]McElroy, *History of Kentucky,* pp. 121-5; Marshall, *History of Kentucky,* I, 206; Littell, *op. cit.,* pp. 61-63.
[5]Marshall, *op. cit.,* I, 360; Littell, *op. cit.,* pp. 63-5.
[6]Smith, *Kentucky,* p. 246; Collins, *Kentucky,* I, 354.
[7]Robertson, *Petitions, Kentucky to Virginia,* pp. 79-81.
[8]Hening, *Virginia Statutes,* XII, 37-40; Littell, *op. cit.,* pp. 72-76.

NOTES TO CHAPTER XXVI

[1]Littell, *Political Transactions,* p. 16; Collins, *Hist. of Kentucky,* I, 261-263; McElroy, *History of Kentucky* p. 120; Kerr (ed.), *Hist. of Kentucky,* I, 241.
[2]Littell, *op. cit.,* pp. 16-17; Thomas Marshall Green, *The Spanish Conspiracy, A Review of Early Spanish Movements in the South-West* (Cincinnati: Robert Clarke & Co., 1891), pp. 67, 76.
[3]Hening, *Virginia Statutes,* XII, 240; Littell, *op. cit.,* Appendix VI, pp. 72-76.
[4]Littell, *op. cit.,* Appendix VII, pp. 78-79; William Jay, *Life of John Jay,* I, 235-238; Edmund Cody Burnett, *Letters of Members of the Continental Congress* (Washington: Carnegie Foundation, 1921), pp. 654-658; Jensen, *The New Nation,* pp. 169-175.
[5]Littell, *op. cit.,* Appendix VIII, pp. 79-80; Burnett, *op. cit.,* pp. 655-658.
[6]Kerr (ed.), *op. cit.,* I, 241, f. n. #11; Albert J. Beveridge, *The Life of John Marshall* (Vol. 4; Boston & New York: Houghton Mifflin Co., 1916-19), III, 282.
[7]Green, *op. cit.,* pp. 120-131; Bodley, *Introduction to Littell,* pp. cxix-cxxxix (Wilkinson's Memorial and Expatriation Declaration), Nathaniel Weyl, *Treason: The Story of Disloyalty and Betrayal in American History* (Washington: Public Affairs Press, 1950), pp. 33, 119, 121.
[8]Elizabeth Warren, "Benjamin Sebastian and the Spanish Conspiracy," *Hist. Quart.,* Apr., 1946, pp. 112, 113; Green *op. cit.,* pp. iv-viii, 285, 286; Bodley, *George Rogers Clark,* 314-328; Kerr (ed.), *op. cit.,* I, 272; *The Gazette,* Jy. 4, 1789.
[9]Thomas Speed, *The Political Club, Danville, Kentucky, 1786-1790,* The Filson Club Publications, No. 9 (Louisville: J. P. Morton & Co., 1894), pp. 39, 56; Bodley, *Hist. of Kentucky,* I, 380-383; Maude Ward Lafferty, "Danville Political Club," *Danville Daily Messenger,* May 12, 1921; Ann Price (Mrs. Sydney S.) Combs, "Notes on the Political Club of Danville and its Members," *Hist. Quart.,* Oct. 1961, pp. 333-352.
[10]Burnett, *op. cit.,* pp. 663, 667, 671-678, 690-695.

NOTES TO CHAPTER XXVII

[1]C. Frank Dunn, "John Bradford Bicentennial, *Hist. Quart.,* Jy., 1948, pp. 158, 161; *The Gazette,* Jan. 16, 1800; William Henry Perrin, *The Pioneer Press of Kentucky,* The Filson Club Publications No. 3 (Louisville: J. P. Morton & Co., 1888), pp. 8-14; Samuel M. Wilson, "John Bradford, Kentucky's First Printer," *Hist. Quart.,* Oct., 1937, pp. 260-269.

[2]Smith, *Hist. of Kentucky,* p. 276; Kerr (ed.), *Hist. of Kentucky,* I, 242.
[3]*The Gazette,* Aug. 15, 1787. (No copy of the first issue of *The Kentucke
Gazette* is known to exist. Its date was presumably August 11, 1787. Refer-
ences to the *Gazette* are from original and photostatic copies in the Filson
Club in Louisville and in the Lexington Public Library.)
[4]C. Frank Dunn, *op. cit.,* p. 159; Lucien Beckner (ed.), "Shane's Interview with William Clinkenbeard," *Hist. Quart.,* Apr. 1928, p. 114.
[5]*The Kentucke Gazette,* Aug. 18, 1787.
[6]*Ibid.,* Feb. 2, 1788.
[7]*Ibid.,* Oct. 6, 1787.
[8]*Ibid.,* Oct. 13, 1787.
[9]Bodley, *Hist. of Kentucky,* I, 249; f. n. #2 (*Draper MSS* No. 9DD46),
Kerr (ed.), *Hist. of Kentucky,* I, 244.
[10]Burnett, *The Continental Congress,* pp. 707-709; Marshall, *Hist. of
Kentucky,* I, 299; Kerr (ed.), *op. cit.,* I, 254.

NOTES TO CHAPTER XXVIII

[1]McElroy, *History of Kentucky,* pp. 139-140; Kerr, (ed.), *Kentucky,* I,
256-259; Collins, *Kentucky,* I, 267.
[2]Mary Verhoeff, *The Kentucky River Navigation,* The Filson Club Publications No. 28 (Louisville: John P. Morton & Co., 1917), pp. 57, 58;
The Gazette, Dec. 16, 1787.
[3]Kerr (ed.), *op. cit.,* I, 260-261, 270 (f.n. #11).
[4]*Ibid.,* I, 270-271; *West Virginia Historical Magazine,* Vol. II, No. 4,
p. 254; Bodley, *Kentucky,* I, 439-440; (f. n. #19).
[5]Kerr (ed.), *op. cit.,* I, 260-261; (f. n. #1), John Bach McMaster, *A
History of the People of the United States* (Vol. 8; New York: D. Appleton & Co., 1915), I, 519; Carl Russell Fish, *American Diplomacy, Fourth
Edition* (New York: Henry Holt & Co., 1923) pp. 72-78.
[6]Tapp, *Kentucky,* I, 265; *The Gazette,* Oct. 15, 1788; Kerr (ed.), *op. cit.,*
I, 262-263; Marshall, *Kentucky,* I, 296-297.
[7]*The Gazette,* Nov. 15, 1788; Brown, *Political Beginnings,* pp. 259-263;
Kerr (ed.), *op. cit.,* I, 263 (f. n. #11) 265-268 (f. n. #5).
[8]Marshall, *op. cit.,* I, 318; Smith, *Kentucky,* pp. 285-287.
[9]*The Gazette,* Jan. 30, Feb. 5, 1789; Smith, *op. cit.,* pp. 286-289.
[10]Kerr (ed.), *op. cit.,* I, 272; (f. n. #16)
[11]Hening, *Virginia Statutes,* III, 788-791; *The Gazette,* Feb. 14, 1789.
[12]Bureau of the Census, *A Century of Population Growth,* (Washington:
Government Printing Office, 1905), pp. 9, 121, 132, 200, 207, 220. (Of
the total number in Kentucky, 61,133 were whites, 12,430 were Negro
slaves, 114 were free Negroes. The Census listed five towns: Lexington,
with 834 people; Washington, first county seat of Mason, 462; Bardstown,
216; Louisville, 200; Danville, the District capital for ten years, 150).
[13]Pratt Byrd, "The Kentucky Frontier in 1792, *Hist. Quart.,* Jy., 1951,
pp. 182, 184, 189-190; Oct., 1951, pp. 288, 291; Niels Henry Sonne,
Liberal Kentucky, 1780-1828 (New York: Columbia University Press,
1939), pp. 26, 78.
[14]Hening, *Virginia Statutes,* XIII, 17-21.

[15]Kerr (ed.), *op. cit.*, I, 274, 278; Brown, *op. cit.*, pp. 220-222; Collins, *op. cit.*, I, 271-272

[16]Joseph Gales, Sr. (compiler), *Debates and Proceedings in the Congress of the United States,* Vol. II (Washington: Gales & Seaton, 1834), cols. 2372-2373; Noel Gaines, "Washington Approved Kentucky First," *Kentucky Progress Magazine,* Jy., 1929, p. 24;*The Kentucke Gazette,* Apr. 16, 1791, p. 2, col. 2. (The name, *The Kentucke Gazette,* was changed to *The Kentucky Gazette* in the issue of March 14, 1791, ". . . due to requirement by the Legislature of Virginia that certain advertisements be inserted in the *Kentucky Gazette.*")

[17]McMaster, *op. cit.*, II, 35; Kerr (ed.), *op. cit.*, I, 280; Burnett, *The Continental Congress,* pp. 502, 655, 707-708.

NOTES TO CHAPTER XXIX

[1]*A Century of Population Growth, 1790-1900,* From the First Census of the United States to the Twelfth (Government Printing Office, Washington, 1909), p. 80, Table 11; p. 82, 83, Table 17; p. 117, Table 45; p. 129.

[2]*Ibid.,* p. 117; p. 123, Table 45, pp. 128-129.

[3]*Ibid.,* pp. 37, 132, Table 108.

[4]*Ibid.,* p. 117, Table 45; pp; 123, 128-9.

[5]William Chauncy Langdon, *Everyday Things in American Life,* New York: Scribner & Sons. (Vol. I, [1607-1776] 1937; Vol II, [1776-1876] 1941) II, p. 308.

[6]*A Century of Population Growth, op. cit.,* pp. 40, 45.

[7]*Ibid.,* pp. 38, 39-41, 45.

[8]Langdon, *op. cit.,* Vol. II, pp. 304-9.

[9]*Ibid.,* Vol. II, p. 9.

[10]*Ibid.,* Vol. II, p. 256.

[11]*Ibid.,* Vol. I, p. 13.

[12]*Voice,* (Publication devoted to the Walking Horse), Chattanooga, Tennessee, May, 1964.

[13]*A Century of Population Growth, op. cit.,* pp. 11, 78.

[14]*Ibid.,* pp. 11, 98.

[15]Langdon, *op. cit.,* Vol. II, pp. 176-191.

[16]*A Century of Population Growth, op. cit.,* pp. 27-28, 43; Langdon, *op. cit.,* II, pp. 284-285.

[17]*A Century of Population Growth, op. cit.,* p. 43; Langdon, *op. cit.,* Vol. I, pp. 284-5.

[18]Langdon, *op. cit., Vol. II,* p. 281.

[19]*Ibid.,* Vol. I, p. 27; Vol. II, p. 256.

[20]*A Century of Population Growth, op. cit.,* pp. 5-6, 21, 73.

[21]*Ibid.,* pp. 3, 21, 22.

[22]*Ibid.,* pp. 27-29; Capt. Alan Villiers and Others: *Men, Ships and the Sea,* (National Geographic Society, Washington: 1962), pp. 195-197.

[23]*A Century of Population Growth, op. cit.,* pp. 12, 29-31.

[24]*Ibid.,* pp. 32, 33.

[25]*Ibid.,* pp. 1, 2, 22, 23.

[26]*Ibid.,* pp. 20-21.

[27]*Ibid.*, pp. 14, 32, 81.

[28]Ellwood P. Cubberley, *The History of Education*, (Houghton Mifflin Co., Boston: 1920), pp. 363, 374, 494.

[29]Copies of the State Constitutions in effect in 1792, Law Library, University of Louisville, Louisville, Kentucky; correspondence with several State Archivists; some photostatic negatives from several constitutions (sections relating to the franchise and to elective office). All of this material has been given to the Law Library.

NOTES TO CHAPTER XXX

[1]Kerr (ed.), *Kentucky*, I, 282-285; Collins, *Kentucky*, I, 355; Journal of the First Constitutional Convention of Kentucky, Danville, April 2-19, 1782, Pamphlet (Lexington: State Bar Association of Kentucky, 1942).

[2]*The Gazette*, Oct. 29, 1791, p. 2, col. 3; May 5, May 12, 1792. (Bullock's schedule took him to Bourbon Court House on the first and fifteenth of each month; on successive days to Boonesborough, Madison Court House, Lincoln Court House, Danville, Harrodsburg, Bardstown. He was due in Louisville on the ninth and twenty-third; "from thence up Brashier's Creek, through Spring Station on the Beargrass, Floyd's, Low Dutch, Sturgis' and Linn's Stations to Squire Boone's, near Shelbyville; then along Big Benson Creek to Lee's Town on the Kentucky River below Frankfort; from there by way of Richard Cole's tavern to Lexington.")

[3]Pratt Byrd, "The Kentucky Frontier in 1792," *Hist. Quart.*, Jy., 1951, pp. 182, 184, 189-190; Oct., 1951, pp. 286-292; Tapp, *Kentucky*, I, 155-216.

[4]Smith, *Kentucky*, pp. 301-303; Marshall, *Kentucky*, I, 414.

[5]Collins, *op. cit.*, II. 712-713; Reuben T. Durrett (ed.), *The Centenary of Kentucky*, The Filson Club Publications No. 7, (Louisville: John P. Morton & Co., 1892), p. 131; *Appleton's Cyclopaedia of American Biography, Revised Edition* (Vol. 6; New York: D. Appleton & Co., 1888), V, 491-492.

[6]Gilbert Imlay, *A Topographical Description of the Western Territory of North America, Third Edition* (London: J. Debrett, 1787), p. 168 (adapted).

[7]Tapp, *op. cit.*, I, 222.

[8]State Bar Association of Kentucky, *op. cit., Journal of Convention*, p. 17; (Constitution of 1792, Art. 7th, Sec. I)

[9]*The Gazette*, June 9, 1792; George W. Ranck, "How Kentucky Became a State," *Harper's New Monthly Magazine*, June, 1892, pp. 46-49.

[10]C. Frank Dunn, Lexington, Letter of July 5, 1951; C. Frank Dunn, "John Bradford Bicentennial," *Hist. Quart.*, Jy., 1948, pp. 161, 163-4; (Reprint) *Lexington Leader*, May 31, 1951, p. 26.

[11]*The Gazette*, June 23, 1792.

[12]*Ibid.*, June 23, 1792.

[13]"Acts of the First General Assembly," p. 9, Chapter VI, Section 1," (Printed by John Bradford, Lexington, 1792.)

[14]C. Frank Dunn, Lexington, Unpublished Notes, and Letter of July 5, 1951; Collins, *op. cit.*, II, 182.

[15]*Register*, Vol. I, (1903), p. 31; Vol. 22 (1924), pp. 93-96; *The Gazette*, Sept. 26, 1798; C. Frank Dunn, Unpublished Notes.

[16]*The Gazette*, Nov. 17, 1792, p. 2, col. 3; Collins, *op. cit.*, II, p. 32.

[17]*Ibid.*, Nov. 17, 1792, p. 2, col. 1.

Selected Bibliography

Alden, John Richard. *Southern Colonial Frontier, 1754-1775.* Ann Arbor: University of Michigan Press, 1944.

Alvord, Clarence W. *The Mississippi Valley and British Politics.* Vol. 2. Cleveland: The A. H. Clark Company, 1917.

Ayres, William. *Historical Sketches.* Pikeville: Sun Publishing Company, 1925.

Bakeless, John. *Daniel Boone, Master of the Wilderness.* New York: Wm. Morrow & Company, 1939.

Baldwin, Leland D. *The Keelboat Age on Western Waters.* Pittsburgh: University of Pittsburgh Press, 1941.

Barnhard, John D., ed., *Henry Hamilton and George Rogers Clark in the American Revolution.* Crawfordsville: R. E. Banta, 1951.

Bartholomew, Henry S., ed., *Michigan Pioneer Collections.* Vols. IX, X. 2nd ed. Lansing.: Wynkoop, Hallenbeck, Crawford, 1908.

Beattie, George W. and Helen P. "Benjamin Linn—Hunter, Explorer, Preacher." *The Filson Club History Quarterly,* April 1946, pp. 139-144.

Beattie, George W. and Helen P. "Benjamin Linn—Hunter, Ex- *The Filson Club History Quarterly,* July 1946, pp. 223-226, 231.

Beckner, Lucien. "Eskippakithiki, the Last Indian Town in Kentucky." *The Filson Club History Quarterly,* October 1932, pp. 355-382.

Becker, Lucien. "John Findley, the First Pathfinder of Kentucky." *The Filson Club History Quarterly,* April 1927, pp. 213-219.

Beckner, Lucien. "Captain James Harrod's Company." *Kentucky Historical Society Register,* September 1922, pp. 280-282.

Beckner, Lucien. "The Henderson Company Ledger by John D. Shane." *The Filson Club History Quarterly,* January 1947, pp. 22-46.

Beckner, Lucien. "Shane's Interview with William Clinkenbeard." *The Filson Club History Quarterly,* April 1928, pp. 98, 104, 106-112, 114, 119, 124, 126-127.

Beckner, Lucien. "Shane's Interview with Jeptha Kemper." *The Filson Club History Quarterly*, July 1938, pp. 155, 156, 157.

Beckner, Lucien: "Shane's Interview with Mrs. Sarah Graham." *The Filson Club History Quarterly*, October 1935, p. 236.

Bernstadt, Carl. "Certain Phases of the Origin of Louisville." *The Filson Club History Quarterly*, July 1930, pp. 107-151.

Bemis, Samuel F. *A. Diplomatic History of the United States*. New York: Henry Holt & Company, 1936.

Beveridge, Albert J. *The Life of John Marshall*. Vol. 4. Boston and New York: Houghton Mifflin Company, 1916.

Bodley, Temple. *History of Kentucky*. Vol. 4. Chicago and Louisville: S. J. Clarke Publishing Company, 1928.

Bodley, Temple. *George Rogers Clark, His Life and Public Services* Boston: Houghton Mifflin Company, 1926.

Bodley, Temple. *Our First Great West—in Revolutionary War, Diplomacy and Politics*. Louisville: J. P. Morton & Company, 1936.

Bradford, John. "Notes on Kentucky." Sec. 14. *The Kentucke Gazette*, November 24, 1826.

Bradford, John. "Historical Notes." Sec. 9, 10. *The Kentucke Gazette*, October 20, 27, 1826.

Bradford, John. "Notes on Kentucky." Sec. 13. *The Kentucke Gazette*, November 17, 1826.

Brown, John Mason. *The Political Beginnings of Kentucky*. Louisville: J. P. Morton & Company, 1889.

Bryan, Charles W. "Richard Calloway, Kentucky Pioneer." *The Filson Club History Quarterly*, January 1935, pp. 35-50.

Bryan, Edward. "Notes on Bryan's Station." *Kentucky Historical Society Register*, July 1944, p. 269.

Burnett, Edmund Cody. *Letters of Members of the Continental Congress*. Washington: Carnegie Foundation, 1921.

Burnett, Samuel Cody. *The Continental Congress*. New York: The Macmillan Company, 1941.

Burton, M. Agnes, ed., *Michigan Pioneer Collections*. Vol. XIX. Lansing: Wynkoop, Hallenbeck, Crawford, 1908.

Butler, Mann. *A History of the Commonwealth of Kentucky*. Louisville: Wilcox, Dickerman & Company, 1834.

Byrd, Pratt. "The Kentucky Frontier in 1792." *The Filson Club History Quarterly*, July 1951, pp. 182, 184, 189-190.

Calk, William. "His Jornal." Photostat copy, Library of the Filson Club, Louisville, Kentucky.

A Century of Population Growth, 1790-1900. Washington: Government Printing Office, 1909.

Chinn, Mrs. Jennie M. "Early Churches of Kentucky." Typescript. Kentucky Historical Society Library. Frankfort, 1930.

Clore, Julia Alves. "Personnel of the Transylvania Company." *Kentucky Progress Magazine*, Summer 1934, pp. 336-337, 400.

Coleman, J. Winston, Jr. *The British Invasion of Kentucky*. Lexington: Winburn Press, 1951.

Collins, Richard H. *History of Kentucky*. Vol. 2. Rev. ed. Louisville: J. P. Morton & Company, 1876.

Combs, Ann Price. "Notes on the Political Club of Danville and its Members." *The Filson Club History Quarterly*, October 1961, pp. 333-352.

Commanger, Henry Steele, ed. *Documents of American History*. 3rd ed. New York: Columbia University Press, 1944.

Conkwright, S. J. *History of the Churches of Boone's Creek Baptist Association of Kentucky*. Winchester, 1923.

Cubberley, Elwood P. *The History of Education*. Boston: Houghton Mifflin Company, 1920.

Dandridge, Denske. *George Michael Bedinger, A Kentucky Pioneer*. Charlottesville: The Michie Company, 1909.

Doddridge, Joseph. *Notes on the Settlements and Indian Wars of the Western Parts of Virginia and Pennsylvania*. Pittsburgh: Ritenour and Lindsey, 1912.

Dunbar, Seymour. *History of Travel in America*. Indianapolis: Bobbs-Merrill Company, 1915.

Duncan, Fannie Casseday. *When Kentucky Was Young.* Louisville: J. P. Morton & Company, 1928.

Dunn, C. Frank. "John Bradford Bicentennial." *The Filson Club History Quarterly,* July 1948, pp. 158, 161, 163-164.

Dunn, C. Frank. "Transylvania Seminary—Where?" *The Kentucky Historical Society Register,* October 1947, p. 323.

Durrett, Reuben T. *Bryant's Station.* Louisville: J. P. Morton & Company, 1897.

Durrett, Reuben T., ed., *The Centenary of Kentucky.* Louisville: J. P. Morton & Company, 1892.

Durrett, Reuben T. *The Centenary of Louisville.* Louisville: J. P. Morton & Company, 1893.

Durrett, Reuben T. *John Filson, The First Historian of Kentucky.* Cincinnati: Robert Clarke & Company, 1884.

Durrett, Reuben T. "First Christmas Day in Louisville." *The Courier-Journal,* August 2, 1893.

English, William H. *The Conquest of the Territory Northwest of The River Ohio, 1778-1785 and Life of General George Rogers Clark.* Indianapolis: Bobbs-Merrill Company, 1897.

Fackler, Calvin Morgan. *Early Days in Danville.* Louisville: Standard Printing Company, 1941.

Field, Thomas P. "Place Names of Kentucky." *The Filson Club History Quarterly,* July 1960, p. 243.

Filson, John. *The Discovery, Settlement and Present State of Kentucke.* Wilmington: James Adams, 1784.

Fish, Carl Russell. *American Diplomacy.* 4th ed. New York: Henry Holt & Company, 1923.

Force, Peter. *American Archives.* Fourth Series. Vol. 6. Washington: M. St. Clair Clarke and Peter Force, 1837-1843.

Ford, W. C., ed. *Journals of the Continental Congress.* Washington: Government Printing Office, 1907.

Gaines, Noel. "Washington Approved Kentucky First." *Kentucky Progress Magazine,* July 1929, p. 24.

Gales, Joseph, Sr. *Debates and Proceedings in the Congress of the United States*. Washington: Gales & Seaton, 1834.

Green, Thomas Marshall. *The Spanish Conspiracy, A Review of Early Spanish Movements in the South-West*. Cincinnati: Robert Clarke & Company, 1891.

Hamilton, Sir Henry. *Journal of the Vincennes Expedition, 1778-1779*. Photostat copy. The Filson Club, Louisville, Kentucky.

Hanna, Charles A. *The Wilderness Trail*. Vol. 2. New York: G. P. Putnam's Sons, 1911.

Haywood, John. *History of Tennessee*. Knoxville: Heiskell & Brown, 1823.

Henderson, Archibald. *The Conquest of the Old Southwest*. New York: Century Company, 1920.

Henderson, Archibald. "Creative Forces in American History: Henderson and Boone." *American Historical Society Review*, XX, p. 105.

Henderson, Archibald. "The Transylvania Company Personnel." *The Filson Club History Quarterly*, October 1947, pp. 327-328, 331.

Henderson, Archibald. "Transylvania Company Personnel—James Hogg." *The Filson Club History Quarterly*, January 1947, pp. 3-21.

Hening, William Waller, ed., *Laws of Virginia, Statutes at Large*. Vol. 13. Richmond: Franklin Press, 1820.

Henry, William Wirt, *Patrick Henry—Life, Correspondence and Speeches*. New York: Charles Scribner's Sons, 1891.

Horine, Emmet Field, ed., *Pioneer Life in Kentucky, 1785-1800, by Daniel Drake, M.D.* New York: Henry Schuman, 1948.

Howard, George Elliott. *Preliminaries of the Revolution, 1763-1775, in The American Nation: A History*. Edited by A. B. Hart. New York: Harper & Bros., 1905.

Hulbert, Archer Butler. *Boone's Wilderness Road*. Cleveland: A. H. Clark Company, 1903.

Hulbert, Archer Butler. *The Ohio River, A Course of Empire*. New York: G. P. Putnam's Sons, 1906.

Hunt, Gaillard, ed., *Journals of the Continental Congress,* XXII. Washington: Government Printing Office, 1909.

Imlay, Gilbert. *A Topographical Description of the Western Territory of North America.* 3rd ed. London: J. Debrett, 1787.

James, James Alton, ed., *Collections of Illinois State Historical Society, George Rogers Clark Papers, 1771-1778.* Springfield: Illinois State Historical Library, 1912.

Jay, Williams. *Life of John Jay.* New York: J. & J. Harper, 1833.

Jenson, Merrill. "The Cession of the Old Northwest." *Miss. Valley Historical Society Review.* June 1936, pp. 27-48.

Jenson, Merrill. *The New Nation: A History of the United States During the Confederation, 1781-1789.* New York: Alfred A. Knopf, 1950.

Jillson, Willard Rouse. *Filson's Kentucke.* Louisville: John P. Morton & Company, 1929.

Jillson, Willard Rouse. *Tales of the Dark and Bloody Ground.* Louisville: C. T. Dearing Printing Co., 1930.

Jillson, Willard Rouse. *The Topography of Kentucky.* Frankfort: State Journal Company, 1927.

Johnston, J. Stoddard. *Memorial History of Louisville.* Chicago: American Biographical Publishing Company, 1896.

Joyes, Morton V., Sr. "Letter by Colonel John Todd, Jr., 1778." *The Filson Club History Quarterly,* July 1928, p. 157.

Kellogg, Louise Phelps. *Frontier Advance on the Upper Ohio, 1778-1779.* Madison: 1916.

Kennedy, John P., ed., *Journals of the House of Burgesses of Virginia, 1770-1772.* Richmond: Virginia State Library, 1906.

Kentucky Progress Magazine, Summer 1935.

Kerr, Judge Charles, ed., *History of Kentucky* by Wm. E. Connelley and E. Merton Coulter. Chicago: American Historical Society, 1922.

Kilpatrick, Lewis H. "William Calk, Kentucky Pioneer." *Kentucky Magazine,* January 1918, pp. 33-42.

Kilpatrick, Lewis H. "The Journal of William Calk, Kentucky Pioneer." *Miss. Valley Historical Society Review,* March 1921, pp. 363-377.

Kincaid, Robert F. *The Wilderness Road.* Indianapolis: Bobbs-Merrill Company, 1947.

Lafferty, Maud Ward. "Danville Political Club." *Danville Daily Messenger,* May 12, 1921.

Lafferty, Maude Ward. "A Revolutionary Tragedy: The Destruction of Ruddle's and Martin's Forts." Typescript. The Filson Club, 1931.

Langdon, William Chauncey. *Everyday Things in American Life.* New York: Charles Scribner's Sons, 1937.

Littell, William. *Political Transactions in and Concerning Kentucky.* Louisville: J. P. Morton & Company, 1926.

Macdonald, William, ed., *Documentary Source Book of American History,* 1616-1926. 3rd ed. New York: The Macmillan Company, 1933.

Marshall, Humphrey. *History of Kentucky.* 2nd ed. Frankfort: George S. Robinson, 1824.

Marshall, W. F. "Robert Trent, River Pilot." *The Challenge.* Nashville, Tennessee, November 1, 1936, pp. 1, 6, 7.

Mason, Kathryn Harrod. *James Harrod of Kentucky.* Baton Rouge: Louisiana State University Press, 1951.

Mason, Kathryn Harrod. "Harrod's Men—1774." *The Filson Club History Quarterly,* July 1950, pp. 230-233.

McElroy, Robert M. *Kentucky in the Nation's History.* New York: Moffat, Yard & Company, 1909.

McMaster, John Bach. *A History of the People of the United States.* New York: D. Appleton & Company, 1915.

Miller, Arthur McQuiston. *The Geology of Kentucky.* Frankfort: State Journal Company, 1919.

Morehead, James T. *Address in Commemoration of the First Settlement of Kentucky.* Frankfort: A. G. Hodges, State Printer, 1840.

Palmer, W. P. and McRae, S., eds., *Calendar of Virginia State Papers*. Richmond: James E. Goode, 1881.

Palmer, W. P., ed., *Calendar of Virginia State Papers, II*. Richmond: R. F. Walker, 1875.

Perrin, William Henry. *History of Fayette County, Kentucky*. Chicago: O. L. Baskin & Company, 1882.

Perrin, William Henry. *The Pioneer Press of Kentucky*. Louisville: J. P. Morton & Company, 1888.

Perrin, W. H., Settle, J. H., Kniffen, G. C. *Kentucky, A History of the State*. 4th ed. Louisville and Chicago: P. A. Battey & Company, 1887.

Phillips, Josephine E. "Flatboating on the Great Thoroughfare." *Bulletin*. Ohio Historical and Philosophical Society, June 1947, pp. 11-24.

Phillips, P. Lee. *The First Map of Kentucky by John Filson*. Washington: W. H. Lowdermilk & Companly, 1908.

Pirtle, Alfred. "Where Louisville Started." Louisville: The Standard Printing Company, 1921, pp. 1-5.

Pusey, William Allen. *The Wilderness Road to Kentucky*. New York: George H. Doran Company, 1921.

Quaife, Milo M. "When Detroit Invaded Kentucky." *The Filson Club History Quarterly*, January 1927, pp. 60-63.

Ranck, George W. *Boonesborough*. Louisville: John P. Morton & Company, 1901.

Ranck, George W. "How Kentucky Became a State." *Harper's New Monthly Magazine*, June 1892, pp. 46-49.

Ranck, George W. "The Travelling Church." Louisville: Baptist Book Concern, 1891.

Robertson, George. *Scrap Book on Law and Politics, Men and Times*. Lexington: A. W. Elder, 1885.

Robertson, James Rood. *Petitions of the Early Inhabitants of Kentucky*. Louisville: J. P. Morton & Company, 1914.

Robertson, James Rood. "New Light on Kentucky History." *Proceedings Mississippi Valley Historical Association*, IX, Part I (1915-1916), pp. 90-92.

Rothert, Otto A. "John Floyd—Pioneer and Hero." *The Filson Club History Quarterly,* July 1928, p. 173.

Saunders, William L., ed., *The Colonial and State Records of North Carolina.* Vol. 20. Raleigh, 1890.

Semple, Ellen Churchill. *American History and its Geographic Conditions.* Boston: Houghton Mifflin Company, 1903.

Skinner, Constance Lindsey. *Pioneers of the Old Southwest.* New Haven: Yale University Press, 1919.

Smith, Zachary F. *History of Kentucky.* Louisville: *Courier-Journal* Job Printing Company, 1886.

Sonne, Niels Henry. *Liberal Kentucky,* 1780-1828. New York: Columbia University Press, 1939.

Sparks, Jared. *The Life of Governeur Morris.* Vol. 3. Boston: Gray & Bowen, 1832.

Spaulding, M. J. *Sketches of the Early Catholic Missions of Kentucky.* Louisville: B. J. Webb and Brother, 1844.

Speed, Thomas. *The Political Club, Danville, Kentucky,* 1786-1790. Louisville: J. P. Morton & Company, 1894.

Speed, Thomas. *The Wilderness Road.* Louisville: John P. Morton & Company, 1886.

Spencer, J. H. *A History of Kentucky Baptists from 1769-1885.* Cincinnati: J. R. Baumes, 1885.

Staples, Charles R. *The History of Pioneer Lexington.* Lexington: Transylvania Press, 1935.

Staples, Charles R. "Pioneer Kentucky Preachers and Pulpits." *The Filson Club History Quarterly,* July 1935, pp. 130, 139, 148, 153.

Talbert, Charles G. "Kentucky Invades Ohio—1779." *Kentucky Historical Society Register,* July 1953, p. 228.

Talbert, Charles G. "Kentucky Invades Ohio—1780." *Kentucky Historical Society Register,* October 1954.

Talbert, Charles G. "Kentucky Invades Ohio—1792." *Kentucky Historical Society Register,* October 1955, pp. 293-298.

Talbert, Charles G. "A Roof for Kentucky." *The Filson Club History Quarterly,* April 1955.

Talbert, Charles G. "William Whitley, 1749-1813." *The Filson Club History Quarterly,* April 1951, pp. 103-106, 107.

Tapp, Hambleton. *The Sesqui-Centennial History of Kentucky.* Vol. 5. Chicago: American Historical Society, 1946.

Taylor, John. *A History of Ten Baptist Churches.* 2nd ed. Bloomfield: Will H. Holmes, 1827.

Thruston, R. C. Ballard. Family Papers and Personal Interviews. The Filson Club. Louisville, 1938.

Thruston, R. C. Ballard. "Filson's History and Map of Kentucky." *The Filson Club History Quarterly,* January 1934, pp. 17-38.

Thwaites, Reuben Gold and Kellogg, Louise Phelps, eds., *Documentary History of Dunmore's War.* Collections Wisconsin State Historical Society. Madison: 1905.

Thwaites, Reuben Gold. *Daniel Boone.* New York: D. Appleton & Company, 1902.

Thwaites, Reuben Gold and Kellogg, Louise Phelps, eds., *The Revolution on the Upper Ohio.* Collections Wisconsin State Historical Society. Madison: 1908.

Turner, Frederick J. "Western State-Making in the Revolutionary Era." *American Historical Society Review,* I, pp. 76-81.

Verhoeff, Mary. *The Kentucky River Navigation.* Louisville: John P. Morton & Company, 1917.

Villiers, Capt. Alan et al. *Men, Ships and the Sea.* National Geographic Society. Washington, 1962.

Warren, Elizabeth. "Benjamin Sebastian and the Spanish Conspiracy." *The Filson Club History Quarterly,* April 1946, pp. 112, 113.

Webb, Benjamin J. *Centenary of Catholicity in Kentucky.* Louisville: Charles A. Rogers, 1884.

Weyl, Nathaniel. *Treason: The Story of Disloyalty and Betrayal in American History.* Washington: Public Affairs Press, 1950.

Wharton, Francis, ed., *The Revolutionary Diplomatic Correspondence of the United States.* Washington: Government Printing Office, 1889.

Wilson, Samuel M. *Battle of the Blue Licks.* Lexington: 1927.

Wilson, Samuel M. "John Bradford, Kentucky's First Printer." *The Filson Club History Quarterly,* October 1937, pp. 260-269.

Wilson, Samuel M. "Daniel Boone, 1734-1934." *The Filson Club History Quarterly,* October 1934, p. 151.

Wilson, Samuel M. "John Filson in Pennsylvania." *The Filson Club History Quarterly,* October 1939, pp. 179-201.

Wilson, Samuel M. *First Land Court of Kentucky, 1779-1780.* Lexington: 1923.

Winsor, Justin, ed., *Narrative and Critical History of the United States.* Vol. 8. Boston and New York: Houghton Mifflin Company, 1881-1897.

World Almanac. New York: New York *World-Telegram,* 1958.

Index

Ruby Addison Henry unfortunately died before this, her only book, was published. Her story is as fascinating as that which she relates. Born in 1873, she was reared in the old tradition of the South. She studied at the School of International Studies, Geneva, Switzerland; Cambridge University in England; the University of Michigan; and the University of Chicago, and received a degree from the University of Louisville. L i t e r a t e , charming, well traveled, she epitomized the classic tradition of gentility and culture which one still finds as part of Southern aristocratic heritage. A teacher all of her life, she devoted herself to scholarly and cultural pursuits and was particularly active in many historical associations.

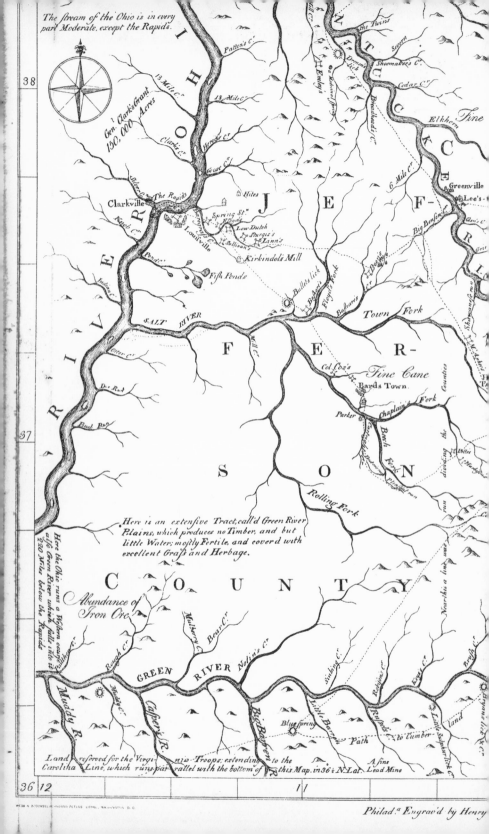

The stream of the Ohio is in every part Moderate, except the Rapids.

38

37

36 12

Gen.l Clarks Grant 150,000 Acres

18 Mile Cr.

18 Mile Cr.

Pattens Cr.

Clark Cr.

Mercer Cr.

Goose Cr.

Clarkville

The Rapids

Hites

Louisville

Spring St.r Floyds

Lew Dutch

Sturgis's

Sullivan's

Lann's

Kirkindol's Mill

Fish Ponds

Pond Cr.

Indian Cr.

SALT RIVER

Mill Cr.

Otter Cr.

Doe Run

Buck Run

Bullets lick

Beshars

Floyds Fork

Beshars Cr.

Town Fork

Col. Cox's

Fine Cane

Bards Town

Parker

Chaplain's Fork

Beech Fork

Rolling Fork

Here is an extensive Tract, call'd Green River Plains, which produces no Timber, and but little Water, mostly Fertile, and cover'd with excellent Grass and Herbage.

C O U N T Y

Abundance of Iron Ore

Here the Ohio runs a Western course, also Green River which falls into it 220 Miles below the Rapids

Mulberry Cr.

Bear Cr.

Rough Cr.

GREEN RIVER Nolin's Cr.

Muddy R.

Muddy Cr.

Calpeper's R.

Big Barren

Blue spring

Little Barren

Sinking Cr.

Ridiford's Cr.

Ezel Cr.

Paybody Cr.

to Timber

Path

A fine Lead Mine

Little sulphur lick Cr.

Land reserved for the Virgi-   nia Troops, extending to the
Carolina Line, which runs parallel with the bottom of   this Map in 36½ N.Lat.

Dreanons lick

Kentucky Springs

Shoemakers Cr.

Severn

Cedar Cr.

Broad heads Cr.

Elkhorn

Fine

Greenville

Lee's

Glen's Cr.

6 Mile Cr.

Big Benson Cr.

H. Dogles

H. Dogles Cr.

Shawanese men

the Counties

dividing

the

Nari-his line way

run

Philad.a Engrav'd by Henry